Jalan-Jalan: A Journey of Wanderlust and Motherhood

by Margo Weinstein

ISBN 978-1-64663-664-8

REVIEW COPY: This is an advanced printing subject to corrections and revisions.

Published by

◤köehlerbooks™

3705 Shore Drive
Virginia Beach, VA 23455
800-435-4811
www.koehlerbooks.com

JALAN-
Jalan

*A Journey of Wanderlust
and Motherhood*

MARGO WEINSTEIN

VIRGINIA BEACH
CAPE CHARLES

For Jake, who changed my *jalan-jalan*.

Table of Contents

Introduction

"JALAN-JALAN?" ASKED PUTU WHEN he saw me lacing up my sneakers instead of slipping on my flip-flops. "*Jalan-jalan?*" asked Komang when I walked out the villa's teak doors and past the car without asking him to drive me anywhere. Putu and Komang used this Indonesian phrase to ask me whether I was going for a walk, something I did most days during the two years my son, Jake, and I lived in Bali. Our Balinese staff and neighbors had become used to seeing me on my walks through the rice paddies and along the steep, winding roads of Ubud. And I had learned the hard way to wear sneakers for these walks after developing plantar fasciitis, an injury common among expats in Bali who happily adopt Balinese footwear but keep their Western walking habits.

What led me, a class action lawyer and single mom from Chicago, to walk away from a successful career and drag nine-year-old Jake to the other side of the world? Or, in a mashup of English and Indonesian, what was my *jalan-jalan*? *Jalan-jalan*—the polysemous Indonesian word I co-opted for my book's title—is ubiquitous in Bali. At Green School, the international school Jake attended, *Jalan-Jalan* was the program where students could step out of their comfort zones and try something new. During one *Jalan-Jalan*, Jake's class rescued sharks from tanks at a

Denpasar nightclub and released them into the ocean off the Gili Islands. (Two of three sharks survived the transfer.) Green School's adoption of the word fits perfectly within the spirit of its dictionary definition. As a verb, *jalan-jalan* means to take a walk, but also to go on, to go forward, to pass. As a noun, it means road. We lived on Jalan Sri Wedari, just north of Jalan Raya Ubud, the main road through central Ubud. But *jalan-jalan* also means (literally and figuratively) a route used for traveling between places, a course taken, and a path chosen in life or career.

My *Jalan-Jalan*—both my path and this book—has two parts. Part I, before Jake was born, is my travel to remote regions of the world, rafting, kayaking, trekking, and climbing in wild places, and experiencing different cultures. This travel provided needed escapes from my demanding job, and adventures that challenged and pushed me to expand my abilities and perspective. I took risks that later led Jake to exclaim, when he read Part I, "Mom! How was I ever even born?"

Part II is the story of how Jake changed my path and my travel. My risk threshold, which had been high (especially for a lawyer), needed to adapt to include a child I did not want to get killed or leave motherless. My travel destinations moved from the rugged mountains of Pakistan to the more stroller-friendly boulevards of Paris. Instead of paddling a river raft or ocean kayak, Jake and I took Disney cruises. These trips were fun, and Jake loved hugging Mickey Mouse and playing Ping-Pong with Goofy, but they were not enough. I needed to find and follow a new path that could accommodate motherhood *and* satisfy my wanderlust. Instead of a series of exciting but disparate adventures like those in Part I, Jake and I embarked on more sustained adventures. We did not climb mountains, but we took significant risks. We left home for months, and then years, moving first to Shanghai and then to Bali. Through travel, we changed our lives and ourselves.

Regardless of where you are on your path, if you share my wanderlust, I hope this book inspires your travel. Or, after reading about my near-death experiences traveling in Pakistan and Burma and how I dragged my young son to live on the other side of the world (twice), you may be glad you stayed home with a travel book.

Margo hiking in the Dolomites the year before Jake was born

Part I

BEFORE

Margo with a jeep (deflated river raft in its rear, river guides relaxing in its shade) in northern Pakistan

Margo and a Kalash woman in the Kalash Valley, Pakistan

Courtesy of Joani Carpenter, reprinted with permission

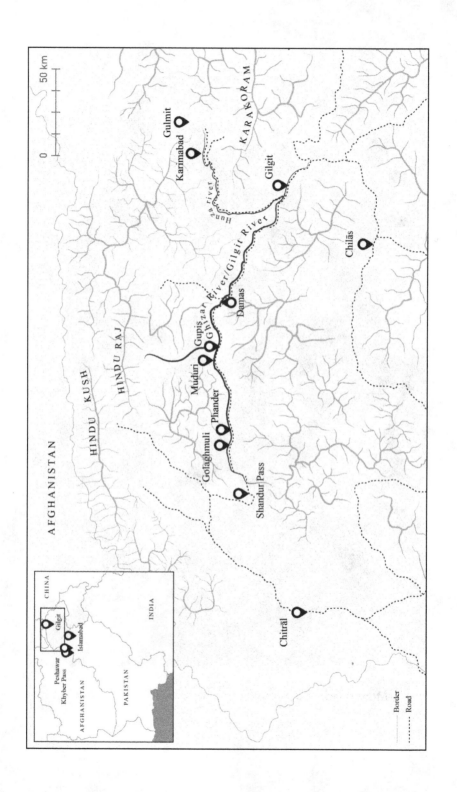

Chapter One

ALLAH HOO ALLAH HOO
TRAVELING THROUGH PURDAH IN PAKISTAN

THE CAPSIZE HAPPENED FAST. I hit the water with my mouth wide open—probably from screaming—and icy river water slammed down my windpipe. As the water filled my lungs, my life jacket propelled me to the surface, but I couldn't catch my breath. I had popped up under the capsized raft and was trapped in the shallow air pocket between the river and the raft's floor, which bounced just above my head. Struggling to clear my lungs and take a breath in the tight space, I inhaled more water than air.

And I couldn't see anything except the solid, shapeless color blue—azure blue, not slate blue like the river or slate gray like the raft. After a second of panic and confusion, I realized that when the raft upended and flipped, I must have landed in the water before it did, and the crashing tube hit me on the head, jamming my azure-blue helmet down over my eyes. I tried to push the helmet up. When it didn't budge, I knew I had to focus instead on my bigger problem—getting out from under the raft before I was sucked into a hole, pulled deep underwater, and drowned. Adrenaline and a primitive survival instinct pushed me to do something, anything, to save myself. But I needed to think and not act rashly or out of fear. If I emerged downstream of the raft at the wrong time, I risked being crushed between the moving raft and a stationary boulder or canyon wall—not a good outcome anywhere, but especially not here in a remote and rugged region of northern Pakistan.

I headed for what I hoped was the upstream edge of the raft. I raised my arms toward the floor of the capsized raft and tried to hand walk across the rubber bottom, like doing a handstand and walking on my hands, except upright in the water. I moved a few inches and got a face full of freezing water so far up my nose it felt like my eyeballs were floating. Blowing out the water, I tried swimming freestyle (the front crawl)—my stroke when I swam on my high school swim team. Against the momentum of the rapid propelling the raft and me in the opposite direction, I was swimming in place, wasting energy, going nowhere. Then, a slight shift and easing of the rapid allowed me to surge forward and grab the line secured to the upstream edge of the raft.

My sense of relief lasted only a second. I was still under the raft. To get out, I needed to go under the tube and come up on the other side. I tried diving down, but my life jacket's life-saving buoyancy prevented me from submerging long enough and deep enough to swim under the tube that formed the raft's sides. Two futile attempts depleted the air in my lungs and left me gasping. Tamping down panic, I grabbed the line, tilted my head up to refill my lungs with air, and reassessed. I could not swim down with my life jacket on, and I would most likely drown if I took my life jacket off. I needed to try something else. Instead of swimming, maybe I could pull myself down and around the raft, holding on to the line so that I did not float up. I took a deep breath, put my head back in the water, and hand-over-hand pulled myself under. It worked. I unclenched my grip on the line, surfaced outside and behind the raft, and pushed my helmet up and off my eyes so I finally could see.

Mike, our lead river guide, was there, ready to grab me. When I first surfaced under the raft just after we capsized, Mike had heard me gagging and was relieved to know where I was. But then I didn't come out. I was taking too long. With increasing concern, Mike scanned the river, watching for me to emerge from under the raft. As soon as he spotted me, before I even knew what was happening, Mike grabbed the shoulder of my life jacket and hurled me on top of the upside-down raft. The raft's bottom was flat, wet, and slick, and the raft was bouncing through a class V rapid. When I hit the surface, I kept going and slid right back into the river. As I went over the edge, I somehow had the presence of mind to grab a line. Mike reached down, grabbed hold of my life jacket, pulled me out of the river again, and—with a look that said, "Stay!"—set me down on the bottom of the raft. I stayed.

My fellow paddlers—Attaullah, a Pakistani river guide, and Jahangir, our Pakistani jeep driver (transferred from his jeep to our raft as the ballast we need to run these rapids)—were already there. When the raft flipped, they had landed in the river nearby, and Mike pulled them on top before I emerged from under the raft. With everyone out of the water, we were relatively safe, but we were still on an upside-down raft on the wild Ghizar River in the Hindu Kush region of northern Pakistan.

As we rounded a bend and headed into the next series of class V rapids, Attaullah and Jahangir lay flat on their stomachs next to each other at one end of the raft, gripping a line. Attaullah craned forward, trying to see what was ahead and anticipate the raft's movement. Jahangir kept his head down, trying not to see what was coming and probably praying. I crouched on the other end, focused only on not falling off. As the raft spun in the rapids, sometimes Attaullah and Jahangir were in the front and got the brunt of the waves; sometimes I was in front and took the hit. Mike, who had lost his helmet in the capsize, was in constant motion. He hurled himself across the raft, side to side and front to back. I didn't know whether his frantic efforts to level and steer the raft without oars or a paddle worked, or if the river gods decided we'd had enough. But the raft got into the current, went sideways around the edge of the first hole, pivoted, and floated through the long wave train without getting wrapped on a boulder, slammed against the canyon wall, or sucked into a hole.

Then I heard Mike shout over the roar of the rapids, "I am going to re-flip the raft!" As the raft approached the relative calm at the end of the rapid, Mike looked at me and yelled, "Jump off!"

At first, I figured I hadn't heard correctly. Go back in the river? I don't think so.

"Now!" Mike shouted.

As I hesitated, I landed in the water. Mike needed to regain control of the raft before we hit the next rapid, and he could not reflip the raft with me desperately clinging to the bottom. So, he threw me off. With Attaullah, Jahangir, and me floating in the river, Mike re-flipped the raft so that it was upright and grabbed the oars. He rowed over and quickly pulled me in. As I crawled off the raft floor and sat on the tube, Mike reached over the edge and hauled Jahangir in by the shoulders of his life jacket. From the other side, Attaullah pulled himself up and into the raft. With a few purposeful strokes, Mike rowed to shore before the current swept the raft into the next set of rapids.

This death-defying melodrama was not what I had envisioned nine months earlier when I first heard about a new rafting trip in Pakistan. Then, a sunny and cold January morning in Chicago, I sat in my law office on the seventy-seventh floor of the Sears Tower, staring at my computer screen, trying to edit a legal brief that had to be filed in court the next day. I could not focus. My mind kept wandering to my recent trip rafting the Biobío River in Chile. *I'd so rather be rafting*, I thought. Then, as if someone at Mountain Travel Sobek's office in Oakland, California, had read my mind, the phone rang.

"Hey, Margo," came the voice. "How was the Biobío? I heard you guys had great weather. Are you up for an even bigger river?"

"Maybe. Probably. Where?" I asked.

"Pakistan. We're planning the first commercial rafting trip down the Ghizar River in Pakistan. It will be epic. And you'll get to hike in the Hunza Valley and drive the Karakoram Highway. How about it?"

Why did Mountain Travel Sobek call *me* about this Pakistan trip? When not traveling, I spent my days indoors wearing a business suit and heels, not in the wild wearing a Farmer Jane wetsuit and rubber booties. And at five feet, two inches tall (in those rubber booties), I may not have seemed the likeliest candidate for a rugged trip rafting in a remote region of Pakistan. But personal, professional, and financial circumstances changed the calculus.

On a group trip, a good attitude, determination, enthusiasm, and flexibility go a long way to compensate for a lack of physical strength and technical expertise. When plan A failed, as it so often did, I was all in for plan B, C, or D, and probably up to plan H before I complained (much). Because I did not yet have a child, I could travel to remote regions where I would be out of touch for weeks (smartphones did not exist yet) without guilt or worry about what was happening at home. And as a partner at a large national and later multinational law firm, so-called BigLaw, I had unlimited vacation time—within reason, though perhaps I did interpret this differently than other lawyers who seldom even took a three-day weekend—and could arrange my schedule and delegate my work to allow me to take extended trips. That January morning, I was eager for another adventure far from home. Of course Mountain Travel Sobek called me. Of course I said yes.

After agreeing to join the trip, I was excited to see it featured in *Men's Journal,* the lifestyle magazine for men of action, and labeled "cutting edge." Who was adventurous enough to sign up for what *Men's Journal* deemed a cutting-edge trip? Four women: Joani, Michèle, Mary Jane, and me. In September and October 1997, I traveled through Pakistan with three adventuresome American women, two American men (both river guides), and eight Pakistani men—two river guides, four jeep drivers, a cook, and one camp crew.

My first impression of Pakistan was of a country with no women. As a class action lawyer defending lawsuits across the US, including in Southern towns like Beaumont, Texas, Columbus, Georgia, and Texarkana, Arkansas, I was used to being the only woman in a room full of men. I made my living and spent much of my life in what was still a man's realm. But a conference room or courtroom with no women was a far cry from a country with no women, or at least no visible women. Except for us, no women walked freely down the sidewalks of Rawalpindi, shopped in the crowded bazaars in Peshawar, sat in the stands at a polo match in Gilgit, or watched the smugglers coming through the Khyber Pass from Afghanistan.

To move through a country with virtually no visible women in the public sphere, we dressed like Pakistani men. Almost every Pakistani man wore *shalwar kameez* every day. (*Shalwar* is a baggy pant; *kameez* is a long tunic.) Although Pakistani women also wore *shalwar kameez* in the privacy of their homes, the women's style was impractical for hiking and rafting; it fit too tightly, was made from nonbreathable fabrics, and was decorated with embroidery and beads. Also, the women's version included scarves, and the idea of wearing a long scarf while driving on the Karakoram Highway in an open jeep conjured images of Isadora Duncan strangled to death by her flowing scarf while riding in a convertible. So, we four women purchased and then wore the men's *shalwar kameez* as we traveled and hiked throughout Pakistan. We even wore *shalwar kameez* over our wet suits and paddle gear and under our life jackets when rafting through populated areas. We did this in an effort to dress respectfully and modestly while still being able to move safely and comfortably. But we didn't look androgynous . . . we just looked odd.

Still wearing our Western clothes (we did not buy the *shalwar kameez* until the next day), our first stop was the Khyber Pass. We almost missed the opportunity because our small group was running late. The delay had started twenty-four hours earlier when the pilots for my British Airways flight from Manchester, England, to Islamabad, Pakistan, "went illegal," over the limit for the number of hours they could work. The passengers and crew from the packed 747 jumbo jet all got off the plane and spent the night in Manchester hotels (courtesy of the airline). The next morning, we finally flew to Islamabad, arriving nineteen hours late. Unbeknownst to me, Michèle and Mary Jane were on the same flight. We checked into the Pearl Continental Hotel in Rawalpindi (the twin city adjacent to Islamabad and part of the same metro area) at 1:30 a.m. the day after our scheduled arrival.

I was exhausted. The weeks before I left for Pakistan had been consumed by one work "crisis" after another. The weekend before I left, I had spent every waking minute, including straight through the night on Sunday, sitting at my desk in my office, organizing, finishing, or delegating everything I needed to get off my plate before I could leave on vacation and be unreachable for almost one month. Early Monday morning, I went home, took a quick nap, showered, packed, and headed to the airport to catch my flight to London. During the two-day layover, I had planned to see friends, relax, and adjust to the time difference. Instead, I raced around London, buying things I forgot to pack in the rush to catch my plane.

Once in Pakistan, the lack of sleep caught up with me. We were supposed to be out of the hotel and on the road only a few hours after checking in, but I could not get up and moving on time. (I was not the only one.) It was a four-hour drive from Islamabad to the Khyber Pass. If we did not make it to the Khyber Guards police station to pick up the mandatory security guard before the 10 a.m. check-in deadline, we could not proceed to the Khyber Pass.

It was close. Arriving at the checkpoint a few minutes after ten o'clock, we were allowed to pick up our guard—a skinny, stern, mustached man armed with what I was told was an AK-47. The AK-47, the so-called Kalashnikov, is a Soviet assault rifle with a cyclic firing rate of 600 rounds per minute. Despite being from Chicago, I had never seen an assault rifle. In the past, when I had told people in other countries I was from Chicago, they often shaped their hands into a machine gun and did their best imitation of the Valentine's Day Massacre while repeating "Al Capone, Al Capone" between simulated machine-gun noises. (Later, Michael Jordan replaced Al Capone as the personification of Chicago—a much better image—although more recently, Chicago is again known for its gun violence.) Why did the guard need a Soviet assault rifle? And why did we need him?

Now hyperalert, I did not object when the armed guard ordered me to stay close to him and pay attention. However, when he advised me to watch for any car that appeared to be following me, especially a luxury car, I did ask, "Why?" In response, he mumbled something about Pathan people and kidnappings. Maybe the four men in the white Toyota Camry were trailing me, looking for an opportunity to snatch me if I stepped away from the guard. Maybe they were just going the same direction, driving slowly because of the crowds. Taking no chances, I stuck close to the armed guard as we moved through the crowded bazaar, weaving around merchants, trucks, and camels. Even in this brief respite between the Mujahideen and Taliban eras, American tourists like us probably did not belong in this milieu. Yet, there we were, protected by a single guard and his AK-47.

Despite the potential danger of the situation, I was thrilled to be at the Khyber Pass, a strategic gateway for thousands of years. The Macedonians, Mongols, and British invaders are long gone, but I could visualize Alexander the Great in 326 BCE, Genghis Khan in the thirteenth century, and British troops in the nineteenth and twentieth centuries marching, riding, and rolling through the Khyber Pass. The camel caravans still wound through the pass using a lane designated just for camels, separated from the dangerously overloaded trucks. As I watched a long line of camels fitted with big metal carriers on either side of their humps carrying Sony televisions through the pass from Afghanistan into Pakistan, I imagined I was watching the camel caravans that traveled the ancient Silk Road through the Khyber Pass carrying goods (including silk, of course), animals, religion, ideas, and disease back and forth between Asia and Europe

Bringing me back to the present, one of the guides told this riddle: A border guard on the Pakistani side of the pass grew increasingly frustrated at his inability to catch a teenager the guard knew was smuggling something. Every day about the same time, the boy rode a bike through the pass and approached Pakistani customs. Every day, the guard thoroughly searched the boy, his belongings, and the bicycle, but found no contraband. This pattern continued for weeks. Finally, on the border guard's day off, his replacement arrested the boy. What was he smuggling?

I did not need to ponder the answer. It was right in front of me. As I watched, young boys pedaled one bicycle while towing one or two other bicycles alongside or behind them through the pass and across the border into Pakistan. What were they doing? Smuggling bikes.

———— ᨠᨿᨿᨿᨿᨿ ————

We survived the trip to the Khyber Pass without incident and drove to Peshawar, leaving our armed guard and his AK-47 back at the police station. In Peshawar, we shopped for our *shalwar kameez*. In addition to several dull men's *shalwar kameez* I planned to wear while rafting, hiking, and camping, I bought a bold red women's version with intricate embroidery. I wore the red outfit once in Pakistan, for dinner that night at our five-star hotel in Peshawar. Beautifully dressed, I posed for a photo next to a large sign in the lobby stating, in English,

---

HOTEL POLICY

Arms cannot be brought inside the hotel premises.
Personal Guards or Gunmen are required
to deposit their weapons with the Hotel Security.
We seek your cooperation.
Management

Although we had left our armed guard behind, apparently enough other guests traveled with personal guards or gunmen to warrant this sign. I doubted they deposited all their weapons with hotel security. What is a gunman without his gun? With so many guns and guards in the hotel, I did not know if I was safer or more at risk of being shot as collateral damage. As I lay in bed that night, on alert for sounds of gunfire, I wondered whether the bathtub was bulletproof.

After a surprisingly peaceful night, I awoke to the clear weather needed for our scheduled flight to take off. The forty-five-minute flight from Peshawar to Chitral navigated through some of the highest mountains in the world outside the Himalayas and was only possible on a clear day. If the weather had been bad, we would have endured a difficult twelve-hour drive. Instead, we flew and—probably because we were American women—the pilots invited us into the cockpit to see and film spectacular views of Mount Tirich Mir (at 25,289 feet, the highest mountain in the Hindu Kush range). After landing in Chitral, we drove into the Kalash Valley near the Afghanistan border, surrounded by the Hindu Kush mountains.

Suddenly, it felt like we had entered a different country—one with women. Women were out and about in the village and mingling with men. We were still in Pakistan, but among members of a distinct religious and ethnic minority. Unlike 95 to 98 percent of Pakistanis, the Kalash people are not Muslim. They practice a unique religion that is polytheistic, animist, and pagan. Kalash women have more freedom than Pakistani Muslim women do—freedom to date and marry whom they choose, freedom to divorce, and freedom to take part in society and be out and seen in public (except when they are menstruating, when they must remain in a women's house, the *bashaleni*).

The indigenous people of the Kalash Valley also look different from the darker-skinned Muslim Pakistanis. Many Kalash people have fair skin, blue eyes, and sandy-colored hair. For centuries, they claimed to be the descendants of Alexander the Great and his Macedonian Army. For centuries, historians dismissed these claims. When I visited, my guidebook described this purported connection to Alexander the Great's army as nothing more than folklore. But subsequent DNA evidence and data established that the genetic link to Alexander the Great's army might be real. In 2014, the journal *Science* reported that researchers had found genetic evidence for hundreds of examples of large-scale mixing of human populations. Chunks of DNA from an ancient European population were found in the Kalash people. Statistical evidence suggests this DNA is from a mixing event that occurred before 210 BCE, possibly even from the army of Alexander the Great. Data now support the ancient stories of these indigenous people.

Soon after stepping out of the jeep, I found myself in the middle of a group of Kalash women, beautifully attired in their unique and traditional dress. Women and girls wore black skirts and black shirts, elaborately embroidered with intricate designs in bold colors: fuchsia, blood red, deep blue, and sunny yellow. The women wore orange and yellow beaded necklaces—not just one or two necklaces, but twenty to fifty necklaces stacked high on their chests. On their heads and flowing down their backs, they wore headdresses embroidered and decorated with beads, cowrie shells, and coins. Wearing my baggy *shalwar kameez* and no jewelry, I looked drab and dowdy standing next to the splendidly dressed Kalash women. As I walked around the village and sat with them in their homes, it felt as though I had worn cheap yoga pants and a hoodie to a cocktail party. But I did wear one item that caught their attention—wraparound sunglasses secured with a neoprene lanyard. A line of Kalash women took turns trying on my shades and posing for photos.

Once we left the Kalash Valley, we were back in Muslim Pakistan. Purdah, the complex Islamic rules that govern interactions between genders, affected our interactions with the people we met. Purdah divides men from women, and thus, public from private. Private interior spaces were for women. Commerce, politics, and the public exterior spaces (roads and markets) were primarily reserved for men. In these outdoor spaces, men were everywhere, crammed inside and hanging off the sides of buses, squatting and smoking on the sidewalks, buying and selling goods from shops and stalls. The very few women I saw in these public spaces were completely covered by burkas.

Most of these women wore black burkas, which typically have three pieces: the heavy coat, a separate head covering, and the *niqab* (the veil that contains a slip for the eyes). However, I also saw some women—including several sitting on the flatbed of a pickup truck that blocked traffic in front of us—wearing the more restrictive, blue-colored burka, sometimes called the shuttlecock. The shuttlecock burka (which comes in other colors as well) covers a woman's body with a single piece of cloth and has lattice-like cutouts over the face instead of an open slit for the eyes, making it more difficult to see and breathe. Although the heavy, black burka might seem more restrictive, apparently, it is not, which likely is why the Taliban favors the shuttlecock style. Not surprisingly, I had no opportunity to interact with any of the burka-clad women I saw.

However, the purdah rules seemed more relaxed the farther north we went in Pakistan and the farther we moved from the big cities. In the villages we floated through on our rafts, the women did not wear burkas, only hijabs—scarves to cover their heads but not their faces. Except among young children, genders remained separated, but we saw women working in the fields and teaching in girls' schools. As we rafted down the river, we camped in villages, and I had the time and opportunity to meet the women who lived there.

The little girls liked me, perhaps because I looked like them. I had long dark hair and brown eyes, and my face was tan from the days outside in the open jeep and on the river. I was also the youngest of the four women in our group, and the combination of my looks and age may have made me appear the most approachable. With short, curly, blond hair and blue eyes, Mary Jane looked foreign, nothing like the girls in this part of Pakistan. Michèle and Joani are both tall, with short hair. One afternoon, when Michèle perched on a boulder and tried to read a book, twenty little boys swarmed her. With short hair, and wearing pants, she must have looked like a boy to them. When they realized she was a woman, they burst out laughing and ran away.

Our American river guides would have liked the opportunity to interact more with the Pakistani girls and women who lived in the villages we traveled through, but the guides were men. Culture and religion, purdah, kept men out of the places where the women lived and spent their days. I, however, was invited in. The women living in these small, isolated villages welcomed me into their homes with warm hospitality. They always offered me tea and something to eat, often chapati but occasionally locally grown grapes or pomegranates.

One Sunday morning when we camped near the village of Muduri, Mike found a way to join me when I visited with a large group in a private home. That morning, I unzipped the flap of my tent and found a group of girls silently sitting inches from the mesh screen, waiting for me to emerge. When I did, they started giggling and could not stop. One of the girls took my hand, and the group led me from the campsite along the river up into their village. We stopped outside a small, one-room home with a wood-burning stove in the center that provided heat and the only light, except what came through the open door. We entered, followed by a crowd of thirty to forty Pakistani women and children who squeezed into every available space on the floor and around the room. Everyone stared at me with curiosity. Who was I? What was I doing there? And what was I wearing? Smiling and laughing, we communicated basic information through the children who knew some English. Then, the woman of the house, dressed in a forest-green *shalwar kameez* and emerald hijab, offered me a seat on a cushion and served sweet chai and chapati.

As we shared the food and drink, some of the women and children were a little shy, hiding behind someone's skirt or behind a group standing together. Then I heard Mike's Alabama/Pakistani-accented English coming through the door seconds before he did. Mike had convinced a young boy to show him where I was. Mike slipped into the room, and before anyone could ask him to leave, plopped himself down on the floor and started shouting out greetings in Urdu (one of Pakistan's two official languages), Pashto (the predominant language in the North-West Frontier Province where we were), and maybe another local dialect he had learned. (Pakistanis speak seventy-four different languages, with less than 8 percent speaking Urdu.) I didn't know what language and dialect they spoke in this village or even whether anyone understood what Mike was saying, but he was allowed to stay.

At Mike's urging, the young boy who had led Mike into the home sang a song in English that he probably learned in school. The song's refrain was "on a summer day." Each verse was a different activity you could do on a summer day. The boy acted out each activity as he sang. The crowd cheered him on, clapping, laughing, and joining in to sing the refrain. With each verse, the boy gained confidence. When the "summer day" activity was dancing, he assumed the perfect pose and danced, delighting everyone in the room, as well as the men who had gathered in the doorway, probably attracted by the singing and laughter within. Although we did not share enough of a common language to engage in substantive conversation, it still felt like we had shared something meaningful—the tradition of hospitality to strangers, food, music, and a little joy.

That night, our group camped farther downstream on the grounds of a girls' school in the village of Damas. In the morning, when the girls arrived, I walked into school with them. I was not sure what to expect, but the head of the school and the teachers, all women, welcomed me. The headmistress and teachers spoke English, which was (and remains) the second official language of Pakistan—a holdover from Pakistan's colonial history under the British Empire. With a common language, we could have a substantive conversation and go beyond pleasantries. I had not had this opportunity with the other Pakistani women I had met. (Although our Pakistan river guides and crew could have translated for us, they were not present when I went into women's homes, and I doubt Pakistani women would have spoken freely through men they did not know.) This was my first opportunity to really speak with Pakistani women, but the teachers' fluency in English was not unexpected. Few Pakistanis spoke English as their first language, but a majority spoke it as a second language, making English—not Urdu or any of the other seventy-four native languages—the most widely spoken language in Pakistan.

I was excited to get to know these women and learn about the school they ran. The feeling was mutual. I was probably the only American, and perhaps the only foreigner, to visit this small local school, and they were excited to show it off. We started with a tour of the school. As we walked through the building and peeked into classrooms, the teachers described with pride the curriculum and the students' achievements. The teachers also told me about themselves, how and why they became teachers and the barriers they confronted.

After the tour, the headmistress asked me if I would speak to the students. I replied that, of course, I would be delighted. I asked what she would like me to talk about; what would interest the girls? She suggested I tell them something about my life, education, and job, but warned that only the older girls spoke more than rudimentary English. As I quickly organized my thoughts, the entire student body, about 160 girls, gathered and sat on the floor in front of me. Using simple words I hoped the younger girls could understand, I tried to communicate how pleased I was to meet them and visit their school. I told the girls a little about myself and asked about them. I spent most of the time answering their many questions as best I could. However, I had no good explanation for the strange mix of Pakistani and American clothes and rafting gear I wore and no simple answer to the question of why I was not married. With a glance at the headmistress, I ended by encouraging the girls to continue their education.

Educational opportunities for girls in this region of Pakistan deteriorated rapidly over the following few years as the Taliban took over the North-West Frontier Province (renamed Khyber Pakhtunkhwa [KPK] in 2010). Although the Pakistani constitution gives female citizens the right to an education, patriarchy, extremism, and poverty keep girls out of school. Nationwide, less than 50 percent of women in Pakistan are literate, with a much lower percentage in rural areas. Girls' schools in Pakistan that continue to hold classes, including in the KPK, are attacked, burned, and bombed by militants. Malala Yousafzai, the Pakistani Nobel laureate and education advocate, was raised and went to school in this area. The Taliban targeted Malala for her advocacy of education for girls and shot her in the head as she rode the school bus home. Years later, following the bombing and torching of schools in Chilas along the Karakoram Highway, Malala tweeted, "The extremists have shown what frightens them most—a girl with a book."

Although this was a rafting trip, we spent as much time traveling in a jeep as in a raft. On the rafts, we had safety equipment—life jackets, helmets, and throw bags with lines that could be tossed to someone who fell overboard. Every time we got in the jeeps, though, we tempted fate.

We had no safety equipment—no hardtops, roll bars, or airbags. But it hardly mattered because there were no seat belts either, and we would have been thrown from the jeep before airbags or a roll bar could have protected us. And a hardtop would have ruined the experience.

I loved standing on the back seat of the jeep, my head higher than the windshield, holding on to a flimsy frame (intended to hold the canvas top, not to serve as a roll bar), riding with the wind in my face and an unobstructed view of some of the tallest mountains in the world. And it was far better to look up at the mountains than down at the road beneath us. The unpaved dirt-and-gravel road was as twisted and treacherous as any river. At one point, the jeeps stopped so we could take pictures of a series of short switchbacks going up the face of the mountain. It looked like San Francisco's Lombard Street (the self-proclaimed "crookedest street in the world") on steroids, except if you missed a turn here, you died rather than hit a flowerpot or a car parked in a driveway. In the end, neither the treacherous road nor the hazardous jeeps determined our fates. All that mattered was the driver. And we had excellent ones who saved our lives at every blind curve and sheer drop.

As we drove into the Hindu Raj mountains, with the Hindu Kush mountain range to the west and the Karakoram range to the east, across the high passes and along narrow dirt roads, the *qawwali* music of Nusrat Fateh Ali Khan blasted from the jeeps' tape decks. Khan was the Pakistani vocal master of *qawwali*, a South Asian style of music involving sung poetry accompanied by rhythmic clapping, percussion instruments, and one or two harmoniums (a small reed organ played while seated, sometimes called the Indian accordion). *Qawwali* began on the Indian subcontinent in the thirteenth century as the music of Sufism, Islamic mysticism. In the late twentieth century, Nusrat Fateh Ali Khan brought *qawwali* music to the West through his many performances in the US and Europe. Khan was also well known for his Grammy-nominated collaborations with Peter Gabriel and his soundtracks for films directed by Martin Scorsese and Oliver Stone. Despite Khan's considerable fame in the West, I had never heard his *qawwali* music or his distinct voice until I traveled to Pakistan.

And then it was everywhere.

Nusrat Fateh Ali Khan died in August 1997, a month before I arrived in Pakistan. Wherever we went, Pakistanis were celebrating his life and music. It was like being in the US after Prince died and hearing "Purple Rain" everywhere. Khan's *qawwali* music continually blasted out of terrible, tinny speakers from every shop and square. We bought cassette tapes of his music from small kiosks and played the tapes at peak volume in the open jeeps as we traveled.

Qawwali songs are all about the buildup and are long—fifteen to thirty minutes is typical—perfect for hours of driving. And the lyrics repeat often, allowing non-Urdu speakers plenty of opportunities to sort out and learn the words. My favorite song for disappearing into the beauty of the mountains was one of Khan's signature songs, the haunting and mystical "Allah Hoo Allah Hoo." For standing on the back seat and bouncing to the rhythm of the holes and bumps in the road, "Mustt Mustt" was my go-to song. As we drove up and across the Shandur Pass, the site of the world's highest polo field at 12,300 feet, and then down to the watershed where the rivers flow together to form the Ghizar River, we clapped and chanted along with Nusrat Fateh Ali Khan: "Akhi ja malanga akhi da malanga akhi ja malanga tu Ali Ali Ali Ali . . . must must must must" and "Allah Hoo, Allah Hoo, Allah Hoo, Allah Hoo, Allah Hoo, Allah Hoo."

As we traveled through Pakistan, I noticed our river guide and fearless leader Mike using a communication trick I had learned from my friend Diane when we traveled through Europe after our college graduation. Our travels started in Yugoslavia (now Croatia, Serbia, and Bosnia and Herzegovina), where we were hosted and feted by Diane's extensive network of family and friends. A few knew English, but no one understood me when I tried to speak with them in English. Then I listened to Diane. When she spoke English, Diane did her best imitation of her Serbian-born father's strong accent. When I first heard this, I elbowed Diane, nudged her under the table, and gave her a dirty look. When she spoke that way in Chicago, she was mocking her dad. What was she doing now, insulting our hosts? But no one was offended. No one commented on Diane's accent. And no one else knew Diane was mimicking her father. They simply understood Diane's English better than they would have without the accent. I was reluctant to try a Serbian accent. I did not want to be rude, and I was not as good at it as Diane, who had perfected the accent over her childhood. But slowly, I began to imitate Diane imitating her father. It worked. The Yugoslavians smiled broadly, finally understanding me when I spoke English.

Listening to Mike switch between two distinct and strong accents, I knew he had perfected the technique. Despite years living in Denali National Park, Alaska, when he was not traveling the world working as a river guide, Mike still spoke with a twangy Alabama accent. Or at least that's how he spoke to Americans. When Mike spoke English to Pakistanis in Pakistan, he spoke with an Alabama imitation of a heavy Pakistani accent. To me, it sounded like Mike was acting in a cheesy, racist, and offensive comedy sketch. To the Pakistani river guides, drivers, and crew who traveled with us, Mike spoke clear, easy-to-comprehend English. Using the lesson I learned in Yugoslavia, I imitated Mike imitating the Pakistanis' English, without the Alabama twang. The technique worked as well in Pakistan as it had in Yugoslavia.

We transferred from jeeps to rafts and put in on the Phundar River. The first few days of rafting before the confluence of the Phundar and other rivers become the Ghizar River were easy class II and III rapids. Trying to assess our rafting abilities and figure out how we would run the big rapids with so few of us, our two American guides tried different combinations of the four women adventurers and two Pakistani river guides in Mike's oar boat and John's paddleboat.

My prior rafting experiences had all been in paddleboats, where I could actively take part in the action. Even though I could not read the river, gauge the rapids, or pick a line to run, all I needed to do in order to help rather than hinder progress in a paddleboat was to paddle in sync, follow instructions—"forward," "back," "left back," "right back," "stop," "HIGHSIDE!"—and not fall out. On previous rafting trips, I had viewed riding in the oar boat as too passive, doing nothing most of the time and then crouching on the bottom of the raft and holding on for dear life for a few minutes in the biggest rapids. But this river had long stretches of flat water where paddling was tiring and not particularly exciting. Lying back in the sun on the tube of the raft while someone else rowed these stretches was appealing.

I started spending time in the oar boat. When I wasn't feeling so lazy, I tried to learn how to row the raft. I was an American Red Cross–certified instructor in rowing, canoeing, and sailing—a prerequisite for a summer job teaching sailing at an overnight camp in Connecticut. Rowing a raft in a river, however, is not the same as rowing a boat on a lake, even without the rapids. River raft oars are longer and heavier and often are supposed to move independently in opposite directions. As you move down the river, most of the time, you are pushing the oars rather than pulling the oars, like when you face backward in a rowboat. My right arm was much stronger than my left, and I struggled to push with the same force on both sides and keep the raft on a straight course. It felt good when I got it right for a few consecutive strokes.

One quiet afternoon, as I slowly rowed downstream, I took advantage of the downtime to ask Mike about a story I had heard a few years earlier while hanging out at the small hotel bar at the Drake Bay Wilderness Resort on the Osa Peninsula in Costa Rica. A guest I did not know told a hilarious yet horrifying story of a raft trip on the Boh River in Borneo. Mountain Travel Sobek had categorized the trip as a level III cultural trip (on a scale of I to V), with three days of moderate rafting through a gorge. It turned into twelve death-defying days of unnavigable rapids, floods, foot rot, and flipped boats, all while covered head to toe, morning to night, by bees. I did not know if, or how much of, the story was true, but it entertained the crowd.

Back in Chicago after the Costa Rica trip, while spending a rainy Sunday afternoon browsing the travel section at a local bookstore, a book titled *Shooting the Boh* caught my eye. Remembering the outrageous story, I bought the book. It had more details, and was not as funny, but it definitely was the same Mountain Travel Sobek rafting trip. There could not be more than one such trip on the Boh River. But was the storyteller I met in Costa Rica on that trip? Or had he simply read the book and recounted the tale as his own?

After I signed on for the Pakistan trip, Mountain Travel Sobek sent out the twenty-two-day itinerary and identified the guides, including Mike. I wondered if this was the same Mike who had guided the Boh trip in Borneo. I flipped through my copy of *Shooting the Boh* and found where the author had identified the guides by their full names. It was the same Mike, the same guide. Now, floating down a river in Pakistan with Mike, I got an answer to my question about whether the storyteller had been on the Boh. Yes, he was, and his name is Bill. Mike remembered receiving a postcard from Bill sent from Costa Rica at the same time I was there and confirmed other details I remembered. I loved discovering connections formed through travel and the closing of this travel circle.

As Mike and I talked about the Boh River, a small group of boys ran along the shore, racing our raft. Competing against my inept rowing, the boys easily won. I rowed up to the shore to congratulate them. A group of kids gathered. Everyone wanted to shake my blue-gloved hand, but no one was brave enough to come aboard, despite Mike's boisterous invitation. We were about to push off from shore when an old man nimbly climbed aboard, followed by two little boys and two girls, emboldened by his move. The man had a tanned, deeply lined face with a long gray goatee. He wore *shalwar kameez* (of course) and the typical *pakol* or Chitrali cap—a soft, round-topped wool hat. The man motioned for me to move out of the way. After glancing at Mike for the okay before turning his boat over to a stranger, I moved aside. The old man took my place on the cooler that did double duty as a seat, confidently took hold of the oars, and expertly rowed the boat away from the shore.

Attaullah, who had been lounging on the back tube as I rowed, sat up and translated so that Mike and I could communicate with our guest rower. From his strokes, which were much better than mine, it was clear that the raft was in the hands of a professional. Attaullah confirmed that it was not our guest's first time rowing a boat on that river. For decades, he had rowed the ferry that shuttled people, goods, and animals across the river. Now, he was having a good time, showing off his prowess as he rowed back and forth between the banks of the slow-moving river, taking care not to move too far downstream—he and the kids had to walk back home after the ride.

These were our only guests bold enough to board either raft, but floating down the river, we frequently attracted huge groups of boys who would run along the shore beside us, waving and shouting as they raced the rafts downstream. One morning, as we floated by a boys' school, hundreds of boys streamed out of the building and started running along the shore, chased by a teacher with a switch trying vainly to herd them back to class. Reaching a long, rickety suspension bridge over the river before we did, the boys spilled onto the bridge, cramming every inch. As we passed under the bridge, the boys leaned first over one side and then the other, cheering us on. We shouted and waved back and hoped the bridge would not collapse.

Unlike the girls who invited me into their space, the boys invited themselves into ours. One day, when we stopped for a picnic lunch on some boulders along the shore, a group of about seventy-five boys in gray *shalwar kameez* surrounded us, staring at us intently. As we ate, the boys inched closer and closer, tightening the circle around us until we could feel their breaths on our necks—time to get back on the river. That night, we ate dinner in the large dining tent with front flaps pulled back and open. Out front, dozens of kids sat in rows, staggered like stadium seating at a theater, with the little ones in the front rows and the bigger ones in the back rows. They stared at us as though they were watching a movie or television. Finally, Mike suggested, "Think of yourself as the Discovery Channel." We were the show, featuring a different culture and species, one with strange dress—especially the life jackets, paddle gear, and helmets.

———— �ᨠᩈᩫᨶᨧᩥ᩠ᨦ —————

As the tributaries we rafted flowed together into the Ghizar River, the river and the intensity of its rapids changed. Some of the rapids were now too big or too risky for us to run safely. Depending on the rapid and surrounding topography, the guides chose one of two options to get the rafts past the unrunnable rapids: lining or portaging.

Lining keeps the raft in the river and is usually simpler and faster than portaging. With no one on board, the raft is pulled downriver using taut lines at the bow and stern. To do this safely and efficiently, the persons pulling the lines from the shore need excellent balance and the ability to leap between boulders as the raft moves downstream. It also helps to be strong because rafts are heavy, and the current is powerful. On the Ghizar, the four male river guides lined the rafts while the four female clients sat on the shore and watched. It was hard work for the guides and boring for the ones deemed incapable of assisting.

The alternative to lining the rafts was portaging them. Portaging requires taking the rafts out of the water and carrying them on land past the point where the river is too dangerous to run. Portaging is usually more difficult than lining and is only done when lining is not feasible. But on this trip, we could take advantage of the road that ran parallel to the river. We only had to find an accessible point where we could carry the rafts up to the road and tie the still-inflated rafts to the tops of the jeeps. We then slid into the jeeps, ducking under the rafts, and were driven down the road, past the rapids too dangerous to run.

Our last day on the river had the biggest rapids deemed runnable. After some fun, easy class III wave trains, we pulled to the shore to scout the two rapids Mike and John had named Love It and Leave It on their first descent of the Ghizar River. Love It (where my raft flipped) was the shorter of the two. Then, around a bend, the river went immediately into Leave It (where we rode on top of the capsized raft). Both were class V rapids, the most challenging category of extreme yet runnable rapids and the upper limit of what is possible in a commercial raft. According to the classification criteria, class V rapids are long, obstructed, very violent, or all three. Holes—where the river passes over the top of a rock or other obstacle near the surface, travels deep toward the bottom of the river, and then reverses back onto itself—may be unavoidable. Drops are large, routes are complex and demanding, and precise maneuvers are required. Mistakes are often unrecoverable. Swims (when the paddler is out of the raft) are dangerous, and rescue is often difficult.

Based on what they saw scouting the current conditions, and their prior experience on these rapids, Mike and John decided we could run Love It and Leave It, but we would need more paddlers in the rafts for power and propulsion and more weight and bodies in the rafts for high siding. (High siding, also called tube crashing, is when everyone throws their weight to one side of the raft to avoid an obstacle and try to keep the raft upright.) Attaullah, Jahangir, and I would paddle in Mike's oar boat. Joanie, Michèle, Mary Jane, and Assan (a second Pakistani river guide) would paddle in John's raft.

Qudrat, another of our Pakistani jeep drivers, offered to take my video camera and film the rafts going through the rapids. After debating whether he should film Love It or Leave It, we decided on Leave It. That second rapid was longer, and Qudrat could get a better panoramic shot. As I headed down to the river, Qudrat headed up to find the perfect spot for filming. (The description at the beginning of this chapter of our run upside down through the rapids relies on the video Qudrat shot, which captured details I missed as I tried not to drown.)

I climbed into the raft and took my place in the starboard bow, sitting on the tube that forms the sides of a self-bailing raft. I jammed my foot as far under that tube as it would go, hoping this would keep me inside the raft in the rapids ahead. Then, life jacket tightened, helmet secured, heart racing, and paddle in hand, I nodded to Mike that I was ready to go. Mike rowed the raft away from shore, and we moved into the first rapid. Immediately, diagonal waves coming from the right shifted the raft to the left and lined us up straight into the first hole, rather than around the hole, where we needed to go. We didn't stand a chance. The left side of the bow slammed into the hole. I was sitting on the right side of the bow. As the boat went up in the air, my foot stayed wedged under the tube. Briefly, my body flew perpendicular to the raft, rooted by my foothold. And then the raft flipped . . .

From that harrowing moment until I stepped onto dry land, I functioned on adrenaline. Once I was safe on shore, the adrenaline drained as quickly as it had kicked in. My muscles seemed to melt. I collapsed on the ground. While in the river and on the capsized raft, I was impervious to the cold. But onshore, the cold registered, and I started to shiver uncontrollably. Whatever had kept me going, it was gone.

If the capsize had happened deep in a gorge with no way out except by continuing downriver, I hope I would have found the strength, muscle control, and mental state necessary to get back in the raft and paddle. But I did not have to try. The road followed the river, and our jeeps were nearby. Without much discussion and no dissension, we ended our rafting adventure. We loaded the rafts onto the jeeps, climbed in, and headed into the town of Gilgit by road rather than by river. By the time we arrived in Gilgit, I had warmed up and calmed down.

Since my first rafting trip on the Green River in Utah when I was a teenager, I had known I could wind up under a capsized raft and had trained for the possibility. Fortunately, good guides and good luck had kept me in the raft or floating alongside it—until the Ghizar River got the better of us. I was not glad that we capsized in such a dangerous river in so remote an area or that I had wound up under the raft, and I would not willingly do it again, but I was relieved that it happened. I had handled it (with help) and survived unharmed. Strangely, the experience was empowering.

We arrived in Gilgit in time to watch several polo matches. Pakistani polo is not Palm Beach polo, or the polo played by Prince Charles and Prince William. The Pakistanis claim they invented polo and that the British co-opted and ruined the game by imposing rules. As played in Gilgit, there were no rules and no referees. Most of the time, I had no idea what was happening on the field as the horses galloped past me, but it was thrilling to watch. Sitting in the stands, perched on the edge of the bench, I leaned backward and forward, to the right and to the left, as though my movements could save the player whose helmet-less head was directly in the path of a swinging mallet. My motion was wasted, and my concern unmerited. No heads were smashed by mallets—at least not in the matches we watched.

Across the field from us, a row of musicians sat cross-legged, playing the shehnai (a double-reed wind instrument) and drums. The loud, grating sound they made had little in common with Nusrat Fateh Ali Khan's melodious voice and music. And they played nonstop, except when the call to prayer broadcast from the minaret of a nearby mosque would have drowned them out. The polo did not stop during the call to prayer. It continued at the same furious pace until the end of the match. Then, fans of the winning team—all men—joined the players on the field for a celebratory dance. It looked much like the joyous dance performed by the little boy in the village of Muduri as he sang "on a summer day."

From Gilgit, we headed out on the Karakoram Highway (KKH), driving from Gilgit to Karimabad, on to Gulmit, and then back to Islamabad. This drive was at least as dangerous as Pakistani polo. The Karakoram Highway runs 808 miles (1,300 kilometers) from Islamabad, Pakistan, to Kashgar, China. It took the Pakistani and Chinese governments over twenty years to blast through the intersection of three massive mountain ranges (the Himalayas, the Karakoram, and the Hindu Kush) and build the KKH. Over 1,000 men died during the construction, mostly from landslides. The resulting road remains treacherous, with hairpin curves and steep drops—no guardrails providing even an illusion of protection. The views from the road, however, are breathtakingly beautiful.

And riding in a jeep on the Karakoram Highway, I literally held my breath (like when my parents drove past a cemetery when I was a kid) each time our jeep drivers navigated a hairpin turn, exhaling only after they avoided the deadly plunge. Unfortunately, even the most skilled driver cannot avoid what is still the biggest danger on the Karakoram Highway: landslides that take the road and anyone on it crashing down into the valley or river. One of the worst landslides occurred a dozen years after we were there. On January 4, 2010, a massive landslide between Gulmit and Karimabad—exactly where we had been—obliterated the road and killed dozens of people. The debris from the landslide and the road was so extensive that it dammed the Hunza River and created a new lake, Attabad Lake, more than 300 feet deep and thirteen miles long.

On the last day of our trip, while driving the Karakoram Highway from Chilas to Islamabad, we encountered debris from a less severe landslide. The road was only blocked, not obliterated, but it was not expected to be cleared any time soon. It could have been weeks or months before the road reopened. This was such a common occurrence on the Karakoram Highway that workarounds had developed. Travelers and cargo would swap vehicles on either side of the landslide, or, if there were two landslides, travelers and cargo would be ferried between the slides by vehicles trapped in the middle, and swap vehicles on either end. When our jeeps arrived at the part of the road blocked by the landslide, we followed suit. We unloaded our gear, climbed to the top of the rubble, and walked across the debris to the other side of the landslide. Our jeeps, which had been such an integral part of the trip, were left behind. We loaded our gear onto a waiting bus and climbed in for the final miles of our journey.

In *qawwali*, by repeatedly and hypnotically chanting phrases, the audience is transported to a spiritual nirvana. Now, when I click on Spotify and hear Nusrat Fateh Ali Khan chant "Mustt Mustt," or "Allah Hoo Allah Hoo," I am transported, but only back to Pakistan as it was before 9/11, before the Taliban took over KPK, before Muslim bans and anti-Muslim rhetoric in the US. Back to a time when a Jewish American woman could travel to Pakistan, visit a girls' school, and sit in a villager's home and share tea and chapati, or just take a jeep and a rafting trip with three other adventuresome American women, two skilled American guides, and eight welcoming Pakistani men.

Margo rowing on a calm stretch of the river

The bunkhouse at Camp Muir, 10,080 feet up Mount Rainier

Chapter Two

"MAN AND HIS LAND"
TEEN TRAVEL

"WHY?" THE RISK-AVERSE, CAREER-DRIVEN lawyers at my firm would ask. Why would I travel somewhere that I needed to be protected by a guard armed with an AK-47? Why did I risk drowning under a capsized raft in class V rapids on a river in a remote region of Pakistan? They were baffled, and occasionally appalled, by my choices.

Why did I—a full-time working lawyer *without* great physical strength, stamina, conditioning, flexibility, coordination, power, speed, agility, or training—assume that I could go directly from an office high in the Sears Tower to a village high in the Himalayas? What made me think that Stairmaster sessions in the Sears Tower's basement gym were sufficient training for trekking in the Alps, Andes, Karakorum, Hindu Kush, and Himalayas? And why did I expect some free-weight routines to sufficiently strengthen my arms and shoulders for paddling ocean kayaks in Palau, Papua New Guinea, and Baja, and whitewater rafts in Pakistan, Chile, China, and Costa Rica? The answer to these questions likely goes back to my childhood and what I learned and experienced on my first adventure travel trips when I was a teenager.

———— ꦫꦮꦸꦗ꧀ꦮꦸꦩꦟ꧀꧀꧉ ————

Teen trips and so-called service trips are ubiquitous now, but they were not so when I was a teen. Nelson Wieters, chairman of the Department of Leisure and Environmental Resources Administration at George Williams College in suburban Downers Grove, Illinois, developed one of the first wilderness adventure programs for teens and managed it through an organization called Man and His Land Expeditions. I still have the spiral-bound document Man and His Land used to market these trips in 1974 and '75. Amid the photos and itineraries, Wieters included educational goals, methods, and objectives that seem to be aimed more at convincing parents to let their teens go than convincing teens to sign up. Despite the dense language, Wieters's innovative ideas about the powerful impact these summer trips could have on teenagers come through: "With adventure and intrigue provided through contrasting travel, geography, and people, the individual should constantly be exposed to unique and broadening media. It was also felt that a small group of young people of similar interest, working with and depending on each other, sharing adventuresome, aesthetic, AND difficult experiences, planning and decision-making together, should create the important potential of social growth."

And despite what now might seem an exclusionary and sexist name, *Man* and *His* Land was progressive on gender equality, ahead of its time. The trips were coed, with teenage girls and boys traveling together, taking on the same physical challenges, and assuming the same responsibilities. On the Western trip, girls and boys climbed the same mountain, on the same route, on the same rope teams. For nine weeks, girls and boys pitched their own tents, did their own laundry, and shopped and cooked together on the same cook crews. On the Caribbean program, girls and boys crewed on the same boats, took the same scuba certification course, and similarly tried to avoid cooking and cleaning duties. Such equality between the sexes was not the norm in the early to mid-seventies when schools required girls to take home economics and boys to take shop.

At thirteen, I wanted to join Man and His Land's nine-week camping trip across the Western United States, but the Man and His Land directors said no—I was too young. I had to complete a year of high school first. Instead, they offered me a place on the Caribbean trip with teenagers going into ninth through twelfth grades. What I wanted most was to get away from the Chicago suburb where I lived, so I agreed. My parents agreed, too. They were delighted to have me go away for the summer—anywhere would be fine.

The next year, I was old enough to join the Western trip. Over the decades since and through many moves, I somehow managed to hold on to two spiral-bound notebooks containing the detailed journal I kept that summer. Doing research for this book, I opened my journal for the first time since the trip ended and found a treasure trove—hundreds of pages crammed full of dates, places, people, details, descriptions, and sketches showing how to tie on crampons and laying out the three-tiered sleeping shelves in the bunkhouse at Camp Muir, 10,080 feet up Mount Rainier. Reading the journal as an adult and as the parent of a teenager, I cringed occasionally at my teenage self, but mostly I was proud of who I was and what I accomplished that summer. The details in the journal are the foundation of this chapter, but the experiences the journal relates are the foundation for my lifetime of travel and adventure.

Wieters claimed to have purposefully designed both the Caribbean and Western trips based on experimentation and research to accelerate learning. From my perspective as a teenage participant on both trips, they could not have been more different in design and execution. (In keeping with the differences between the two trips, in contrast to the hundreds of pages I wrote on the Western trip, on the Caribbean trip, I filled only three pages, front and back, with sketchy notes.) During the two-day orientation before heading out for our expeditions, I quickly got a sense of just how different.

On the Caribbean trip, meals had been as haphazard as everything else. The range of food available in the British Virgin Islands was limited, as was refrigeration on the boats. Around dinnertime, someone might ask, "Margo, are you hungry?" If I replied, "Yes," the response would be, "Okay, make some mac and cheese for everybody." And I would. But the next day, I would do the same thing to someone else. On one of my cooking days, digging around in the cabinet above the stove in the small galley, I found a stack of pads with detailed menu planners. I had no idea what these were for. We never used them.

On the Western trip, we used those planners for every meal. Rather than eating whatever was available, whenever we wanted it, cooked by whoever was unlucky enough to get hungry first, meals were planned and shopped for in advance. The guides divided the twenty-nine teenagers into cook crews. With a tight budget—$7 for breakfast and $20 for dinner to feed thirty-seven people, including the eight guides—and those meal-planning sheets, each cook crew was responsible for planning, shopping for, and cooking a certain number of breakfasts and dinners for the next portion of the trip—for example, Monday breakfast, Wednesday dinner, and Friday dinner. (One crew only did lunch and did it every day.) Between expeditions, we would pull into a town with a large grocery store and a laundromat. While our clothes were in the wash, we would hit the grocery store with our meal planners.

My journal describes our first shopping experience on the Western trip. My cook crew "headed for the produce department since we had that night's dinner and were serving a chef's salad, fresh fruit salad, and French bread. It was a really different way to shop. Besides shopping for 37 people, price was important. Instead of picking the best salad dressing, we picked the cheapest (it came down to Italian vs. creamy garlic and a democratic vote decided on creamy garlic). We fed 37 people dinner for around $19. Next, we shopped for our other meal of the week, breakfast. That was easy: 37 oranges and 5 different types of granola."

As we shopped, we loaded the ingredients for each meal into a separate cart. Then we headed for the dog-food aisle, usually the least busy aisle in the grocery store. There, we parked the loaded carts in reverse chronological order—the cart with ingredients for the meal farthest away was first in line. The bagged groceries then went into the trailer or cooler in reverse chronological order. At mealtime, the assigned crew would head to the trailer, grab the dry and cold bags sitting in front of the rows of groceries on the shelf and in the cooler, and start cooking the meal they planned. The only significant issue with the system was the impact the daily specials at the grocery store had on our diet. The cook crews had a tight budget and, depending on what was on sale that day, all the cook crews might have purchased powdered donuts, chicken, and corn. The fourth morning of powdered donuts for breakfast was not as good as the first.

Decades later, I still flash back to that summer every time I walk down the dog-food aisle of a grocery store. And I smile.

For me, the Western trip's high point, literally and experientially, was climbing Mount Rainier. It all started in Paradise. Everyone's climb of Mount Rainier starts in Paradise—the area on the south slope of Mount Rainier and the location of the Paradise Inn, Paradise Guide House, and a popular visitor center. According to the National Park Service, the origin of the name is prosaic. James Longmire, an early settler in what is now Mount Rainier National Park, brought his daughter-in-law Martha to the south slope of Mount Rainier, where she exclaimed, "Oh, what a paradise!"

Mount Rainier is a 14,410-foot active volcano. You cannot simply hike to the top. You need crampons, an ice ax, and a rope team to navigate the glaciers and keep you from plummeting into one of the massive crevasses. People have died attempting to climb Rainier. One terrible Sunday morning in June 1981, ten climbers and their guide were swept to their deaths by an avalanche while ascending to the summit. As I stood in Paradise, awed by the panorama, I was fourteen years old, weighed 102 pounds, and had little upper-body strength. I had no mountaineering experience. Yet, I had no doubt I could climb the mountain.

Our expedition guides were from Rainier Mountaineering Inc.

(RMI). In 1975, and for decades after that, RMI was the only company granted a concession contract by the National Park Service to guide climbs on Mount Rainer. Although the first female climbing guide on Mount Rainier, Alma Wagen, was hired in 1918 when most of the men went off to war, all six climbing guides for our group were men. At that time, RMI had no female guides. There was one woman on our team, Mary Martha. She was the cook.

We met our lead guide, Dan, and another guide, also named Dan, at the guide hut in Paradise. (Mary Martha later married one of the Dans.) The Dans handed each of us an ice ax and told us to put on sunglasses and lots of sunscreen, and follow them. Wearing cotton blue jeans and cotton T-shirts—not wicking, high-performance pants and shirts, which hadn't yet been invented—we hiked about half a mile to a permanent snowfield near Panorama Point. We dropped our packs and donned our cheap plastic rain gear—Robert Gore did not sell his first commercial order of Gore-Tex fabric until the following year.

Training started with self-arrests, the method for stopping your slide before you plummet into a crevasse or off a cliff. I practiced lying on my back, ice ax across my body, and quickly flipping over into a half-pike position with the pick of my ice ax in the snow, my shoulder on the ice ax, and my feet dug into the snow. Once I had the basic motion mastered from a static position lying on the ground, the next step was to repeat the movement while sliding down on my back, feet first. From there, I progressed to sliding headfirst on my stomach and performing a self-arrest, and then feetfirst and doing the same. It was not hard to stop sliding on the gentle slope, so I focused on mastering how to flip into a half-pike position without stabbing myself with the ice ax. It was fun but seemed excessive, as I did not really need the ice ax to stop; digging my boots into the snow as I flipped was enough.

About the time I became overconfident, Dan and Dan directed us to stop practicing and start climbing. We climbed up the snowfield to where the slope was steep and boots alone no longer stopped a slide. I flew down in various positions: on my back, stomach, and side, feet in front, feet in back, and feet to the side, performing self-arrests until I reached the bottom. Once we knew how to stop a fall, we learned how to come down a mountain without falling. We walked up and then walked down, trying to use the proper techniques. Back up the snowfield and back down, over and over.

After lunch, Dan and Dan broke us into groups of four and five. They spaced us about twenty-five feet apart and tied us into the rope and to each other. Above 10,000 feet, Mount Rainier is all glaciers and crevasses, so rope teams are essential for safety. If one person on the rope team falls into a crevasse, the others can save her by doing self-arrests and anchoring the team. On the other hand, if one person falls into a crevasse and her rope team cannot do self-arrests to stop her fall, she will take everyone down with her—off the cliff or into the crevasse. A rope team of four or five has greater stopping power—more weight—and provides more safety near crevasses than a smaller rope team. For our group of inexperienced climbers, more people on the rope team also meant more backup. If one person could not quickly self-arrest and anchor the rope securely, the others on the rope team could do it, making it less likely that the entire team would be dragged into the crevasse.

Low on the mountain, there were no crevasses on the snowfield, so we could learn without risking anyone's life. The rope teams practiced walking together at the same pace, keeping a constant amount of slack between each person. We tried to keep the rope almost taut between us, leaving enough slack that no one was dragged. Then we practiced having one person fall and the others perform self-arrests, saving each other.

When the guides decided we were good enough, we headed back to our campsite near Paradise. That evening, most of the group went to a talent show put on by employees at the Paradise Inn. I was tired from the day on the mountain and excited for the upcoming climb, so I stayed at camp, relaxed, and got a good night's sleep while I could.

The next morning, the guides fitted each of us with crampons, steel spikes that strapped onto our hiking boots for traction on the glaciers. We then packed the crampons for use higher on the mountain and started the long hike up to Camp Muir, our high camp at 10,080 feet. Camp Muir consisted of three small and basic buildings: the historic guide shelter (a.k.a. "the cook shack") built in 1916, the public shelter built in 1921 on the east end of the ridge, and the bunkhouse, a prefabricated wooden building flown up to Camp Muir and erected in 1971. RMI's clients, including our group, stayed in the bunkhouse.

Inside, the bunkhouse is about fifteen feet by thirty feet and fitted with three extended wooden shelves around the perimeter on three sides, forming a triple-layer *U*. Each shelf held sleeping bags, lined up side by side. At night, when the bags were filled with climbers, if one person on the shelf rolled over, everyone else had to roll, too. The space between the shelves was barely high enough to sit up. I don't know how the tall or big guys even got into or stayed on the shelves. For two nights, thirty-seven of us slept (or lay wide awake) in this tiny hut.

The afternoon before our ascent, the guides explained the climb to the summit. They described the route and what to expect at each stage. They also told us what would happen if any of us could not climb all the way to the top. There was no turning around. It was too dangerous to allow anyone to go back to Camp Muir by themselves without a full rope team, and the guides were not going to turn around an entire rope team because one person could not make it. If you could not climb farther, you would stay where you were. Each guide carried a sleeping bag in his backpack. If you could not climb further, he would pull out the sleeping bag and direct you to climb in. Then, he would stake the sleeping bag—with you in it—to the glacier, so it did not slide into a crevasse or off a cliff. For hours, you would lie in the sleeping bag, alone, staked to a glacier, high on a mountain, in the dark, with no shelter, in the freezing cold, while your rope team continued climbing without you. If all went well—you did not climb out to pee, the stake did not fail, and you did not freak out—the guide would pick you up on the way down.

Today, as a lawyer and the parent of a teenager, I am appalled that the National Park Service allowed RMI to leave exhausted, scared, and inexperienced children on the side of a mountain, in a sleeping bag, staked to a glacier. Perhaps my current disapproval stems from changed sensibilities, changed perceptions of liability and legal responsibility for minors, or changed notions of personal responsibility in the wilderness. But the climbing policy changed, too. In 1998, RMI guides started to provide a tent for any climber left behind. Sometime after that, guides occasionally rearranged rope teams so that one guide could lead a rope team of tired climbers back down to Camp Muir. Finally, in 2007, in the renewal of RMI's ten-year concession to guide climbers to the summit, the National Park Service expressly prohibited leaving climbers on guided summited attempts alone on a glacier.

In 1975, I was a fourteen-year-old rising high school sophomore, and it did not dawn on me that anything was wrong with the practice. But I certainly knew I was not going to be left behind, alone at night, in a sleeping bag staked to a glacier. Climbing to the summit was my only option.

The guides divided our group into the rope teams for the climb to the summit. I was on Gary's rope team, Red Dog Three, with my friend and tentmate Karen, plus Rich and Bob. Red Dog Three met briefly for a rope-team pep talk, and then it was time for an early dinner and an early bedtime.

In late July, groups heading for the summit left Camp Muir by about 1 a.m. Once the sun came up, the snow began to melt, and the risk of avalanche increased. Climbers needed to reach the summit and be back at Camp Muir before the snow turned to slush. Because we needed to wake up at midnight, we were in our sleeping bags by 6 p.m. Between the early hour and the terrible sleeping arrangements, I don't know how much anyone slept. I must have dozed off at some point, though, because I jumped when the guides woke us a little after midnight.

It was a perfect night for the climb, one of only a handful of nights that whole summer with such ideal conditions. The air was crisp and clear, and the temperature was warm. The moon was full, and there were no clouds. The reflection of the moon off the snowfields and glaciers was so bright that we were able to climb and even cross crevasses without using our headlamps. It was a great start to what would be a long night and day, and this boost at the beginning added to the reserves (physical and mental) I would need over the next twelve hours.

Leaving Camp Muir, we slowly climbed in a rising traverse across the Cowlitz Glacier to the top of Cathedral Gap at 10,800 feet. To keep going at a steady pace, I used a modified version of the rest step I learned a few weeks earlier while hiking in Rocky Mountain National Park. At altitude and on steep slopes, the rest step slows your cadence, relaxes your muscles, and conserves energy. Done correctly, it takes the pressure and strain off your muscles and transfers it to your bone structure. I never mastered the shift from muscle to bone—even harder with crampons in the snow—but I did master the other part of the rest step, pacing myself based on my breaths. I inhaled deeply and exhaled fully between each step. Earlier in the climb, at lower altitudes, I took one deep breath between steps. Moving higher, two deep breaths between steps. And higher, three deep breaths between steps. I knew the key to reaching the summit was maintaining a slow, steady pace, always moving forward. At first, it seemed excruciatingly slow, but it conserved energy and was easier, and ultimately faster than rushing until I was breathless or could not move, then taking a break and restarting.

We followed the Disappointment Cleaver route, the easiest and most popular route to the summit. Back at Camp Muir, our teenage imaginations created and spread stories of ax murderers wielding "disappointment cleavers" to kill climbers before they reached the summit. Or maybe the name was in honor of a climber that escaped the cleaver-wielding murderer and made it to the summit, hence "disappointment cleaver." Fortunately, neither version is how the route got its name. *Cleaver* is the geological term for a narrow ridge of rock that separates the flow of glacial ice into two glaciers flanking and flowing parallel to the ridge. Someone with an active imagination, maybe a teenager, thought this geological formation resembled a meat cleaver slicing a hunk of meat into two sections. The *Disappointment* part of the name comes from where it occurs on the climb.

For many novice climbers, the top of Disappointment Cleaver, at 12,300 feet, is the hardest part of the climb, and typically a crucial point for deciding whether to continue to the summit. From Ingraham Flats, the top of the Cleaver appears to be the summit of the mountain. When you look up the glacier, you are climbing toward the highest point on the horizon. You see nothing higher. The 1,200-foot climb from Ingraham Flats to the top of Disappointment Cleaver is one of the steepest slopes on the entire route. After an arduous climb, perhaps using their last bits of physical and mental energy, some climbers reach the top of Disappointment Cleaver and are surprised to discover it is not the summit. They are only halfway there. In their disappointment, they can't go on.

I had the opposite reaction. It helped that we had been well prepped on the route, and, always the good student, I paid close attention. According to my contemporaneous journal, "When I got to the top of Disappointment Cleaver, and I was still moving and breathing, I was ecstatic—over halfway there!" The difference between disappointment and excitement at reaching the halfway point often determined a climber's success. At the top of the Cleaver, we took a break. As we climbed higher, the temperature had plummeted. I took off my backpack, pulled out my remaining layers, and put them on to stay warm.

At the top of Disappointment Cleaver, Red Dog Three was strong. We left the rest break with excitement and energy, ready to conquer the next half of the climb. Then, fifteen minutes later, Karen stopped and said she could not go any farther. Not wanting to see her left alone on the glacier, I tried to encourage her to keep going. Gary interrupted me and asked Karen whether she could make it to the summit. No, she could not. That was it. Just as they had explained the previous day, Gary pulled a sleeping bag from his backpack, secured Karen inside, and staked the bag to the mountain. With a stern warning to Karen that she must not get out of the sleeping bag for any reason, and an estimate of what time we would return, we turned our backs on Karen and kept climbing.

Above Disappointment Cleaver, the Ingraham and Emmons Glaciers meet. From the top of Disappointment Cleaver to the crater rim, the mountain is an uninterrupted maze of large crevasses and steep slopes. Climbing this unbelievably gorgeous part of the mountain was terrifying, if I thought about it. So I didn't. I just kept going at the same steady, slow pace—one foot and then the other.

The shifting crevasses determine the changing route on this section of the mountain. That night, the safest route was steep. On the switchbacks, my feet were at a fifteen-degree angle to my legs. My crampons gripped the snow, and I was steady, but it was hard on my ankles and slowed me down even more. And I still had not seen the summit, which was discouraging. Then, at our next rest stop, I looked up, and there it was—the summit of Mount Rainier. I must have been watching my feet, not the horizon, so I did not see the summit until we stopped. The excitement did not last long. Continuing the climb with the summit now in sight but seemingly not getting any closer, I started to drag, physically and mentally. My earlier enthusiasm and energy disappeared. For me, this was the most challenging stretch of the climb.

Then we hit a wall—an actual wall, not a metaphorical one. Gary climbed up, kicking in with his crampons and swinging his ice ax. Our ice axes were primarily for self-arrests, to stop ourselves from plummeting into a crevasse and pulling our rope team in with us, but during the full day we had spent at Camp Muir, we had learned how to climb with them. I paused a minute, getting ready to start up, when I felt a pull around my waist. Without asking me, or even telling me, Gary pulled me up the wall. Before I knew what was happening, I was standing on top. I was mad, certain I could have done it myself. Then I watched the two strong teenage boys roped behind me struggle and slide as they slowly climbed the wall. I changed my mind, grateful that Gary had accurately estimated my upper-body strength (or lack thereof). Most of the climb had been one foot after another, just keep going, requiring endurance and mental strength. I had those. But scaling the wall required upper-body physical strength I lacked. I could not have done it without help. I had that help, and we kept climbing. The final push was across the crater—a stark reminder that Mount Rainier is a volcano, and a live one at that.

In the early hours of July 22, 1975, I reached the summit of Mount Rainier and was greeted with hugs, laughter, and tears from my friend Karen—a different Karen, not the girl we left in a sleeping bag staked to a glacier. Red Dog Three was one of the first rope teams up the mountain.

Over the next thirty minutes, the remaining rope teams straggled up to the top. I thought it might be discouraging for the teams bringing up the rear to see me—small and weak—on the summit, but they later told me how motivating it was. If I could make it, they certainly could. When Adam, the last man on the last rope team, reached the summit, we all cheered.

I had been sure I would make it the top. From the other guides' reactions when they summited with later rope teams and saw my smiling face, I knew they had been as sure that I would not. What they failed to appreciate when they misjudged me was not my determination to summit the mountain but my determination not to be left alone in the dark in a sleeping bag staked to a glacier.

We didn't stay long at the summit. Once we stopped moving, it was hard to keep warm. And we needed to get down before the rising sun started to melt the glaciers and the slope turned to slush. After taking time to appreciate the amazing views looking *down* on the Cascade Range and Olympic Mountains and posing for plenty of photos, we started our descent.

Going down was hard on the knees, even young knees. I kept falling. When I fell, it was easier to simply slide, glissading down on my butt, than to get up and start walking again. And it was faster. But it was also dangerous. Every time I did it, Gary yelled, "Margo, get off your ass and walk." On one of the slides, my ankle slammed hard against a rock, twisting and bruising it just enough to make the rest of the descent even harder.

We stopped to pick up the Karen left behind. Her relief was palpable. Gary roped Karen back in with us, and Red Dog Three climbed down to Camp Muir. Once we got to Camp Muir, it was a free-for-all. Untied from our rope teams, free of the crampons, and without the risk of crevasses, some of the kids fairly flew down the mountain. I did not have the speed or energy to keep up with them. I had lost the motivation and awe that had kept me going on the ascent. At one point, to get me moving faster, one of the Dans took my backpack and ice ax and gave me his ski poles. I might have sped up a little after that, but I was still the last one in our group to get down. I didn't care. I had summited a 14,410-foot glaciated volcano with an average summit success rate of only 50 percent. In 1975,

6,143 climbers attempted the climb. Only 3,564, including me, succeeded and summited. I climbed that mountain.

After a few days of reflection, I wrote, "It's probably the most exciting experience I'll ever have in my life." I was fourteen when I summited and had just turned fifteen when I wrote that, and, fortunately, it was not true. But a framed copy of my certificate of achievement memorializing my ascent of Mount Rainier, signed by all the guides, hung in my powder room for years next to my diplomas from Yale College and Northwestern University School of Law. And forty-one years later, when I hiked the trails just above Paradise with my son, Jake, I was still in awe that I had climbed that mountain.

In his introduction for the Man and His Land trips, Nelson Wieters wrote, "An acceleration of the self-confidence level through successful confrontation with adventure, a realignment of the learning attitudes, and a dramatic awareness of man's environment on his life. These are the objectives of this program." Objectives achieved.

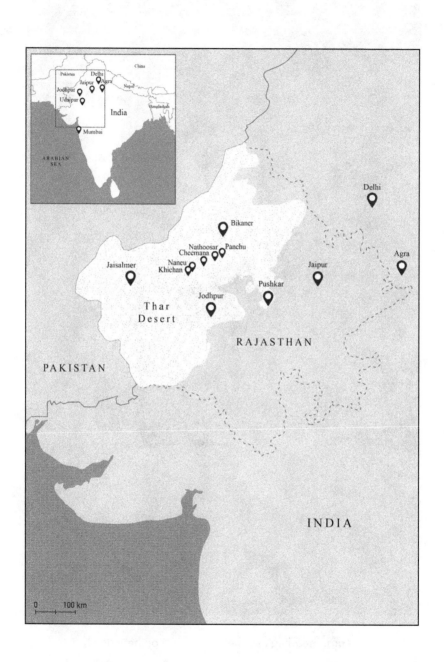

Margo heading into the Thar Desert on her camel

Courtesy of Andrew Meissner, reprinted with permission

Negotiations at the Pushkar Fair

Courtesy of Andrew Meissner, reprinted with permission

Chapter Three

HORN OK PLEASE
TRAVEL IN INDIA "INDEFINITELY DELAYED"

DURING MY FIRST YEAR of law school, I escaped the tedium of torts and contract law by traveling to India. Sort of. Since I had no money or time to actually fly to India, I traveled vicariously while watching *The Jewel in the Crown*. Absorbed by the doomed romance and the private and public violence marking the end of colonialism in India, I sat glued to the television for the fourteen-part, fifteen-hour Masterpiece Theatre serialization of *The Raj Quartet* novels by Paul Scott. Oh, how it made me want to travel to India—in person.

A decade later, I finally did. I made plans to travel to India with my friend Andrew, whom I met the year before, trekking in Nepal. Not all good friends are good travel companions. Not all good travel companions become good friends. But based on weeks hiking together high in the Himalayas, I knew Andrew was both. And as an LA-based vegetarian who practiced yoga and meditated, Andrew had the laid-back and flexible attitude needed to enjoy a trip to India.

To help us cope with the massive transportation and logistical issues we anticipated, we signed up for a three-week small-group tour of Rajasthan. The final bulletin for the trip contained multiple warnings and instructions. Most addressed potential travel issues due to overbooked, delayed, or canceled transportation, as well as extremely tight accommodations that might require hotel changes at the last minute. It bluntly concluded, "Therefore, we advise you come to India fully aware that such delays and changes can occur." Okay, we were forewarned.

Andrew and I planned to arrive in Delhi a few days before the tour started so we could go to Agra and visit the Taj Mahal, India's iconic monument to eternal love. (Located in Uttar Pradesh, it wasn't on our Rajasthan itinerary.) Andrew and I flew separately from the US, but our flights were both due to land in New Delhi on the same day, around 2 a.m. Why do international flights to New Delhi typically land between one and three in the morning? I suspect that it has nothing to do with logistics or the distances traveled from the other side of the world. No, it is an intentional trial by fire. Foreign tourists, arriving jet-lagged and disoriented, are thrust into the teeming crowds and chaos of an Indian airport and city in the middle of the night. If you cannot navigate your way out of the airport and find your hotel, you cannot handle India.

Andrew's flight arrived relatively on time. He checked the arrival board for information on my flight and saw "Indefinitely Delayed." Yes, *indefinitely delayed*. Not canceled, which would have required Air India to put passengers on another flight. Not delayed for several hours, which would have meant the flight had a definite departure time or at least a definite departure day. No . . . just indefinitely delayed.

On the other end of the "indefinite delay," I sat in Hong Kong International Airport. When it became apparent that my flight would not leave that day, or even the next, and that Air India would not transfer me to another airline or pay for a hotel room during the indefinite delay, I deferred the refund battle until I returned to the US and started searching for alternatives. The only flight I could find was standby on Gulf Air from Hong Kong to Bangkok, connecting to an Aeroflot flight (one of the few airlines with a safety rating even lower than Air India) to New Delhi. Yes, I wanted to see the Taj Mahal, but I also wanted to live. I kept looking. A resourceful Cathay Pacific ticket agent found a flight for the next day on Cathay Pacific from Hong Kong to Bangkok, connecting there to a Thai

Airways flight to New Delhi. These flights seemed more likely to leave and land safely. I booked and paid for this second set of tickets from Hong Kong to New Delhi. Defeated yet triumphant, I took a taxi back to the Hong Kong hotel where I had checked out just a few hours earlier. When I got to my room, I looked out the window and saw that the desk clerk, having realized that a travel snafu had caused my return, had upgraded me to a spectacular harbor-view room. I appreciated the view, but before I could enjoy it, I had to get in touch with Andrew.

This was in the days before cell phones and international texts, and even before use-anywhere internet email, so I sent a fax to Andrew at his hotel in New Delhi and hoped someone would deliver it to him. I explained what had happened with my Air India flight and told Andrew to go ahead without me, not to miss the Taj Mahal. I gave him my new flight information and said I would meet him in Agra if I could.

My two flights were on schedule, and I arrived in New Delhi between 1 and 2 a.m., of course. I took a taxi to the Claridges Hotel, where I had prepaid for a nonrefundable room for the previous night, which I forfeited when my Air India flight was indefinitely delayed. I also had a prepaid, nonrefundable reservation for the following night, when I was supposed to return from Agra. I did not, however, have a reservation for the night I arrived, and the hotel was full. It went downhill from there. Because I was not a current hotel guest, the staff refused to cash my traveler's checks, which, in the pre-ATM era, left me with no local currency. In fact, the staff flatly refused to assist me in any way. They acted as though I were a vagrant loitering in their lobby, rather than a quasi-guest in need. It was the middle of the night, I was exhausted from jet lag and long flights, and I had no hotel room or cash. If they were going to treat me like a vagrant, I told them, then I would sleep in the lobby. They believed me. The hotel staff placed a phone call for me to the tour company's local representative in Delhi.

When he arrived, I apologized for calling him in the middle of the night. No need to apologize, he said; he was awake and working. The hours between midnight and 4 a.m.—when flustered international travelers arrived and departed—were his busiest hours. He provided a clear explanation of the situation and offered a possible solution. There was not a hotel room to be had in Delhi that night, and the morning tourist train to Agra was sold out. He had, however, arranged for a taxi to drive me to Agra, leaving immediately and arriving about dawn. I could pay the driver when we arrived at my hotel in Agra—where I had a room for the night I was about to spend in the back seat of a taxi—and could exchange my traveler's checks.

I blame my decision to get in that taxi on jet lag and a desire not to leave India without seeing the Taj Mahal. The desire to live that had kept me off the Aeroflot flight had waned. With no other better option at that moment, I left my duffel bag with the tour company's Delhi representative (the hotel, of course, would not hold it for me until my return that evening), grabbed my daypack, and climbed into the back seat of a beat-up taxi with bald tires and no seat belts to drive for hours through the countryside at night.

Any danger I faced as a woman, alone, at night, in a foreign country, with no local currency and no cell phone (again, they had not been invented yet) was nothing compared to the danger I faced riding in a taxi in India, with its deplorable roads and equally deplorable accident rate. When you drive in an Indian city, there are no lanes. Cars, trucks, motorcycles, cycle-rickshaws, and cows fill in all available space, jockeying for position like runners at the start of a road race. Outside of the cities, driving is even deadlier. Highways, where vehicles travel at high speeds, are often a single lane with traffic running in both directions. The roads did not start like that, but the pavement, which is laid on gravel or dirt, erodes over time on both sides, getting narrower and narrower until it is the width of one car, though it's still a two-way road. When cars or trucks approach each other from opposite directions, if they see each other, they engage in a terrifying game of chicken. Too often, neither yields, and everyone dies. If they don't see each other, everyone dies.

Once the taxi moved out of Delhi, I could see nothing but the dark sky and the dim yellow beam of the headlights on the road ahead. I lay down on the back seat and tried to take a nap. I must have drifted off, because I woke abruptly when the taxi shuddered and stopped in the middle of the road, in the middle of nowhere. Based on the time and the pitch darkness, I figured we were still about an hour short of Agra. Before I could ask what happened, the driver got out of the car, opened the hood, and started banging the engine with a wrench. I could not imagine how hitting the engine would restart the car, but the driver seemed confident that this would work. As time passed, I knew I had to get out of that taxi, which was sitting right in the middle of an unlighted, one-lane, two-way road. I kept envisioning a brightly painted truck, decorated with tassels and marigolds and bearing a sign saying "Horn OK Please," plowing head-on into the taxi, killing the driver and me on impact.

How did I know that the truck that killed us would say "Horn OK Please"? Because virtually every truck in India had this grammatically incorrect phrase painted across its back. "Horn OK Please" was the most ubiquitous phrase in India. "Horn OK Please" was synonymous with India.

"Could we push the taxi to the side, out of the center of the road?" I asked the driver.

"*Koi baat nahi. Koi baat nahi.* No problem. No problem," he replied, as though repeating it in Hindi and English would make it true.

Indians are fatalistic, which may be why they continue to travel on such roads. But I am not Hindu.

"I am going to wait in the field over there," I told him, pointing in a general direction off the road.

In the darkness, I slowly walked away from the taxi until the road began to disappear beneath my feet. Then I walked just a little farther. Miraculously, soon after I stepped into the field, the taxi sprang to life. With the taxi's headlights now on to light the way, I sprinted back to the road and climbed into the back seat again. Without further incident, we drove the rest of the way to Agra.

The taxi dropped me off at the hotel where I had paid for the night and where Andrew managed to spend the night. This hotel exchanged my traveler's checks for Indian rupees without problem, and I paid the waiting taxi driver. With local currency in my pocket, I did not feel so vulnerable in case something else went wrong—which it would. This was India. From the lobby telephone, I called Andrew's room.

"Hi, I'm here."

"What time is it?" he replied.

"Early, but I need to go to the Taj Mahal. If I sit down, I won't be able to get up and out the door again. Will you meet me in the lobby, please?"

"When?"

"Now."

The Taj Mahal opens for tourists at sunrise. Andrew, my easygoing travel companion, and I arrived at the gate soon after it opened.

The Mughal emperor Shah Jahan built the Taj Mahal as a mausoleum for the remains of his favorite wife, Mumtaz Mahal. (He had two other wives while she was alive.) Mumtaz Mahal died in 1631 after giving birth to her fourteenth child in nineteen years!

The iconic image of the Taj Mahal is recognizable worldwide, but the millions of photographs of the Taj Mahal fail to capture the perfection of the design and the optical illusions you see in person. Only by standing in the arch of the Great Gate, the *Darwaza-i-rauza*, looking down the central reflecting pool leading to the mausoleum and minarets, can you fully appreciate its beauty and symmetry. From a distance, the minarets at each of the four corners appear vertical to the eye, look vertical in the reflecting pool, and look vertical in the millions of photographs taken from this vantage point. But as you approach each minaret, you can see that it actually leans slightly outward, away from the main building. This angle serves two purposes. The optical illusion created by the leaning minarets presents a symmetrical and perfect scene, and the leaning minarets also protect the central mausoleum. In the event of an earthquake or attack, due to the angle, a collapsing minaret likely would fall away from the mausoleum.

Seeing the Taj Mahal in person, I also realized that the varying colors of the marble seen in photos is not simply due to filters enhancing the image. In just a few hours of being there, we saw several color changes. In the dawn light, the Taj Mahal's marble exterior appeared pink, and even glowed. When we returned at noon after touring the nearby (and nearly as spectacular) Red Fort, the building's marble appeared pure white in the harsh light. The changing hues of the marble are genuine and truly astonishing. The Taj Mahal exceeded the hype. No question: it was worth all that effort to get there.

That afternoon, Andrew and I took the train to Delhi and back to the inhospitable Claridges Hotel. The next morning, we joined the ten other Americans in our group and our Indian guide. The tour had been scheduled around the Pushkar Fair, held each November at the time of the Kartik Purnima full moon. (Kartik is the month in the Hindu calendar that falls in November and December. Kartik Purnima is the fifteenth lunar day—the full-moon day—of the month of Kartik, and it is celebrated by Hindus as the day Lord Shiva defeated the demon Tripurasura.)

One of the oldest cities in India, Pushkar is a holy place sited around a sacred lake. Legends say that the lake was created when the god Brahma killed a demon with a lotus flower, and the petals floated down to earth, forming the lake. Once a year for eight days, this small city is transformed. Camel traders from all over rural India gather in Pushkar for what purports to be the world's largest camel fair. Tens of thousands of camels are brought here for sale, along with horses, cows, goats, sheep, textiles, and food. Musicians, snake charmers, dancers, fortune-tellers, magicians, and others provide entertainment. Toward the end of the fair, the camel traders, entertainers, and tourists are joined by Hindu pilgrims who travel to Pushkar to bathe in the sacred waters of the lake under the full moon.

Most Western tourists in India succumb to "Delhi belly" at some point in their travels. My time came while I was at the Pushkar Fair. In some ways, it was not the worst place to be so sick. As I walked around, when I felt nauseous, I would vomit where I stood, then kick dust over the result. My offering blended in with the sand, dust, and dung of the 50,000 animals that were milling around for sale. The pungent smells of the fair easily overwhelmed any smell from my puking. No one noticed the vomit in the dirt and sand or would have cared if they did.

My memories of the fair may be influenced by my case of Delhi belly. What I remember most is the toilet. We were staying in foreign tourist accommodations set up by the Government of Rajasthan Department of Tourism. The location was perfect, in the desert on the edge of the fairgrounds. Each large tent had two separate "rooms." The front room contained basic furniture, sufficient for sleeping and relaxing, relatively luxurious for a tent in the middle of thousands of camels. The back room, however, is what amazed me. It contained a white porcelain sink and a white porcelain toilet. The sink had running water, and the toilet flushed. In my nauseated state, I was thrilled to have such plumbing. However, after making frequent use of the toilet and sink, I started to think about the mechanics of this plumbing. What and where was the infrastructure? This tent city did not exist the previous week and would not exist the following week. The water was coming from large tanks. Where did the waste go? Two long rows of tents were lined up back-to-back. I walked around my tent and discovered that these sparkling-clean, white porcelain fixtures were draining into the ditch between the two rows of tents. Any smell and lack of sanitation, like my vomit on the fairgrounds, just blended into the overall atmosphere.

Following the Pushkar Fair, our group set off on a four-day, four-night camel trek in the Thar Desert in the area between Bikaner and Jaisalmer. Although we were in the desert, we were in the second-most populous country in the world, and people lived among the dunes and rolling sand. We traveled by camel across the desert and through the remote villages of Panchu, Nathoosar, Cheemana, Naneu, and Khichan.

On the first day, the lead camel driver sized me up and misjudged me based on my size. He assigned me to a small, old, slow female camel that dragged along at the back of the pack, often refusing to move if she was not being led. Because I spent the day in everyone else's dust, I was not aware that, in the front of the pack, someone else was having the opposite problem with his camel. The next morning, I was reassigned to a different camel, a fast male teenager. I don't remember his name, but for the purposes of telling this story, I am going to call him Anirudh, which I believe is a traditional but trendy Rajasthani boy's name that means "unrestrained" or "unstoppable."

Anirudh was not mean. He did not spit, bite, or kick. But he was excitable, stubborn, and hard to control. The minute the handler let go of Anirudh's lead, he was off, with me on his back. Although Anirudh usually went in the correct general direction, staying on track, he walked and galloped ahead of everyone. I couldn't control him: I could not get him to slow down or stop and stand still. The only command I could issue effectively was the command to drop to the ground. A camel drops to the ground in stages. First, he lowers himself to a kneeling position on his front legs while his back legs are still in a standing position. This is not graceful. It is a jerking movement that puts any rider in a precarious position, leaning forward and down. Then the camel kneels on his back legs, another jerking move, but at least to a more level position. Finally, the camel lowers his body to the ground. When Anirudh and I got too far ahead of the group, I would issue the order, and he would kneel and lie down. We would stay there, Anirudh's legs folded beneath him, lying in the sand in the middle of the track, with me sitting on him until the group caught up. I began to wonder whether Anirudh was outsmarting me, running ahead so he could lie down and chew his cud.

Near the end of the trek, when it seemed that Anirudh and I had come to an understanding—he was in charge, but not out of control, and I enjoyed the ride—Anirudh took off, heading toward a village. I could not even get him to obey my one effective command. He sped ahead and then abruptly turned in to a courtyard and stopped. He was home. We were in the village where the crew and camels lived. Thanks to my uncontrollable camel, we (everyone else joined us) had an unplanned and wonderful stop in the village and had a chance to meet the families of our guides and crew.

The camel trek was not glamping, but when we arrived at camp at the end of the day, the tents were pitched and meals were prepared and served.

The first night, the crew thought it would be a treat if they set up our tents on top of a small dune with a gorgeous, sweeping view. It was indeed a spectacular site for our first campground, but, after riding a camel all day, it was painful to climb even a small dune. Camels are wider than horses, and the straddle over the saddle is a stretch for anyone who is not a competitive gymnast or yogi. And unlike horse saddles, which have stirrups to support and redistribute some of the rider's weight, providing relief for knees and hips, we sat on cushions that had no stirrups. When I climbed off the camel that first night, my legs hurt and wobbled. I struggled to lift one foot after the other as I headed up the dune through the shifting sand to my tent pitched at the top. Although I was focusing on my own progress, I don't remember anyone moving any better than I did. No one complained, but the crew must have noticed our struggles. The remaining nights, the crew set up camp beside the dunes, not on top of them.

As a vegetarian, in the days before the HappyCow app directed me to vegetarian and vegan restaurants around the world, I used to struggle to find local food I could eat. A vegetarian meal was often nothing more than the meal served to the omnivores—but without the entrée. And then, after one bite of the side dishes, I usually suspected the vegetables were cooked in animal fat. But India was a huge exception. India has more vegetarians than the rest of the world combined. About 32 percent of Indians are vegetarians. In 1995, that was more than 300 million vegetarians, more than 430 million today. Indian cuisine embraces vegetarianism. And I embrace Indian food.

The first evening in the desert, I climbed down the dune from my tent, drawn to the cook tent by the wonderful smell of simmering Indian spices. When the crew served dinner, however, none of the food matched those aromas. Instead, it was what Indians thought Western tourists wanted to eat—Western food. What I had smelled cooking was being prepared for the Indian crew, not for us tourists. When I went over to the cook tent to see if there might be a bit of Indian food to share, I saw a row of chutneys in varieties I had never tasted before. This was the kind of food I had hoped for in the Thar Desert.

Luckily, switching my menu from blah Western food to flavorful vegetarian Indian food was easy. I simply had to ask. Some in our group were concerned that if they switched to Indian food, they would succumb to Delhi belly—not something they wanted to deal with while riding a camel and camping in the desert without even fake plumbing like we had in Pushkar. But I figured the choice of cuisine made no difference. The same person cooked all the food under the same conditions. If he was healthy, the food-prep area was clean, and only bottled water was used to wash vegetables and cook, no one would get sick, regardless of whether they ate Western or Indian food. And, fortunately, no one in our group got sick during our desert trek.

I loved being in the desert, soaking up the heat and disappearing into the sweeping vistas. But I may have been the only one who enjoyed the four days and four nights of intense heat, endless sand, and unpredictable camels. Although the tour company continued to run the Rajasthan trip, it never again included such a long camel trek, limiting that portion of the tour to two days and one night.

Following the camel trek, we were off to Jaisalmer—a 140-kilometer drive through a monotonous flat landscape of sand and scrub. Occasionally, the interminable yellow sand was punctuated by brilliant bursts of color—fuchsia, magenta, red, and orange—as we drove past women dressed in vibrant colored saris standing out against the stark terrain. Then, suddenly, we saw the spectacular Jaisalmer Fort rising out of the desert. From a distance, it probably looks much as it did in 1156, when it was built along the caravan routes from Egypt, Arabia, Persia, and Central Asia to Delhi and Gujarat. The fort, also known as Sonar Quila (Golden Fort), is built from golden-colored, locally quarried sandstone and sits atop a plateau 250 feet above the surrounding landscape. When I first spotted the fort through the heat coming off the paved road, the sandstone shimmered. I could easily imagine weary traders along the Silk Road dismissing the image as a mirage seeming to float above the desert floor.

The Jaisalmer Fort is a labyrinth of houses, shops, and temples. More than 2,000 people still live within the walls, making it the last "living fort" in India. Inside these walls, I learned of the existence of an ancient religion, Jainism, a predecessor to Hinduism and Buddhism, that I knew nothing about. I also was able to visit some of the seven Jain temples still inside the fort. When I got home, I did some research and learned there were Jain temples throughout the US. In 1993, two years before I visited the Jain temples in Jaisalmer, the Jain Society of Metropolitan Chicago built a large Jain temple in a western suburb of Chicago. As so often occurs, I went to the other side of the world and learned something about what is in my backyard.

————— ᩅᩤ᩠ᩅᨣᩪᩅᩢᨾᩥᩢᩁ —————

In 1995, having a guide seemed essential to travel around India without losing days and nights waiting and sleeping in train stations or airports. Virtually every one of our booked buses, trains, and planes failed to depart as scheduled, or failed to depart with us on board. Our guide Akbar was particularly helpful because he was the local operator and point person for several of the large international travel companies offering India trips. He had good connections and good relationships. That did not immunize us from trouble, but it helped us move along.

Our last domestic flight provided the ultimate example of Akbar's creative guiding know-how. Our group arrived at the Jodhpur Airport well in advance of the departure time for our flight to New Delhi. We were flying Indian Airlines, which merged with Air India (the airline that indefinitely delayed my flight from Hong Kong) in 2007, but in 1995 was still a separate equally abysmal carrier. There were two main flights on this route, operating almost like a cross-country bus. One went northeast from Mumbai to New Delhi, stopping in Udaipur, Jodhpur (where we were waiting), and Jaipur. The other, heading southwest, went from New Delhi to Mumbai, stopping in Jaipur, Jodhpur, and Udaipur. While our group read, talked, and waited, Akbar moved around, checking boards and talking to various airline personnel, whom he appeared to know well.

As the time when we should have boarded came and went, Akbar returned to tell us that our plane was late. Not a surprise, but a problem.

Regulations at the Jodhpur Airport did not allow planes to land or take off after dusk, and it would be dark before our plane made it there. Due to these regulations, the plane would have to fly over Jodhpur, skipping us entirely, stop in Jaipur, then fly on to New Delhi. There were no tickets for the flight from Jodhpur to New Delhi the following day, which would not have helped anyway, since most of us had international flights that would be departing before that flight would land.

Fortunately, Akbar had a plan. And what a plan. We would begin our flight northeast to New Delhi by flying southwest to Udaipur, landing before the flight heading in the opposite direction arrived. We would then board that plane, fly back northeast over Jodhpur (our current location and the point from which we had tickets), where the airport would be closed, land in Jaipur, and then continue on to New Delhi. We protested our lack of tickets for these flights and the craziness of the plan, but Akbar assured us it would work, and it was the only option. We had to get going. But as Akbar tried to hurry us through security, a cultural conflict arose that almost derailed his plan.

Sue, one of the women in our group, had tampons in her carry-on luggage. Although commonly used by women in Western countries, tampons were seldom used and still taboo in India. Sue was stopped when the guard screening carry-ons could not identify the tampons—he had never seen one before. Sue tried to explain delicately what they were, but Akbar cut her short. Not only were tampons taboo, but menstruation was not openly discussed in India—and never with men. The guard adamantly refused to allow these unknown and possibly dangerous items through security, and Sue refused to leave without the tampons she needed. As the standoff continued, a plane landed. It was the flight from the north, heading southwest—the flight we needed to take. Fortunately, another woman in our group finally realized what was happening, and she walked up to Sue and whispered in her ear, "I have tampons in my checked luggage." That did it. Sue abandoned her allegedly suspicious items and walked through security.

Our group went out to the tarmac where a line of baggage stretched from the terminal to the plane. We were instructed to identify our bags, which were then loaded into the cargo hold. When we boarded the plane, no one asked for our (nonexistent) tickets. We chose seats and buckled up. The security staff may have refused to allow tampons or unidentified bags to be loaded on the plane, but they had no problem allowing passengers to board without tickets.

When we arrived in Udaipur, we disembarked and retrieved our bags on the tarmac before they could disappear into the terminal's baggage-claim area. Per Akbar's plan, we stayed on the tarmac, too, and soon a plane approached from the south. It was the flight that would have picked us up in Jodhpur but for the imminent darkness. When the plane landed and the Udaipur passengers disembarked, we lined up our bags and identified them for security. Then we boarded, sitting in seats that must have been vacated by a group that had just disembarked.

About fifteen minutes later, ticketed passengers from Udaipur began to board. Some had boarding passes for the seats we occupied. After three weeks in India, we were acculturated. We shrugged, acted indifferent, and pretended to read our books. When the plane took off, we remained in those seats. The passengers with boarding passes either sat elsewhere or had been forced to get off the plane. As the sun set, we flew over Jodhpur, where I am certain that tourists without such creative guides were camped overnight in the airport lounge, awaiting the next day's flight.

I could manage travel in India. I could now travel anywhere.

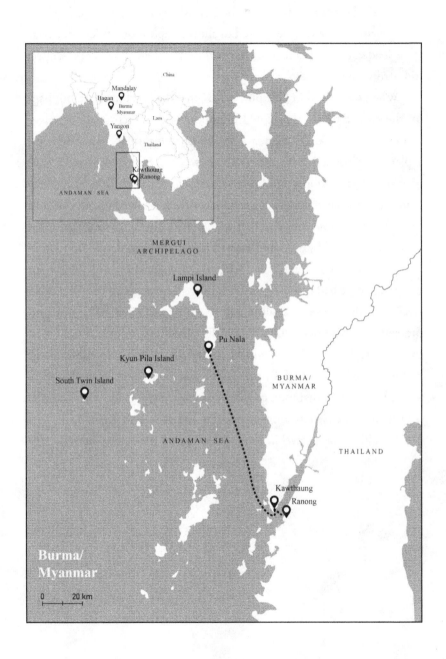

Chapter Four

TO GO OR NOT TO GO?
TRAVEL IN BURMA, OR IS IT MYANMAR?

GO. DON'T GO. I didn't know. I am seldom indecisive. One of my strengths as a litigator is my ability to quickly assess the facts, law, and other relevant factors and reach a conclusion. Rightly or wrongly, I decide quickly. But the question of whether or not to travel to Burma in 1998 had no clear answer, at least not for me.

Aung San Suu Kyi, the nation's famed Nobel laureate, was a vociferous opponent of foreign tourism. "Burma will always be here," she told the *Independent* in a March 1996 interview. "Visitors should come later." In a longer interview she gave to foreign journalists in Rangoon (now Yangon), addressing her opposition to tourism and the military government's "Visit Myanmar Year" campaign, Suu Kyi argued that the arrival of foreign tourists could be seen as tacit support for the SLORC. (The SLORC [State Law and Order Restoration Council] was the military junta that refused to accept the May 1990 election results in which Aung San Suu Kyi's opposition party, the National League for Democracy [NLD], had won a landslide victory.) More directly, foreign tourists gave the SLORC hard currency (US dollars) to fund its war against the Burmese people. Plus, she argued, resources that were badly needed for the Burmese people were being diverted into developing the nascent tourism infrastructure.

When I read this interview in 1998, Suu Kyi spoke with moral authority as the 1991 Nobel Peace Prize winner for her nonviolent struggle for democracy and human rights. Suu Kyi was revered at home and abroad, an icon of democracy, the image of personal sacrifice for her country, and a symbol of peaceful resistance in the face of oppression. I would never have believed that, two decades later, Suu Kyi would become an apologist for the military government's genocidal campaign against the Rohingya Muslim minority. Yet, in 2019, Suu Kyi represented the country at a trial in the International Court of Justice and defended Burma against accusations of ethnic cleansing and genocide. Foreign governments and people outside Burma who once praised her, now accused her of refusing to condemn the military and doing nothing to stop rape and murder. But this twist was yet to come as I considered Suu Kyi's 1996 request that tourists not visit Burma.

I also considered information and advice from other sources, including the US Department of State and guidebooks. The Department of State was neutral, setting forth such facts as "Travel to and within Burma is strictly controlled by the government of Burma," and "Security in tourist areas is generally good." No advice or even comment on the ethical quandary.

In contrast, Lonely Planet's online guide to Myanmar directly addressed the issue. In a "Reality Check" section, under the heading ". . . to go or not to go . . . ," Lonely Planet posed the question I was asking myself. Is it collusion with a repressive military regime if you travel to Burma, or is it ensuring that a gateway (however restricted) to the outside world remains open? The editors of Lonely Planet concluded, "Boycotting Myanmar is not the only possible response to this situation, but it is a legitimate one." As a basis for this conclusion, Lonely Planet said that money going into Myanmar unquestionably would help the SLORC, but it noted that there were still opportunities to support the citizens by taking local transport, staying in private (locally owned) hotels, eating at local restaurants, and buying in markets rather than government-run stores.

On one side of the debate about travel to Burma was the revered Aung San Suu Kyi who said, "**NO**." On the other side was a guidebook for low-budget travelers that said an equivocal "maybe." After weighing the pros and cons, I decided to go anyway. Maybe I was being selfish, but I did not see it that way. Through my research, I had become more interested in the country, its history, politics, and people. I wanted to visit Burma as it was then, not when someone deemed it politically acceptable to visit. The best way to learn about a country, after all, is to go there—to see and be seen.

The application form for a tourist visa was the first direct evidence of the SLORC directly extracting hard currency, cash dollars, from tourists. A section of the visa application stated, "**COMPULSORY EXCHANGE OF US $300.00 ON ARRIVAL IN MYANMAR.** The Foreign Independent Traveller (F.I.T.) holding a Tourist Entry Visa is compulsorily required to exchange on arrival in Myanmar a minimum amount of US $300.00 or its equivalent in Pound Sterling or in specified acceptable travelers' cheques with Foreign Exchange Certificate (FEC) 300 units." But the SLORC did not always get its full $300. Tourists not ethically averse to bribery or afraid of being caught could exchange less than the compulsory $300 by paying part of the difference as a "gift" to the customs officer enforcing the requirement. Based on hearsay, this happened fairly often.

FEC was like Monopoly money, but less useful. Issued by the Central Bank of Myanmar, FEC looked like real money and came in denominations of one, five, ten, and twenty that purportedly were equivalent to US dollars of the same denominations. But FEC was not equivalent to US dollars, not even in Burma, the only place it was negotiable. Almost no business or person in Burma would accept FEC in exchange for hotel rooms, goods, or services. Or, if they did, they would convert the FEC at the "official" exchange rate of US dollars to the local currency, kyats: six kyats to the dollar. This was pennies on the dollar compared to unofficial exchange rates. The private exchange rate, given at hotels, was 250 kyats to 1 USD—forty-two times the official rate. The black-market exchange rate was 350 kyats to 1 USD—fifty-nine times the official rate. The $300 that independent tourists were forced to exchange for FEC was no more than a hard-currency infusion to the SLORC. In the strange morals of such situations, one could regard the amount a tourist paid as a bribe to

avoid exchanging the full $300 as a strike against the military junta—the
cash went directly to a Burmese citizen, not the SLORC.

————  ————

   To go or not to go was not the only question. Hanging over the trip
was the basic question of how to refer to the country. Was it Burma or
Myanmar? Which name was politically, ethically, and morally correct in
1998? In recent decades, when a country changed its name, it typically
was rejecting colonial history and its imposed labels. The new names
denoted independence and were deemed more correct on the moral
barometer of such things. A typical example is British Honduras, a former
British Crown colony that became Belize after independence. An atypical
example is Swaziland. King Mswati III of Swaziland (Africa's last absolute
monarchy) unilaterally changed the country's name to the Kingdom of
Eswatini. The king announced that, in addition to shedding traces of
the country's colonial past, the new name would stop foreigners from
confusing Swaziland and Switzerland. How many people did he think
landed by mistake in Swaziland—a small landlocked country in Southern
Africa—when they had planned to go skiing in the Alps? Regardless, the
country is now the Kingdom of Eswatini.
   But the ethical and moral correctness of Burma's 1989 name change
was not clear. The military junta changed the country's name from Burma
to Myanmar. Aung San Suu Kyi continued to refer to her country as Burma.
If I called the country Myanmar, was I siding with the SLORC? Was it
better, then, to use the old name and call the country Burma? France and
Japan called the country Myanmar. The US and the UK referred to the
country as Burma. (Per the US Department of State website, as of 2022,
"The United States government continues to use the name 'Burma.'")
While in the country, I did my best to avoid using either name.

——— ᩅᩮᩁᩣᩉ᩠ᨂᩣᩅᩮᩁᩣ᩠ᨿ᩠ᨿ᩠ᨿ ———

I crossed the border from Thailand into Burma aboard a souped-up Zodiac. As I stepped off the dock onto the inflated rubber tube and into the small boat, I had no clue what would come next. If I had, I would have stayed right there on the dock, safe ashore.

Three days earlier, Cathay Pacific had repeatedly delayed and rescheduled my flight from Vancouver to Hong Kong, from where I had a connecting flight to Bangkok. Typhoon Zeb had formed in a monsoon trough near the Caroline Islands in Micronesia and was sweeping across Japan, the Philippines, and Taiwan, wreaking havoc with airline schedules throughout Southeast Asia. The plane scheduled to fly me from Vancouver was grounded in Taipei. Typhoon Zeb also delayed the *Wanderlust*, the trimaran on which I'd be spending a week sailing in Burma's Mergui Archipelago. I made it to Bangkok a day late but still in time to catch my flight to Ranong, Thailand. The *Wanderlust*, however, never made it to Ranong, which is what precipitated the asininity that followed.

At Bangkok's Don Mueang International Airport, I met up with my fellow travelers—three flexible and fun tourists and the inflexible, not-so-fun founder of a new and short-lived travel company that had organized this 1998 trip to newly opened Burma. We took a 7 a.m. domestic flight to Ranong, a small Thai border town just east of Burma's southern tip.

From the airport, we headed to the Saphan Plaa jetty, from where we could travel by boat across the border to Kawthaung, Burma. When we arrived, dozens of longtails—traditional Thai wooden boats with small, loud diesel tractor motors connected to long propeller shafts—maneuvered for space at the dock. As we watched, a Zodiac (a rigid inflatable boat) wedged between two of the longtails and pushed its way up to the dock. The Zodiac was for our small group. From out in the harbor, the driver, Graham, had had no trouble picking us out on the busy pier as the American tourists he was waiting for.

The Zodiac had two massive outboard motors, which Graham said could reach speeds up to forty knots (46 mph)—fast for anything except racing speedboats, which are not made of inflatable tubes. The high-backed, roller-coaster-style seats bolted down the middle of the Zodiac were a match for the horsepower of the engines and clearly not designed for leisurely whale-watching tours. We boarded the Zodiac and, in minutes, whipped across the border to Kawthaung, Burma.

Greeting us on the dock as we entered Burma were two big red signs with white lettering, one in Burmese and one in English. I assumed they said the same thing—which was not "Welcome to Burma" or "Welcome to Myanmar." The English sign proclaimed,

---

PEOPLE'S DESIRE

Oppose those relying on external elements, acting as stooges, holding negative views.
Oppose those trying to jeopardize stability of the State and progress of the nation.
Oppose foreign nations interfering in the internal affairs of the State.
Crush all internal and external destructive elements as the common enemy.

Okay, I got the message. But if I somehow forgot for a moment, I would be reminded—often. The "People's Desire" dictum appeared on billboards everywhere we traveled in Burma (except in the Mergui Archipelago), and it was printed daily on the back page of *The New Light of Myanmar*, a government-owned, propaganda-filled newspaper published in English and Burmese. After this warm welcome/warning, we headed over to the small restaurant that did double duty as the Burmese customs office in Kawthaung.

Before leaving the United States, everyone in our group had filled out the forms, paid the fees, and obtained tourist visas from the Embassy of the Union of Myanmar in Washington, DC. With those visas in hand, we should have been in and out of that restaurant/customs office in ten minutes, but we sat there for hours. Was something wrong with our visas? Doubtful. More likely, the customs agents wanted our group—the only tourists in sight—to cough up a bigger bribe than our local agent offered.

Finally, across a restaurant table covered with our passports, visas issued by the Myanmar embassy, duplicate visas issued in Kawthaung, stacks of tens and twenties, in US dollar bill, and large mugs of cold beer, they cut a deal. Our passports and new and old visas were stamped, and we headed back to the Zodiac. Unfortunately, the delay had cost us much more than the bribe. It was getting dark and starting to drizzle.

As he took the wheel and backed the boat away from the dock, Graham boasted that it would have taken the *Wanderlust* ten hours to motor from Pu Nala to meet us here in Kawthaung, but in this Zodiac, we would be able to make it to Pu Nala in just two and a half hours. What? We would be taking this open, inflatable, rubber boat across the Andaman Sea to meet up with the *Wanderlust* in the Mergui Archipelago, not at the mouth of the river as planned! As this began to sink in, it was too late to say anything or hop off. The Zodiac was already headed downriver and out into the Andaman Sea, toward the setting sun.

For the first ninety minutes, it was like riding at night on an unlit roller coaster that never ends. Except for the "never ends" part, it was fun—a little close to the edge, but exciting. Then the drizzle turned into a squall and a violent thunder-and-lightning storm. The wind gusts were so intense I could not breathe while facing forward. The rain pelted us. Wearing only thin cotton pants and a T-shirt, I was pummeled and drenched. Despite the dark sky, I kept my sunglasses on to protect my eyes from the wind and rain, but I could still clearly see sharp lightning strikes slashing the sky. As the lightning got closer and closer, I wondered whether the rubber raft would provide sufficient protection from the electric current if the lightning hit the water, or whether the metal floor to which the seats were bolted would electrocute us. As I tried to remember those details from high school physics, I got distracted by the sea, which had become even more threatening. The swells had grown, and we were slammed every time the boat crashed through a wave.

I looked under and around my seat for a life jacket, which I should have done the minute I boarded. No luck. I shouted up to Graham, but that was useless. He could not hear me. I was afraid to stand up, scared I would

be swept overboard into the inky-black sea—without a life jacket. I tapped
the shoulder of the person seated in front of me and passed the word up to
ask where the life jackets were stowed. The answer came back: "There are
no life jackets. Turn around in your seat and hold on." Gripping the metal
at the top of the seat, I swung one leg over and slowly turned and straddled
my seat. I buried my face in the tall, padded backrest and wrapped my arms
around the seat, hugging it as if my life depended on it, because it did.

For the next hour, traveling at top speed, the small boat crashed through
the swells. Except when suddenly illuminated by lightning, the sky and the
sea were both pitch black. The unrelenting rain hit with horizontal force,
amplified by the speed of the boat. And something near the bow, maybe a
light or an instrument, projected an eerie whistle and shriek in the howling
wind. There was no communication from Graham or chatter among the
passengers. What was there to say? We were all going to die.

Obviously, since I am relating this saga, I did not drown, lost forever
in the Andaman Sea without a body for my family to bury. Although
Graham showed a perilous lack of judgment in taking us out in a storm
like that, he was an able navigator, and he found the *Wanderlust*. As the
Zodiac tied up next to the *Wanderlust* and we started throwing our soaked
bags aboard, I could see the mixture of anger and relief on the captain's
face. Later, just from the tone of a conversation in Thai that I could
not understand, I knew the captain was furious that Graham had even
attempted the crossing that evening. Taking the captain's fury to indicate
that he would not have put us in that life-threatening situation, I felt
better about my safety in the week ahead, sailing on the *Wanderlust*. Still,
the first thing I did after finding my cabin was look for the life jackets.

Tourism in the Mergui Archipelago was very new, only opened by
the Burmese government the previous year. No tourist boats were based
there yet; the *Wanderlust* and her crew were based in Phuket, Thailand,
about 235 miles away. The *Wanderlust* was a fifty-one-foot wooden ketch-
rigged trimaran, which made her more stable and provided more rigging
options during long crossings and bad weather. The belowdecks area was
well designed for sleeping and eating. A double cabin was located toward

the stern of the center pontoon, and each of the side pontoons held a double and a single cabin. My cabin in a side pontoon was narrow but adequate. The boat's wider center area, crossing all three pontoons, held the head (ship speak for toilet) and the shower toward the bow, and the galley and dining area amidships. When the weather was good, the boat felt spacious and comfortable, but when the monsoon rains descended and everyone gathered in the galley/dining area, it was steamy and crowded. (The monsoon season was late that year, and we were caught in several more storms.)

When first introduced to the crew, I was confused by some of their names. Then I realized, of course, they were Thai, not Burmese. Most Thais have a nickname given to them at birth by their parents, and those nicknames stick for life. It is a tradition that comes from the old belief that nicknames fool evil spirits who would otherwise snatch the newborn baby. Animals are common nicknames, perhaps to fool the evil spirits into thinking the baby is not human. Yingluck Shinawatra, Thailand's first female prime minister, is nicknamed Pu, "crab" in Thai. The *Wanderlust*'s captain was Aod, "tadpole" in Thai. Foreign words and names, especially English ones, were also trendy nicknames, maybe for the same rationale, or maybe not. The cook's nickname was A Boy, and the deckhand was Joe. The two Australian dive guides, who also led expeditions and served as ship's crew when needed, were Brandon and Michael. And then there was Graham, the Zodiac driver, whose name should, but does not, mean "reckless, heedless, showing a lack of regard for the safety of others in your care."

A Boy was a fantastic cook. In a tiny galley, he prepared delicious multicourse meals for guests and crew. A typical daily menu included a Western-style breakfast, maybe banana pancakes. Lunch and dinner were multicourse Thai meals, with a perfectly prepared Italian pasta on the side for anyone who wasn't up for Thai food. A Boy accommodated the vegetarians in all entrées and served fresh pineapple and greens with every meal.

While he cooked, A Boy played loud music, mostly Thai rock or disco. But A Boy's favorite CD was *Music of the World Cup: Allez! Ola! Olé!* which had been released in June as the official music for the 1998 World Cup in France. Most of the songs start with a referee whistle and are meant to be chanted by a hundred thousand rabid fans in a stadium, not played nonstop in the tiny galley of a small boat. The songs have inane lyrics, which stuck in my head. The song that most irritated Brandon (the Aussie dive guide) was "Top of the World (*Olé Olé Olé*) (The Name of the Game)," by Estudio Miami Ritmo, especially when they chanted the name of the game: Futbol, futbol, futbol, futbol, futbol! Despite the referee whistle, I did not mind "*Midiwa bôl* (I Love Football)," maybe because the song is from Cameroon, and I did not understand the lyrics. Even A Boy hated "Don't Come Home Too Soon," a whiny Scottish folk song celebrating the Scottish team's qualification that year for the World Cup and asserting that even long shots make it. Not in this case. The Scottish team was as bad as the song and lost in the first round of the World Cup that year.

In addition to the *Wanderlust*'s usual crew for Thailand, we had a Burmese "guide" named Molo. I am fairly certain he was a government spy. Molo did no guiding. Molo did not kayak, hike, swim, or scuba dive. Molo did not assist with handling the *Wanderlust*. Molo sat at the stern of the boat, chain-smoking cigarettes, his eyes hidden behind reflective sunglasses. Was he tasked with determining whether we were "stooges" relying on external elements, trying to jeopardize the stability of the state, as cautioned by the People's Desire billboard? If he decided we were spies, would he "crush" us, as the billboard directed? It took Molo less than twenty-four hours to determine that the "People's Desire" had nothing to do with our small group, and then he ignored us. It took me a little longer to ignore his constant, creepy presence. At the end of the sailing trip, I did not tip the spy.

Based on what I read before coming to Burma, I expected that the guide we were required to hire to tour the mainland would be a government shill, if not a spy like Molo. But our guide, Hein, was neither. Not once during the twelve days he guided us around Burma—in Yangon, Mandalay, Pagan, and Inle Lake—did Hein say anything positive about the ruling military government. Quite the opposite. Hein's swipes and pointed jabs at the SLORC began as soon as we met him. His running commentary on the drive through Yangon from the airport to our hotel was eye-opening and, quite possibly, illegal.

As we drove past Inya Lake, Hein told us that Aung San Suu Kyi had lived under house arrest on the shore of that lake. Hein told us that he loved Suu Kyi and wished he could take us to her home, but he could not because he would lose his guide license. As we passed the shimmering golden stupas of Shwedagon Pagoda, Hein pointed out a second smaller stupa built by General Ne Win (the military dictator who took power in a coup d'état in 1962 and died in 2002 while under house arrest) directly opposite Shwedagon. Hein gloated when he told us, "No one visits the general's pagoda." Then Hein pointed out the "so-called Parliament building"—explaining that it is "so-called" because the Parliament no longer exists. Hein was lucky we were not spies for the SLORC.

Hein's opposition to the military government was longstanding. He had been a student leader in the 1975 protests against Ne Win's military dictatorship. Burmese troops arrested Hein as he protested at Shwedagon Pagoda, standing next to the monument inscribed with the names of eleven Rangoon University student leaders who, in 1920, led the first students' strike against British rule. Troops rounded up and arrested hundreds of other students as well. Military tribunals, not civilian courts, heard the students' cases. Hein was tried and convicted of high treason and sentenced to seven years in prison. Three years later, the military government released him during an amnesty for political prisoners.

Even if the SLORC did not know what Hein was saying as we drove through Yangon in a private van, surely they knew about his political activism and prison sentence. We were astonished that Hein was allowed to guide foreign tourists. Maybe the SLORC did not care so long as we brought US dollars to Burma. Or if they suspected what Hein would say, maybe the SLORC thought it would play well with American tourists who would go home and (wrongly) say free speech exists in Burma. Or maybe Hein just kept his head down and slipped through the bureaucratic cracks. Regardless, we were lucky to have him as a guide and welcomed the political perspective and historical context he provided.

That initial drive through Rangoon was when I first noticed the survival of a strange part of Ne Win's legacy—separate from the political reprisals, economic collapse, xenophobia, and corruption. The van's steering wheel and driver were on the right, like in the UK. But he was driving the van on the right side of the road, like in the US. This felt wrong. If the driver sat on the right side, shouldn't he be driving the car on the left side of the road? I kept waiting for us to have a head-on collision. But all the other vehicles were the same. Why? It's a good story.

On December 6, 1970, General Ne Win unilaterally ordered driving in Burma to switch overnight from the left side of the road to the right side. Drivers immediately switched the side of the road they drove on, but they did not buy new cars. As a result, people drove on the right side of the road, with the steering wheel still on the right side of the car. (Forty-five years later, at the end of 2015, Burma enacted a new law limiting imports to cars with the steering wheel on the left side. Cars with right-side steering wheels that already were in use were allowed to remain, and I suspect many still exist today.)

Why did Ne Win issue this strange edict? One story goes that the general was ill and consulted his wife's astrologer, which would not have been unusual. Burma's army generals often relied on astrologers and numerologists for policy advice. The astrologer told Ne Win that things were not good on the left. The general interpreted this as relating to traffic. He immediately ordered the nation's drivers to switch from the left side of the road to the right side. Perhaps the stars were advising on traffic flow. After ordering the change, the general recovered. However, some Burmese believed that Ne Win misinterpreted the astrologer's meaning. A different switch from left to right was intended—a metaphorical switch, not a literal switch. The move seen by the astrologer was from socialism on the left to a market economy on the right, not switching the side of the road where cars drive. Think how different Burma might be today if this military dictator had interpreted the astrologer's reading of the stars differently.

Relations between the US and Burmese governments were especially tense when I visited. A year earlier, in May 1997, President Clinton had issued Executive Order 13047, imposing further unilateral economic sanctions on Burma. In his accompanying report to Congress, Clinton said, "I have taken these steps in response to a deepening pattern of severe repression by the State Law and Order Restoration Council (SLORC) in Burma. During the past 7 months, the SLORC has arrested and detained large numbers of students and opposition supporters, sentenced dozens to long-term imprisonment, and prevented the expression of political views by the democratic opposition, including Aung San Suu Kyi and the National League for Democracy (NLD)." He continued, "I believe that the actions and policies of the SLORC regime constitute an extraordinary and unusual threat to the security and stability of the region, and therefore to the national security and foreign policy of the United States." According to Hein, the SLORC countered with an intensive propaganda campaign against foreign influences, and in particular against US government policy and American cultural influences.

I did not notice this same hostility from the Burmese people. And the anti-American campaign certainly was not working on the Burmese I met, who, obviously, were not a representative sample because they spoke English and interacted with tourists. One evening, after a delicious Indian dinner at a private restaurant in Mandalay, three of us split into two trishaws for the ride back to the hotel. (A trishaw is a wheeled cart pulled by a person riding a bicycle. A rickshaw is pulled by a person walking or running.) Riding alone, I had a chance to speak to the driver pedaling the trishaw. The driver's brother lived in Westport, Connecticut, so his brother, not the SLORC, was the driver's source of information about America. The driver envied his brother's freedom and told me, "America is the land of the free."

Another time, while slowly climbing up the many, many steps of Mandalay Hill to Sutaungpyei Pagoda, I was joined on my ascent by a novice monk. Climbing the staircase in the heat and humidity, I had little breath left, so he did most of the talking. When we finally reached the top, he admiringly told me, "You come from a very famous country."

And then there was Hein, who wanted desperately to emigrate to the US. Hein pinned his hopes on DV-2000, a US diversity immigration program that offered 50,000 permanent-residence visas each year to applicants chosen through a computer-generated lottery. Entries for the DV-2000 visa lottery were due between October 1 and October 31, 1998. Before meeting us for our tour, Hein had submitted his application. Winners were to be notified between April and July 1999. I don't know whether Hein won the lottery, but I have always hoped that he did.

As participants in a "package tour," our group of four was not required to exchange dollars for FEC. The SLORC got our US dollars in other ways. We were required to hire "guides" like Molo who did no guiding and seemed to be there only to spy on us. We also were required to visit certain sites controlled by the government. For example, in Mandalay, we had to visit the Mandalay Palace and pay $5 cash per person for entry. (FEC was not accepted in payment at this official government site, only US dollars.) During World War II, when the Japanese army maintained a base in the Mandalay Palace, the Allies bombed and destroyed the complex. We paid $5 to visit what was essentially the newly built set of a B movie—little more than a wooden shell, a crudely built reconstruction with amateurish carvings. Based on reading Aung San Suu Kyi's arguments against tourists in Burma, I suspected that this reproduction might have been constructed with "volunteer" labor, which the SLORC used to improve its tourist infrastructure and facilities.

When we made our obligatory stop at the Mandalay Palace, it was too new to have been included in any guidebooks. That the palace was a shoddy, minimal reconstruction was a surprise to me. My contemporaneous notes from this visit predict that "once it's in the guidebooks, no one will go, and the SLORC won't get their cash." I was wrong. According to the current *Lonely Planet Myanmar (Burma)* travel guide, the government continued to expand the reproduction, and it now features more than forty timber buildings and a soaring, multilayered pyramid of gilt filigree above the main throne room. In 2022, TripAdvisor ranked Mandalay Palace number eighteen of forty-nine things to do in Mandalay, and it was getting a mix of reviews, with more "excellent" (212) than "terrible" (60) ones. However, the fact that it is a reproduction is clearly stated in many reviews, so tourists should no longer be caught by surprise.

In addition to mandated tourist sites, we were required to patronize official restaurants. Pretty quickly, though, we realized we did not have to eat at the official restaurants with their drab decor and inedible food—as long as we did not insist on refunds of the money we had paid up front. So, we ate elsewhere. In Mandalay, we found two privately owned restaurants, not on our official itinerary, where they served delicious food, and our US dollars went to the owners and servers, not to the SLORC. My favorite restaurant was Ko's Kitchen, a Thai restaurant on the corner of Nineteenth and Eightieth Streets in the Maygagiri Quarter. We also ate twice at Marie Min, a vegetarian Indian restaurant. Aung San Suu Kyi was correct that tourist dollars supported the SLORC, but in a small yet direct way, we also supported local businesses and individuals.

Before we left Mandalay, I experienced the very best massage of my life—up to that day and since. When I picked up my room key after dinner, the desk clerk at the Emerald Land Inn asked me whether I would like a massage. Yes, I would. The clerk suggested that I put on loose pants and a loose, long-sleeved shirt, and she said the masseur would arrive soon. I hurried to my room and changed clothes. A few minutes later, there was a knock on my door. I opened it to see the clerk standing there with a short, wiry old man. The clerk explained that the man was blind and did not speak English. She would help him get situated in the room and then leave. The cost of the massage would be 400 kyats (about $1.15). I could pay the man directly at the end of the massage. The clerk told me to lie down on my back on the bed. I did. She walked the blind man over to the edge of the bed and put his hand on my ankle. Then she left.

The man climbed up on the bed and got to work. A Burmese massage is nothing like a Swedish massage you might get in a lovely spa—no New

Wave music, no aromatic essential oils, and not the least bit relaxing. But it is so much better. And this slight, old, blind man was an expert. For decades, I have taken every opportunity in other Asian countries with similar massage techniques—Thailand, Laos, and Cambodia—to find a masseur as talented and a massage as amazing. I have not succeeded . . . yet.

Burmese massage focuses on pressure points, which are held for an extended period. This masseur knew anatomy. Without being able to see, he easily found my exact pressure points and arteries. In his most potent individual move, he used his thumb to maintain pressure on my femoral artery to stop the blood flow to my leg. The pressure did not hurt, but it did not feel good either. When he sensed that I couldn't take it any longer, he lifted his thumb. It felt like a powerful force (not just blood) rushed back into my leg. And then he did it again on the other leg. The masseur used his fingers, elbows, and feet to reach and hold other pressure points and stretch my back and limbs. This massage was active. Grasping a leg or an arm or two, he lifted, stretched, and twisted my body into positions I could never have reached on my own, but he never pulled or moved me into a position that was uncomfortable or painful. He sensed how far my spine, neck, or limb could go to achieve the release without pain. After two hours, he climbed off the bed and stood waiting for me to pay him. I handed him the payment and included a huge tip, but I did not know how to tell him that. He could not see the denominations on the bills, and we did not speak a common language. I tried to say thank you in Burmese, but it's a difficult language, and I hope he understood. Then he left and moved on to another room to amaze yet another tourist.

The next morning, I still felt loose, strong, and flexible. The bruises on my calves and arms were a small price to pay for the lasting benefits of the deep massage. I joined my group, and we took the daylong ferry ride from Mandalay up the Irrawaddy River to Pagan (now called Bagan). Founded sometime before the ninth century, Pagan was the capital of the first Burmese kingdom from the eleventh to the fourteenth centuries. The current archaeological site covers fifty square kilometers on the left bank of a bend in the Irrawaddy River. Despite wars, earthquakes, floods, and looting, more than 3,500 temples, stupas, and monasteries remain. In Pagan, you look out on a stunning panorama of thousands of thousand-year-old temples.

We rented decrepit bikes and rode for miles on dirt roads while exploring the site. (Hein stayed with the van. Biking was too much exertion for him.) We had a map, but it proved worthless. Rather than get frustrated trying to navigate toward a particular temple, we got on our bikes and rode in random directions. When we saw an interesting, unusual, or particularly stunning temple, we would stop. Most of the temples had a gatekeeper, who would tell us the temple's name and point to its location on the map. He then would unlock the gate, allowing us to see the wall paintings and glazed decorations adorning the interior walls, as well as the Buddhas and other sculptures filling the niches. Exploring the individual temples was fascinating, but it was the scope of Pagan that overwhelmed me.

Hein had suggested that we watch the sunset from the Shwesandaw Pagoda, with purportedly the best views of the setting sun and the buildings of Pagan. Even without a useful map, Shwesandaw was easy to find—it is one of the highest temples in Pagan and visible from a distance. We even made it in enough time to explore the pagoda before sunset. A pyramid-style pagoda with five terraces below a circular stupa, Shwesandaw has staircases in the center of each of the four sides. Walking around the terraces offered a 360-degree view of the site. Although we could have watched the sunset from any of the terraces, we climbed the narrow, steep steps to the highest level. For the first time that day, we saw other tourists, who also had been directed to Shwesandaw for the sunset. There was plenty of room for everyone. From the fifth terrace, I watched the sun set over the vast complex—truly stunning, with temples and stupas as far as I could see.

In Pagan, I realized that my level of interest went beyond that of my travel companions, who had a terrific day but were ready to move on. I wanted to spend several more days fully exploring this vast and amazing site. One downside of traveling with a group, however small, was that none of us could modify the itinerary on the fly. We could not add days if we found ourselves somewhere astounding or leave early when a place was disappointing. (I certainly would have chosen to leave Mandalay early, as long as I did not miss that massage.)

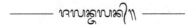

The following year, when I visited the Angkor complex in Siem Riep, Cambodia, I went alone. I spent five days exploring Angkor Wat, Angkor Thom, Bayon, Banteay Srei, and the other temples in the Angkor Archaeological Park. Sometimes I had a guide. Sometimes I just wandered. Early one morning before sunrise, I took a taxi to Ta Prohm, which I had visited with a guide the previous day. Ta Prohm is the only temple the French left as they "discovered" it in 1862, with banyan trees growing through the structure, the temple becoming one with nature. As the light slowly rose through the jungle, I explored the temple before anyone else arrived. Climbing over and through massive roots of ancient banyan trees, I connected to the temple and site in a way I never would have with a guide offering commentary or other tourists shooting photos. Years later, at the Old Town Art Fair in Chicago, I purchased a huge photograph of Ta Prohm (5.5 feet wide by 4.5 feet tall), and it has hung on the wall of my home for the past fifteen years. It is a daily reminder of the power of ancient temples, whether in Angkor or Pagan or elsewhere in the world.

I also see pieces of the temples of Pagan (and Angkor and other temple complexes) at the Art Institute of Chicago, one block from where I live. Unlike my photograph of Ta Prohm, these are not happy reminders. The temples in Pagan have hundreds of empty niches that once sheltered Buddhas. The walls are scarred, and huge chunks are missing where entire frescoes have been removed. Where is it all? Some of it is at the Art Institute, which has an extensive Southeast Asian art collection.

When I walk through the Art Institute's galleries and see pieces from Pagan and other temples in Southeast Asia, I get angry. I lecture Jake and everyone else in earshot that these works of art and the religious and cultural heritage they represent were stolen. Among the stolen works is a standing Buddha from Burma, identified as "Pagan Period, 11th/12th century"—a gift from a wealthy Chicago woman, a so-called patron of the arts. The museum's collection also includes a piece from Burma, dating from 1201 to 1300 and identified as *Bust of Crowned and Adorned Buddha*. I am not an art historian or an archaeologist, but it does not look like a bust to me. It looks like the top half of a statue, lopped off at the waist when it was stolen from a temple niche. This was a gift from the same wealthy patron. How did she obtain these Burmese treasures, and why were they hers to donate?

I asked one of the museum's curators of Southeast Asian art how the Art Institute could justify keeping and exhibiting looted works of art. She hid behind the ridiculous standard adopted in 1970 by UNESCO: the Convention on the Means of Prohibiting and Preventing the Illicit Import, Export and Transfer of Ownership of Cultural Property. To preserve their collections, museums have adopted this self-serving standard that draws a too-recent line in the sand: If the item was already outside its country of modern discovery before November 1970, the museums are absolved of all financial, ethical, and moral obligation to the people and places from whom the work was stolen. If a Buddha or fresco from Pagan was in the Art Institute, in some other museum, or in the hands of a private collector outside Burma in 1969, they get to keep it, and so does anyone who subsequently buys the treasure from them.

Where do the treasures of Pagan belong? In museums in the West where millions can see them? Or in niches in dark corners of temples that are not maintained, not protected from theft or earthquakes, and seldom visited? Except for the number of visitors, this had been the argument against returning the Parthenon marbles (a.k.a. the Elgin marbles, after Lord Elgin who stole them). If the Greeks cannot manage to have the Parthenon marbles returned to Athens, even after building the spectacular new Acropolis Museum, Pagan's treasures likely will never be returned. Fortunately, however, a Western museum may work with a local museum to conserve what remains.

In November 2019, Bagan officials and the Getty Conservation Institute of Los Angeles announced that the Getty would begin a long-term commitment in Bagan to conserve and protect the ancient cultural heritage, working with Myanmar's Department of Archaeology and National Museum. According to the press release, the project will address an array of the site's conservation challenges: repair of buildings damaged by earthquakes (including the major 2016 quake) and work to prevent damage from future earthquakes; conservation of decorative elements of the site; inventory and mapping; strategies to manage the anticipated influx of tourists spurred by Bagan's designation as a UNESCO World Heritage Site in July 2019; and training of local professionals to continue conservation efforts. Although this would be a better approach to preserving Bagan for the next thousand years, I suspect that the COVID-19 pandemic delayed the planned start of the project and that the coup d'état in January 2021 put an end, at least temporarily, to the arrangement.

Exiting Burma was a scarier repeat of entering, but this time we did not pay a bribe. At the end of our trip, my three travel companions and I checked in early for our morning flight on Thai Airways from Yangon to Bangkok. (The unpleasant owner of the fledgling tour company had abandoned us earlier.) With our bags tagged and boarding passes in hand, we waited in the customs line. Suddenly, an armed soldier pulled us out of line and took us to an office and told us to wait there. Someone else in a different uniform—maybe a customs official, maybe not—informed us that we would have to exit Burma from the same point where we had entered. Since we had entered through Kawthaung, we had to leave the same way. We could not fly out of Yangon.

Kawthaung is 800 miles from Yangon. Even if I had believed this officer's threat and wanted to leave from Kawthaung, I could not. I was out of cash. We all were. And credit cards were not accepted anywhere in Burma. "Sir, it is not possible for us to leave from Kawthaung. We have no money and no way to get there," I explained. As a young female lawyer, I had learned to use "sir" (or "Your Honor") as a preface when I argued against a position stated by an older male judge, and I did the same with these officials. It was not a sign of genuine respect and did not mean that I would back down to their authority.

The officer repeated that we could not leave from Yangon, and he gave us a range of ridiculous scenarios for how we could get to Kawthaung. My reply never changed. Eventually, he disappeared and left us alone in the room. Leery that we were being observed, we waited in silence. A different officer came in, and we went through the whole routine again, and then again; the Burmese officials alternated between leaving us alone in the room and making officious pronouncements. For almost three hours, we sat in that room.

I was reasonably sure that this was a farce and that we were being held up to get a bribe. But it was possible that we had inadvertently done something illegal. I remembered reading that the American embassy in Burma did not have a consular treaty with the SLORC. This meant that the embassy could not protect American tourists who ran into trouble traveling in Burma and would not be notified if we were arrested. And embassy staff were not guaranteed access to Americans in jail and could not provide them with food. I did not think the situation would escalate to that level, but as the hours passed, I was not sure.

Our flight was scheduled to leave at 10:40 a.m. At 10:30, with no explanation, an armed officer escorted us out of the room and directly to the boarding gate for our flight. Just before the door closed, we boarded the plane. Moments later, the flight took off. When we arrived in Bangkok, we headed to the baggage carousel. I suspected that our luggage would be there, and it was. The Burmese officials had always intended to allow us to leave on that flight. They just waited until the last minute, hoping to extort a bribe that we could not pay, even if we had been willing to do so.

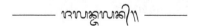

When Aung San Suu Kyi urged tourists to postpone visits because "Burma will always be here," she was wrong. The Burma I saw and experienced in 1998 is no longer there.

Before the global pandemic closed the borders and the military coup in January 2021 sent the country up in flames, the tourist sites I had visited changed. Fleets of charter sailboats and eco-resorts hosted tourists in the Mergui Archipelago, changing the character of the islands. Hot-air balloons filled the skies above the temples of Pagan, changing the panorama at sunrise and sunset. E-bikes replaced the barely mobile pedal bikes we used, taking away part of the fun of exploring this vast archaeological site.

More significantly, the country has changed. Its politics have changed. And Aung San Suu Kyi's position has changed, yet again. In 2019, when she appeared at the International Court of Justice and defended Myanmar against accusations of ethnic cleansing and genocide, Suu Kyi's global reputation and standing plummeted. But she remained popular at home, and her NLD party won a landslide victory in the November 2020 election.

Then on January 31, 2021, in a coup d'état, the military overthrew the country's fragile quasi-democracy and returned the country to full military rule. Suu Kyi was arrested and accused of illegally importing ten walkie-talkies. The charges against her were then upgraded to include breaking a colonial-era official secrets law. On December 5, 2021, Suu Kyi was convicted on charges of inciting public unrest and breaching COVID-19 protocols and sentenced to four years in prison. Within hours, the country's military leader, Senior General Min Aung Hliang, reduced Suu Kyi's sentence to two years. One month later, on January 10, 2022, Suu Kyi was convicted and sentenced to two years in prison for possessing walkie-talkies and two years in prison for a separate count of violating COVID-19 protocols when she walked through a crowd of supporters wearing a face shield but no face mask. As of March 2022, Suu Kyi still faced trial on seven other charges that could result in a sentence of more than eighty-nine years in prison.

When Suu Kyi had the freedom of speech to oppose the SLORC, I ignored her admonition and traveled to Burma. Because I traveled to Burma, met its people, and learned something of its politics and history, decades later, I am closely following the most recent coup there and the growing opposition and protests against the military. Conversely, because

I have not yet traveled to Sudan, Guinea, Niger, or Mali—though I have always wanted to explore Timbuktu—I don't relate to those countries in the same way, and I have not followed the recent military coup d'états in those faraway lands. Of course, I should care about political, socioeconomic, and humanitarian crises everywhere in the world. In truth, I focus my limited bandwidth on the places and people I know and feel a connection to. But the more I travel, the more countries I know, and the broader my world becomes.

The *Wanderlust* in the Mergui Archipelago

Margo searching for game in Botswana from her prime viewing
spot on the Land Cruiser's roof

Courtesy of Andrew Meissner, reprinted with permission

Chapter Five

DON'T THROW BUG SPRAY AT BABOONS
WILD TRAVEL IN ZIMBABWE

MOST VACATIONS, HOWEVER LONG, are still too short. To ease reentry to my workaday reality, I usually tried to plan a few transition days on a beach, at a luxury hotel, or a place with something special to see or do. Victoria Falls, Zimbabwe, provided that opportunity at the end of an extraordinary two-week wildlife safari in Botswana. After camping in the wilderness of the Kalahari Desert, the Okavango Delta, and Chobe National Park, arriving at the Elephant Hills Hotel, a modern resort in Victoria Falls, was jarring (though not as jarring as being back in my office in Chicago would have been). As I waited for my room to be ready, I dared not sit on any of the clean furniture in the lobby or out on the terrace. I was filthy and my clothes were filthy, covered in dirt, dust, and dung from camping and from riding on the roof of a Toyota Land Cruiser. The only showers I had taken for weeks were bucket showers, and the water had been too cold and too limited to get very clean.

Leaning against the terrace railing, I watched a group of spotless tourists, obviously newly arrived in Africa, exclaiming excitedly as they focused on a watering hole so far away that whatever they were seeing through their powerful binocular lenses could not have been more than unidentifiable specks. On the safari I had just taken, we seldom needed binoculars to see the abundant wildlife, and a few of our wildlife encounters were even a little too close. On one game drive in Chobe National Park, I was riding on the roof of the Land Cruiser for a better view of the hundreds of elephants walking and feeding in the fields on either side of the road. Suddenly, a huge elephant, perhaps the matriarch, blocked the dirt road, apparently intent on a game of chicken. She kicked up a cloud of dust, flapped her ears, and swung her trunk—definitely intimidating. I had no idea whether I should sit very still on the roof or try to slide back down into the jeep. No one grabbed my foot to pull me down, so I froze in place. When the elephant got so close I could have reached out and touched her swinging trunk, it stopped being fun and started being scary. I held my breath and hoped someone in the Land Cruiser was taking pictures. Then, as suddenly as she appeared on the road, the elephant disappeared into the bush.

A bellman carrying my massive duffel bag appeared on the terrace and called my name, interrupting my reverie. I followed him to my hotel room, where he showed me around. Stopping next to the sliding glass door to the balcony, he turned and sternly warned me to keep the door closed: "Wild animals are out there." After weeks camping outdoors, the last thing I wanted was confinement in an air-conditioned room. As to the threat of wild animals, I smiled, inwardly scoffing at the idea of wild animals in this big hotel, full of people and far from grazing land and water holes (other than the golf course and the swimming pool).

As soon as the bellman left, I opened the sliding door and kept it open while I took a quick shower and changed into cleaner clothes. I then joined others from my safari for the short walk to the magnificent falls aptly named Mosi-oa-Tunya—"The smoke that thunders." These falls are also known by the colonial name imposed by Dr. David Livingstone (yes, that Dr. Livingstone, you presume correctly) who claimed the right to name one of the seven natural wonders of the world after his British queen—Victoria.

That night, I slept well, thanks to the cool, fresh air coming through the open balcony door. The following morning, with one old friend and one new friend from the safari, I headed off for something completely different from the game drives in the Kalahari Desert, which were inactive and required so much patience, especially while searching for cheetahs. (Our patience was rewarded, though, when we spotted not only cheetahs but also cheetah cubs.) I had convinced my friends to join me rafting the Zambezi River, starting just below the base of Mosi-oa-Tunya. We signed up with a rafting company called Shearwater, purportedly the most safety-conscious of the companies running the river—ha!

Shearwater advertised the trip as the best one-day whitewater experience in the world, running nineteen rapids over seventeen miles of the Zambezi River through the Batoka Gorge. The descriptively named class IV and V rapids included Stairway to Heaven (a class V rapid with one of the largest commercially run drops in the world, thirty vertical feet over a span of fifty feet), the Mother (the mother of all wave trains), Terminator I and II (big, high, and long class V rapids), and Commercial Suicide (commercially unrunnable and the only rapid always portaged). The last rapid, Oblivion, had a crashing hole that flipped approximately 75 percent of the rafts that attempted to run it.

I was not afraid of the mighty Zambezi, a.k.a. the Slambezi. But after the bus ride to the put-in point, during which I had a chance to meet some of the others who had signed up with Shearwater for that day, I was afraid of the inexperienced and blissfully unaware (for the moment) tourists who would be paddling the rafts. This was not a leisurely float to see the Batoka Gorge, punctuated by a few fun wave trains. This was full-on class IV and V rapids, one after another for miles. Yet, Shearwater advertised that no prior rafting experience was necessary for this trip.

Our Shearwater group that day consisted of eight rafts and several safety kayaks whose sole purpose was to pick up swimmers—passengers who fell out of their rafts in the rapids. My two friends and I were assigned to a paddle raft with three of the many neophytes in the group, a man and a woman (a married couple) and their male friend. The two male first-timers were the tallest and heaviest on our raft, and our guide, Turo, positioned them at the front of the raft for ballast and paddling power. My new safari friend Jean sat across from me at the stern, just in front of the guide. Jean was in her sixties, physically fit and tough. A trailblazing woman physicist, she was the founding professor of her university's physics department.

Boats loaded, we paddled into a calm pool for some frenetic practice paddling back and forth, high siding back and forth, jumping out of the rafts into the warm river water, and getting pulled back into the raft. This training was too fun to prepare novices for the rapids to come. From my experience capsizing on the Ghizar River, I knew that saving yourself in the middle of a class V rapid was nothing like pretending to save yourself in a calm practice area. Plus, when quick action and accurate compliance with the guide's commands were required to navigate the rapids, prevent a capsize, or avoid being wrapped on a boulder, some of the international tourists (who spoke limited or no English) could not understand the Zimbabwean-accented English shouted by the guides over the roaring rapids. But Shearwater ran this river every day, with this training and these guides—so it should be okay, right?

Deemed ready to go, our crew high-fived with our paddles and followed the other Shearwater rafts into the current. When we hit the first wave in the first rapid, Jean's physics acumen failed her. She misjudged the force and its impact and flew out of the raft, executing a perfect backflip as she went over the side and into the river. Seconds later, when the raft came down off the wave, the two guys in the front tumbled out of the raft and into the river. In this type of rapid, simply staying in the raft took active effort—paddling hard (the paddle in the water keeps you in the boat), wedging your foot between the tube and bottom of the raft, and sometimes just holding on for dear life. The novices were not prepared for what hit them. Within the first few minutes of a long day on the river, half the paddlers in my raft toppled into the water.

Safety kayaks quickly scooped up all three swimmers. Taking advantage of the calm pool below the rapid, we hauled the two guys back into the raft and they bravely took up their positions in the bow. Jean refused to get back in the raft. She was not physically injured when she backflipped out of the raft, but she was shaken and upset. So fearless in her career, Jean was terrified on this river. But it was too late. We were in a deep gorge.

Other than a helicopter rescue, there was no way out of the gorge until the take-out after rapid 19. For safety, our group of eight rafts all moved to and through the rapids together, so all of the rafts waited in the relatively still water until Jean made her move. With no other realistic option, Jean finally agreed to go into one of the oar boats, where she thought she would be safer. In the oar boat, she would be able to sit on the bottom (rather than on the tube, where you sit while paddling) and just hold on.

With eighteen rapids to go, we were down to five paddlers. Most of the paddle rafts had eight paddlers, giving them extra weight to hold the raft down and extra power to maneuver, but also extra novices to make mistakes. Maybe we would be able to handle the remaining rapids with just five of us. Apparently not. We made it to and through rapid 13 (the Mother) with just five paddlers, but before we hit rapid 16B (Terminator II), we took on another paddler, a guide. I am not sure where he came from, but we probably needed his skilled paddling and the additional weight. No one fell out of our raft, and we stayed upright all the way through Terminator II.

The same was not true in the other rafts. Only four of the eight rafts made it through the Terminator II without losing anyone—or everyone. One of the paddle boats lost two of its seven paddlers. Another lost five of its eight paddlers. And yet another lost three of its seven paddlers and its guide, who did a flying forward somersault off the stern. One of the oar boats made it through, but the other oar boat—the raft where Jean had gone for safety—flipped, dumping everyone into the river. While we waited for all of the swimmers from Terminator II to be scooped up and pulled back into their rafts, I turned to Turo and said, "Let's not flip." We didn't. Our raft made it through the remaining rapids, including Oblivion, upright, with everyone still on board and enjoying the wild ride.

This section of the Zambezi River covers some of the biggest commercially runnable rapids in the world. But I had been on challenging rivers before and since, and I had never seen so many rafts flip and so many swimmers. I am not suggesting that the guides flipped the rafts and tossed the paddlers on purpose, but some features of the Zambezi made this lunacy somewhat safer than it would have been on other rivers. The Zambezi water was warm, each set of rapids dropped into a calm pool instead of flowing directly into the next rapid (allowing time to scoop up swimmers and re-flip rafts), and other rafts and safety kayaks were nearby to help with rescues. As long as no one drowned, the tourists were able to go home with wild tales of surviving the Slambezi. And I have to admit, it was the most thrilling day I have ever spent on the water. I would do it again. Although, I would probably try to bring my own crew of experienced paddlers. And maybe even my own river guide—maybe Mike, who guided for Sobek on the Zambezi, and whom I trust, even though he dumped me into the Ghizar River in Pakistan.

The next morning, I woke up grumpy, sorry to be heading home that afternoon. I dumped the dirty, disorganized contents of my duffel bag onto the floor to sort and repack. I pulled out bottles of sunblock, bug spray, and assorted toiletries I did not want to lug back to Chicago, and I set them on the dresser. Then, after a frustrating minute or so of trying to pack dirty clothes and boots neatly into my duffel, I quit and headed for the shower.

I had just lathered my head with shampoo when I heard noises in my room. I jumped out of the shower, wrapped myself in a towel, and stepped out of the bathroom. Two adult male baboons had entered through the open balcony door and had commandeered the room. The larger baboon sat on the desk. In one hand, he held an apple; in the other, he held my copy of David Lamb's book *The Africans*. (I kept that copy with its baboon handprints for years.) The other baboon sat on the pile of stuff I had dumped out of my duffel and strew my things across the room. As I stood there silently, dripping on the floor and trying to decide what to do next, the baboons ignored me completely.

Baboons are strong, maybe not stronger than I am, but they have sharp teeth. Baboons are also smart. If I had been as smart as a baboon, I would have left the room immediately, abandoning it and its contents to the wild animals. In the moment, however, that is not what I did. I walked to the door opposite the balcony and opened it as a means of egress in case I needed a fast exit. My escape route set, I walked back into the room, determined to clear out the baboons and save my stuff. I grabbed the toiletries I had lined up on the dresser and started hurling them toward the baboons. I aimed to miss them, intending the sunblock missiles as warnings, not weapons. I also started screaming as loudly and harshly as I could: "GET OUT! GO AWAY!" The baboons shrieked in response but did not move, likely inured to humans if their troop lived near this large hotel.

A crowd of tourists en route to breakfast gathered outside the open door, lured by the shrieking—mine and the baboons'. The tourists lingered for the spectacle of a dripping-wet woman in a bath towel hurling bug spray, sunblock, and moisturizer at two full-grown baboons in a small hotel room.

Baboons typically do not attack humans, but they do defend themselves, and, in this case, they probably would have won. About the time it finally dawned on me that confronting the baboons was not the best idea and perhaps I should get out of the room, the baboons left. On his way out, the one that had been tossing my things around the room grabbed a Ziploc bag full of something or other. Carrying the bag, he bounded through the open sliding door, out onto the balcony, and into a tree. The other baboon followed, abandoning my book but taking the apple.

My first thought was to try to figure out what was in that Ziploc bag. Anything I had secured in a Ziploc bag was probably valuable. I started to follow the baboons, but I was only wearing a towel. I went back into the bathroom but didn't finish my shower—something I didn't focus on until hours later, long after I'd left the hotel. I pulled on shorts and a T-shirt and took a moment to put in my contact lenses so I could see clearly. Then I went out onto the balcony to look for the baboon or the bag he might have dropped.

I did not see the baboons anywhere, but I suspected that the couple sitting on lounge chairs on the balcony next door had seen them. They were doubled over in laughter. I think the woman was even crying. I asked if they had seen the baboons. She stopped laughing and turned to look at me.

"Yes, we saw the ba . . . ba . . ." she said. She and her husband doubled over laughing again before she could get out the complete word.

"Did you see what the baboons took from my room?" I asked.

The couple laughed harder. Each time they tried to speak, they exploded in laughter. The woman finally calmed down and wiped her eyes.

She replied, "Tampons. A bag of tampons. The baboon took a bag of tampons."

No longer concerned that the baboon had stolen something vital or irreplaceable (like my passport, camera, or safari videos), I was curious about what had caused the couple's hysterical laughter. In my experience, tampons are not inherently hilarious (although I did find the story of Sue and her tampons at the Jodhpur Airport very funny). Then she explained.

She and her husband had a front-row seat as the baboons jumped off my balcony onto a nearby tree branch, climbed to the ground, and sat on the grass. The baboon with the bag put it on the ground and ripped it open. The pair then took out each tampon, one at a time, and peeled the paper off it, as you would peel a banana. Then the baboons took each tampon out of its cardboard cylinder, dangled it from the string, and smelled it. Realizing it was inedible, they tossed it over their shoulders onto the grass. They repeated this futile exercise until the bag was empty, maybe hoping one of the tampons would be ripe and tasty. I looked down and saw the hotel's manicured lawn littered with cardboard cylinders and cotton tampons. I was sorry I had missed the show. I should have gone out on the balcony in my towel, since half the hotel guests had already seen me mostly naked. I shook my head, laughed, and headed to breakfast.

My ill-advised battle with the baboons disrupted my morning; then I spent too much time at breakfast laughing with guests who had seen the show and explaining what had happened to those who missed it. I was pressed for time. Rushing to get ready to leave for the airport, I quickly shoved everything the baboon had strewn across my room back into my duffel. It was a hot day, so I decided to stay in the shorts and T-shirt I had thrown on for the first leg, a South African Airways flight from Victoria Falls to Johannesburg, South Africa. I tossed a pair of jeans and a jacket into my carry-on day pack so I could change during the five-hour Johannesburg layover before my connecting flight to JFK in New York.

The plane to Johannesburg was small, full of tourists and hunters fresh from photo and hunting safaris, all dressed casually and many not particularly neat or clean. No one glanced twice at me. When I reached the heavily air-conditioned Johannesburg Airport, I headed straight to the women's restroom to change into my warmer clothes. When I pulled the jeans out of my day pack, they reeked. I groaned. I'd worn those jeans for two weeks in the cool evenings as I stood close to the campfire for warmth. Not only did they smell of wood smoke, but they also were filthy and stiff with grime, dirt, and soot. And they didn't fit—the denim had stretched from wear, and I'd lost weight on the trip. So my choices for the upcoming 17.5-hour flight were either the shorts I had on or the filthy, stinky, ill-fitting jeans. I opted for dirty over cold and exposed.

When I landed in New York at 7:30 a.m. local time, I needed to clear customs quickly and then rush from JFK to LaGuardia Airport for my final flight to Chicago, scheduled to depart at 10 a.m. By the time I reached LaGuardia, I'd been traveling for thirty hours. I hadn't washed since the baboons interrupted my shower. My hair was matted because I'd never rinsed the shampoo from it. My filthy, stinky clothes had now also been slept in. Despite my appearance, I was flying first class, courtesy of American Airlines miles earned via dozens of domestic flights for work.

I was assigned seat 3C on the flight to Chicago. A man in a business suit and starched white shirt sat in 3A, the window seat next to me. Across the aisle from me, 3D was empty. Just before the plane door closed, an airline official escorted in a tall, striking woman with long, flowing dark hair. Model and actress Brooke Shields—perfectly dressed, perfectly coiffed, and perfectly made up, her trademark bold eyebrows expertly shaped—sat in 3D. A massive diamond ring from her recent engagement to André Agassi sparkled on her perfectly manicured hand.

The man next to me in 3A (I will call him Joe, since he never introduced himself and I don't know his name) shifted in his seat and tried to catch Brooke's attention. I could sense that Joe wanted to introduce himself to Brooke and start a witty conversation that would cause her to leave her tennis-star fiancé André and move in with him. But I was the obstacle between Joe and the gorgeous actress. In addition to glaring at me, Joe glared at the man in 3F, as though it was somehow that passenger's fault that he was seated next to the supermodel movie star, instead of next to smelly, dirty me. I shut my eyes and pretended to sleep. What I really wanted to do was tell Joe and Brooke (and maybe even the guy in 3F) that I looked like this and smelled like this because I took a chance, took a trip, and found adventure.

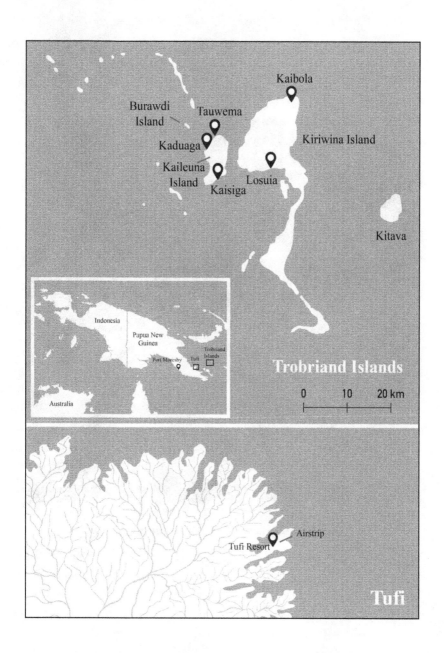

Kaibola

Burawdi
Island   Tauwema

Kaduaga   Kiriwina Island

Kaileuna
Island
          Kaisiga   Losuia

                                    Kitava

Indonesia
          Papua New
          Guinea
                    Trobriand
                    Islands
          Port Moresby Tufi

Australia

Trobriand Islands

0   10   20 km

Tufi Resort   Airstrip

Tufi

Margo kayaking near Tufi, Papua New Guinea

Courtesy of David Nitsch, reprinted with permission

Chapter Six

SAFER IN PORT MORESBY
POST–9/11 TRAVEL IN PAPUA NEW GUINEA

"EXCUSE ME, WOULD IT be possible for me to sit in the cockpit?" I asked the flight attendant, slightly worried she would call the Thai police and have me removed from the plane.

"No, I am sorry," she replied. "Another passenger already asked. But you can sit in the cockpit for landing in Hong Kong."

"That will be great, thank you."

"When it's time, I will come and take you to the cockpit."

Huh, the annoying guy in the pool at the Oriental Hotel in Bangkok had been telling the truth. Surprisingly, Cathay Pacific allowed passengers to sit in the cockpit during takeoff and landing. And now I would be lucky enough to do so while landing at Hong Kong's Kai Tak Airport (which closed a few months later). Surrounded by mountains, water, and apartment buildings, Kai Tak required a technically demanding visual approach, making it one of the world's most challenging airports for landings. On approach, planes flew so low that passengers could peer into apartment windows and see people watching television or eating dinner. Photographers captured these landings from every angle. On a later trip to Hong Kong, after Kai Tak had shut down, I saw a photo exhibit devoted solely to jaw-dropping images of jumbo jets flying between high-rise buildings, somehow slipping through with the smallest margin of error.

Just before the seat belt lights came on, the flight attendant escorted me to the cockpit and showed me to the jump seat behind the copilot, next to the flight engineer. The cockpit windows, which look narrow from the outside, seem expansive from inside the cramped cockpit and provide a spectacular 270-degree panorama. As the pilots navigated the difficult approach and landed the Boeing 747 with hundreds of passengers and crew on the short runway in Kowloon Bay, I sat quietly in my seat, enjoying the thrilling experience. But consider this: No one knew I would behave appropriately in the cockpit. No one screened my background or behavior to confirm that I was not a terrorist, a potential suicide, or a lunatic who might interfere with this tricky landing. One slight deviation and the plane would have flown right through an apartment building. Simply by asking, I was allowed access to the cockpit. But, of course, this was before 9/11.

By 2001, I had rafted with Mountain Travel Sobek in Chile and Pakistan, trekked with them in Nepal and Bhutan, and been the only client to enjoy four days and four nights on a camel safari in the Thar desert. So, when MTS needed clients to join an exploratory kayaking trip in remote areas of Papua New Guinea, they called me, again. Several travel companies already ran organized tours up the Sepik River, where tribes like the Huli Wigmen and Asaro Mudmen staged dances and sing-sings for the tourists. My parents took one of these trips. They had a great time, shot hours of video, and returned home with duffel bags full of life-size carved statues and elaborate tribal masks. (My dad put the statues and masks in a commercial freezer for a month to kill the bugs before bringing this tribal art into my parents' house.) MTS wanted to offer a more adventurous trip to the Tufi coast and the Trobriand Islands, areas not yet discovered by tour groups, but first they needed flexible participants willing to help test logistics and shape the itinerary.

Leo Le Bon was slated to co-lead an exploratory trip in October 2001. Le Bon is one of the co-founders of Mountain Travel and the "Grandfather of Adventure Travel" (as he now refers to himself on his Wanderlust Consulting website). He led the first commercial trek to Nepal and opened new adventure-travel destinations in Tibet, China, Chile, Peru, and Greenland. The MTS salesperson told me that joining Le Bon on this exploratory trip would be a tremendous opportunity to open yet another new adventure travel destination while being among the first tourists to visit these remote areas of Papua New Guinea. Did I want to join? Yes, I did, but not because of Le Bon. Regardless of who was leading the exploratory trip to Papua New Guinea, I would have agreed to join to have the opportunity to explore the area before the itinerary become pat and the experience predictable. Then, just before departure, MTS sent a final bulletin stating, "We are sorry to inform you that Leo Le Bon will not be able to join the trip at this time due to a medical emergency." Maybe the trip would be more of an adventure without Le Bon at the helm.

As I always did before a trip, I read as much as I could about the country and its people. I could not find as much written in English about Papua New Guinea as about India, the Silk Road, or Burma. Most of the books and articles I found on Papua New Guinea were about World War II battles, but I also found a few stories of thrilling and disconcerting encounters between white, foreign men and local tribes.

I learned about a very different exploratory trip in Papua New Guinea in 1930 that became the basis of a book and a documentary film, both titled *First Contact*. The explorers were prospectors, three white Australian men looking for gold, not guides and tourists looking for a new itinerary. The prospectors unwittingly walked into a "first contact" with a Highland tribe. Although the prospectors were not anthropologists or professional filmmakers, they filmed incredible footage of the tribe's first encounters with white men, airplanes, gramophones, tin cans, and guns. The hour-long 1983 documentary combines the original footage of this first contact with interviews conducted fifty years later. In the interviews, locals present during that first contact relate their terrified reactions at seeing white men for the first time. "We believed our dead went over there, turned white, and came back as spirits. That's how we explained the white man: our own dead had returned." Reading the book and watching the documentary was exciting. People who experienced this first contact were still alive. The opportunity to travel in a country not yet homogenized was part of what attracted me to this trip.

A less successful exploration kept popping up in my research. Thirty years after this first contact, Michael Rockefeller (son of then governor of New York and future former vice president Nelson Rockefeller, and scion to one of the wealthiest families in the US) disappeared while collecting primitive art in New Guinea (similar to the art my parents bought a few decades later and stuck in the freezer). Despite extensive and expensive searches by the Rockefeller family and subsequent efforts by journalists, Michael's fate remains unknown. Was he eaten by cannibals as an act of retaliation for a white man's killing of Asmat tribe members? Did he join the Asmat tribe, and was Michael the white man later captured on film? Or did Michael drown when his boat capsized? I didn't think I risked a similar fate (whatever it was) joining this commercial exploratory trip and was not deterred.

To learn more about the people who lived in the Trobriand Islands, rather than the white explorers, I tried to read the best-known work about the Trobriand Islands, Bronislaw Malinowski's 1929 book *The Sexual Life of Savages in North-Western Melanesia: An Ethnographic Account of Courtship, Marriage and Family Life Among the Natives of the Trobriand Islands, British New Guinea*. Malinowski, a Polish anthropologist, spent two years on the island of Kiriwina doing fieldwork. *The Sexual Life of Savages* reports his understanding of Trobriand family life: courtship, marriage, divorce, death, pregnancy, and childbirth, and infamously includes explicit descriptions of sexual behavior that almost caused the book to be banned. The third edition, published in 1932, contains a lengthy "Special Foreword," in which Malinowski complains that the seriousness of his ethnographic work has not been appreciated. Instead, "sensational details were picked out, and wondered or laughed at." Maybe he should have chosen a different title if he wanted to be taken seriously.

My problem with the book was the content, not the title. In the introduction, Malinowski admits that "I am especially aware that my knowledge of obstetrical facts and of the women's attitude at pregnancy and childbirth is rather meagre." Nonetheless, he goes on to write many supposedly authoritative chapters on pregnancy and childbirth among Trobriand Island women. The fact that he was a white Polish man (always fully dressed in Western clothes in the photographs he includes in the book) did not stop him from explaining the sexual practices of black Trobriand Island women (often naked in the photographs in the book). Malinowski expounds on these topics even though he admits to relying heavily on hearsay because he has kept a discrete distance from intimate behavior and never attempted "to spy upon passionate caresses." Malinowski's approach may have been acceptable during his time (or maybe not), but I could not finish reading it.

I forgot about *The Sexual Life of Savages*, until I started writing this book. As I typed descriptions of my limited interactions with Trobriand Islanders and the people who live near Tufi, I started to worry that I might sound like Malinowski, only worse because I only spent weeks, not years, in Papua New Guinea. Should I not describe my interactions with the people I met and pretend we paddled and camped alone, a group of Americans in an uninhabited area? I decided this is a book about travel, and travel is as much about the people you meet as the place you see. So I wrote what I experienced, as I understood it. This concern was not part of my considerations in 2001. At that time, I simply was excited for the adventure to start.

But before that happened, the world changed. On September 11, 2001, al-Qaeda terrorists crashed passenger jets into the two World Trade Center towers, the Pentagon, and a field in Pennsylvania. Just before 8 a.m. Chicago time on September 11, shortly after the first plane struck the north tower of the World Trade Center, my mother called me. For the previous few months, I'd been traveling to New York nearly every week for work. Worried that I might be on a flight to New York, or working in

New York, she was hugely relieved to find me at home. I didn't understand why. She asked whether my television was on. It was not.

I went upstairs to my family room, which had a TV and an unobstructed view of the Chicago skyline, including the Sears Tower, where I worked with hundreds of colleagues and friends. I turned on the TV and, like much of the world, watched in horror as the second plane flew into the South Tower and exploded. Looking out my window and seeing the Sears Tower standing tall behind images of the burning World Trade Center, I grabbed my phone and started dialing. In those days before Twitter and texted news alerts, my friends and colleagues who went into the office early would be sitting at their desks in the Sears Tower, oblivious to the unfolding terrorist attacks.

Clearly, the Sears Tower needed to be evacuated immediately. It was the tallest building in the United States and might be the next target. In this crisis, the building's emergency warning system failed utterly. Before 9/11, the Sears Tower had no building-wide broadcast system to communicate with the more than 10,000 people who worked there. That horrible morning, building management communicated a warning through a broadcast voicemail sent to all phone extensions in the building. In the law firm where I worked, the notice lights on the phones that signaled a waiting voicemail did not light up when a broadcast message was received—even an emergency message to evacuate—unless another (non-broadcast) message was left. Fortunately, some people working in the building heard the news and walked the halls, yelling warnings to evacuate.

Although I was not in my office that day, I experienced firsthand, in the days and weeks that followed, the inadequacies of the building's warning processes and evacuation procedures. Confusing and futile evacuation drills did nothing to reassure employees or prepare adequately for an emergency. My firm's offices were on floors seventy-six to eighty-one. What good was an evacuation drill that walked everyone down one flight of stairs and crowded us into a hallway, waiting for the all clear? How would this drill prepare anyone for a real evacuation down eighty flights of stairs to the street, or up as many as thirty-eight flights to the roof?

When should we evacuate by going down and when should we evacuate by going up? What about my secretary, who had just returned from knee-replacement surgery, not to mention the many other employees who could not walk down several dozen flights of stairs? None of these questions were answered. Then concrete planters—clearly designed to block a vehicle from driving into the building, not to hold flowers—appeared on the sidewalk in front of the building's Franklin Street entrance. Employees quit, some in response to their children, who insisted that they no longer work in the Sears Tower. It felt unsafe.

During this disorienting time, Michelle Higgins, a *Wall Street Journal* reporter, called me. She needed sources and information for a story on whether tourists were still planning adventure-travel trips in the wake of 9/11, the terrorist threats, and the travel restrictions. Higgins had called Mountain Travel Sobek looking for people who might speak with her. Knowing I would talk to anyone if it was about travel, they recommended me.

The *Journal's* feature story focused on how safety concerns affected travel. I think the reporter expected me to say that I was less likely to travel overseas. However, in the aftermath of 9/11 and the continually changing security drills at the Sears Tower, I felt safer about being in Papua New Guinea than at my desk on the seventy-seventh floor of the Tower. A version of what I said appeared in the story published in the *Journal* on October 19, 2001: "Of course, safety doesn't always mean what it used to. Papua New Guinea is so crime-ridden the State Department has issued a 'primer on personal security' for US visitors. But for Margo Weinstein, who works in Chicago's Sears Tower, a two-week kayaking trip sounded like the perfect escape. She says: 'I feel safer there.'" One week later, I left for Papua New Guinea.

The trip was divided into two halves, exploring two geologically and culturally distinct areas of coastal Papua New Guinea: the fjords around Tufi and the Trobriand Islands. We started in Tufi, a small village on the lower slope of Mount Trafalgar, which received its geographically and historically incongruous name (after the naval battle of Trafalgar) from John Moresby, a British Royal Navy officer who explored the New Guinea coast and "discovered" the site of the capital city now named after him. Eruptions from this now-extinct volcano created the spectacular tropical fjords around Tufi when the lava flowed down into the sea. The steep cliffs are layered with tropical rain forests, lush plants, colorful flowers, and orchids. Dramatic waterfalls plunge into the translucent Solomon Sea.

We explored the fjords around Tufi by kayak. To provide a European analogy, this was like touring Copenhagen by bicycle—in short, the perfect way to travel in the area. However, if our kayaks were bicycles, they would have had only one gear, pedal brakes, rusty chains, and hard seats.

The type of kayak we could use was limited by travel logistics. The kayaks (as well as our camping and personal gear) had to be transported on our commercial flight from Tufi to the Trobriand Islands and had to fit in the cargo hold of the small prop plane. This required kayaks that were collapsible or inflatable. We had one collapsible kayak, made by Feathercraft. This was also the only single kayak. The rest of the kayaks were doubles, inflatables made by Innova.

The collapsible kayak had a seat and a rigid frame. It was easy to paddle and steer, moved smoothly through the water, and was fun to use. The inflatables, on the other hand, were maddening. Paddling one of the forest-green inflatable kayaks was like trying to maneuver a water-filled kiddie pool through the ocean. Worse, the inflatable kayaks lacked a built-in elevated seat with a back support. While paddling, you just sat on the bottom of the boat. At my height, if I slumped at all, my armpits barely cleared the sides of the kayak. And there was no footwell or foot brace for leverage while paddling. From this position, it was difficult for me to paddle and impossible for me to use an efficient, powerful stroke.

My frustration with the inflatable kayaks almost became irrelevant, because my first day paddling in Papua New Guinea could have been my last. On our first beach landing, I failed to spot a cluster of sea urchins directly under my kayak. I stepped out of the kayak and right onto several of these barbed creatures. I was wearing Teva sandals, which protected the sole of my foot, but six long spines punctured the soft, tender skin on the side of my arch.

"FUCK! FUCK! FUCK! SHIT!" I screamed as I reached down, resulting in yet another spine puncturing me, this time in my thumb.

David, our guide and the other original co-leader for the trip, came running over with the first aid kit. When he saw the spines protruding from my foot and thumb, he looked worried, very worried. What he knew (and I did not) was that multiple deep puncture wounds from sea-urchin stings can lead to intense fatigue, weakness, muscle aches, shock, paralysis, respiratory failure . . . and death. At the time, all I knew was that it hurt like hell.

As I screamed and swore and David worriedly examined my foot, no one stated the obvious—how could I not have seen the sea urchins under the kayak? I could have said that the sea urchins were dark and hard to see in the shadow of the kayak, but the real reason I missed seeing them was that I was excited and enjoying myself and so failed to take the most basic safety precaution. It was too late—damage done, injury sustained. No one berated me.

The six big spines in my foot had gone too deep to remove with tweezers, and the beach where we landed was a lousy place to start slicing my foot with a scalpel. Plus, my thumb was already swelling and turning blue black. Luckily, we were still close enough to Tufi to go for help, so Brock (the young guide who replaced Leo Le Bon) and I paddled back. When we hit the beach, Brock ran up to the Tufi Dive Resort to get Wayne, the Australian resort manager. Together, they helped me up to the hotel. Wayne was calm, laid back, and knowledgeable about sea urchins. He cleaned and soaked my foot and thumb and then carefully sliced out the spines, making sure none of the creatures' parts were left behind. Examining my now-black thumb, Wayne concluded that the spine was gone, and the remaining color was just sea-urchin dye. Although I knew it would be difficult—okay, impossible— to keep my foot and thumb clean and dry over the next two weeks to prevent infection, I was lucky. I could continue with the trip. Brock and I paddled back to the beach where David waited, having taken the others to the guesthouse up the hill. Before getting out of the kayak, I leaned to the left and peered into the water, then leaned to the right and peered into the water. Lesson learned the hard way.

Paddling in the inflatable kayaks became marginally better as we made a few makeshift adjustments. Pumping them fuller slightly improved the maneuverability so that paddling the kayak was more like propelling an inflatable life ring through the ocean, not an entire kiddie pool full of water. A life jacket provided a sort-of seat that, when I sat on it, raised my armpits above the gunwales and gave me a slightly better angle for paddling. And as we reloaded the kayaks each day, we rearranged some gear into a block I could press my feet against, creating leverage.

Despite the shortcomings of the inflatable kayaks, they were way more comfortable than the traditional wooden outrigger canoes paddled by the villagers. Their canoes were carved from a single tree, sometimes a small tree. In many of the canoes, the hollowed-out area was too narrow for the paddler to sit or kneel inside the canoe. Instead, the paddler would sit with one butt cheek perched on either side of the opening, his butt crack centered in the middle, and his feet squeezed into the narrow hollow of the canoe. Compared to these hard wooden outriggers, the inflatable kayaks' too-soft bottoms were not so bad.

Many of the outriggers had a platform built across the middle of the canoe and supported by spars. These platforms—the local version of a pickup-truck bed—often overflowed with food, supplies, and kids. The one time our group attempted to paddle and ride in a traditional outrigger, we almost sank it. For a start, there were too many of us, and we were too heavy. Waves poured over the gunwales. As an American Red Cross–certified canoeing instructor, I knew we had to bail—fast!—but the only things available to bail with were a coconut half with a hole in the bottom and the top half of a plastic soda bottle. Neither could keep up with the water gushing into the canoe. To keep the canoe from sinking, we periodically grounded it, and our local pilot would bail furiously from the lowered stern. Because there are no roads out of Tufi, only footpaths, it is usually shorter and faster to paddle than to walk between villages—

unless you took on a group of *dim dims* (white people) and had to stop every ten minutes to bail.

Paddling kayaks down a tropical fjord or through the mangroves, we got into the rhythm of the place. Moving slowly (especially in the inflatable kayaks), we saw more. And we were more approachable. Families paddled up to us to sell their goods or fresh fruit or just to say hello. Traveling as the locals did, we fit in, sort of.

On Halloween, we paddled up to Jebo's Guest House on a lovely, white, sandy beach. The guesthouse consisted of a few basic huts and a washhouse equipped with basins of water, a dipper, and clean towels. The staff was delighted to see us. We were their first tourists since David had last been there—eighteen months earlier. As usual, we attracted a crowd.

Before leaving Port Moresby for Tufi, I had sorted my luggage and left a duffel bag at the hotel to pick up when we returned. For the kayak trip, I could take only essentials that would fit in a medium-size dry bag. I left behind two books I had looked forward to reading to have room for a Polaroid camera that took instant photos ("Polaroids"). Now, I dug into my dry bag and pulled out the Polaroid camera. People were reluctant to pose . . . until I took the first photo and handed it to the thrilled subject. Then came the free-for-all. Everyone wanted to pose— alone, with family members, with someone in our group. I obliged, taking photos and handing them the Polaroids, until Lancelot, the headman at the guesthouse, asked me to stop. At first, I was concerned. Had I done something wrong or offended someone? No, quite the opposite. Lancelot wanted to have a photo taken with his family the next day when they could dress in their traditional ceremonial clothes, and he feared I would run out of film before then. (A photo of them in ceremonial clothes—not the Polaroid—appears in this book.)

Although our group, and the income we provided, were very welcome at the small guesthouses where we stayed, our presence exponentially increased the demand for fresh water. The clear, dry weather around Tufi was nearly perfect for paddling, and the resulting lack of bugs was amazing. But the ever-present blue skies and sunshine made the subsistence living conditions even harder. Rain was the villagers' main source of fresh water for drinking and bathing. In its absence, they were living under drought conditions. At one of the guesthouses, a woman named Rachel and two little boys paddled the length of the fjord to a freshwater spring twice each day to fill buckets and containers with water for us. Washhouses with basins full of fresh water for bathing were available for our use, but after seeing the effort needed to obtain that water, we all washed very little. Nonetheless, we still needed to drink a lot of water to replace what we sweated out in the heat.

The residents of the Tufi area could feed themselves with locally grown produce and fish they caught, but they had to buy essentials like clothes, soap, and kerosene (they had no electricity and used kerosene lamps for light). Our local guide on a hike we took one morning wore a shirt that was more holes than fabric, which was not an expensive fashion statement like ripped or distressed jeans. Brock and the guide hit it off during the hike, so I gave Brock the only extra shirt I had with me (a Mountain Travel Sobek T-shirt) to give to the local hiking guide. (The guide was small, and the shirt was large on me, so it fit him.) Rachel, the woman who collected water for us and shared many stories with us, asked me whether I had any pain medication. I gave her all the Advil I had with me, but it was only a small Ziploc bag of ibuprofen. (There is a small medical clinic in Tufi, but a retired doctor in the village told us it often lacks supplies.) These gifts were so little and would not last long, but if the trip went well, perhaps MTS would run more tours and bring additional cash to the area.

I also learned of efforts to provide structural changes that would bring more lasting assistance. A woman I met on the beach one afternoon told me her brother would soon be in Parliament representing that area. He was determined to accomplish three things. First, he wanted to bring water to a central village location so they were not forced to travel every day for water that often was undrinkable. Second, he wanted to bring electricity to the area. Third, he wanted to provide a boat with a motor so that the villagers could take their produce and fish to market and earn cash. I don't know whether he was able to achieve these goals to serve the basic needs of his constituents. I hope he did.

In this beautiful place, life was hard.

Paddling in the kayaks, we were always wet and always in the sun. I usually wore only a bathing suit, shorts, sunglasses, and sunblock, and felt great in the sunshine and on the water. Others in our small group, however, suffered from the constant exposure to the sun and salt water. Several of my travel companions covered themselves from head to toe with hats, long-sleeved shirts, and something thrown over their legs to protect themselves from the sun. Yet somehow, they still managed to get sunburned, and their extra clothes became suffocating, only adding to their heat exhaustion and dehydration. As the days went on, some of them developed blisters and sores that did not heal and were at risk of infection because they could not keep them clean or dry.

Fortunately, between the two legs of the trip, we spent one night at the Tufi Dive Resort (where my sea-urchin wounds were treated that first day). We had beds, electricity, showers, and good food. Wounds and sunburns had a chance to heal before being subjected again to sun and salt water. Even better, the hotel had a washer and a dryer we could use. After a machine wash and dry, most of my clothes were totally clean, dry, and fungus-free—for the moment. It felt luxurious. However, the fungus did not come out of my "wet shirt." (We each had a wet shirt and a dry shirt in our limited personal gear.) But at least I could put on that shirt without wanting to puke from the smell.

The next morning, we got ready to fly to the Trobriand Islands for the second leg of our exploration. We loaded all our gear into a truck for the short drive to a tiny restaurant on a big grassy field at the edge of a cliff that plunged into the Solomon Sea. This was the Tufi Airport.

As we approached the plane that had just landed, the pilot exited from the cockpit and headed toward a barrel with a tube and a crank connected to the top. After inserting the tube into the plane's fuselage, he supervised the hand-cranking of the fuel into the plane. During this refueling, the copilot opened the cargo door and signaled that we should bring our gear over, which included one foldable framed kayak, deflated rubber kayaks, kayak paddles, tents, tarps, water jugs, food (mostly silver bags of freeze-dried meals and Luna bars), safety gear, first aid supplies, and personal luggage. The pile of our stuff was gigantic, and the small rear cargo hold already looked crammed to capacity without our gear.

This did not stop the copilot, who directed us to hand up the boats to load. To our dismay, the copilot started to jam the collapsible kayak into the hold without regard for the frame. Brock quickly jumped into the hold to save the kayak and make space for additional gear. When nothing more could be squeezed into the hold, the copilot started shoving gear under the seats, pushing aside the feet of passengers already on the plane. Eventually, all our gear was loaded somewhere. Our group boarded the plane and found every seat already occupied. The copilot turned his attention to loading passengers in the same way he had loaded gear. A family of four—two parents and two kids—who had been seated in four seats on either side of the central aisle were moved into two seats, a child on each adult's lap. In other rows, three adults were squeezed in seats intended for two. In this way, random seats opened up for our group.

We were on a seriously overloaded plane that was carrying more cargo than it was meant to hold and had almost twice as many passengers as seats. And it had started to rain. Given the drought in the area and the suffering from the lack of local fresh water, I wanted to be happy about the downpour. But I was not. In the pouring rain, the grassy field serving as a runway was quickly turning into mush that could snag a wheel on departure. I briefly considered getting off the plane, but where would I go and what would I do? Despite the obvious and not insignificant risk, I sat down and buckled up. I held my breath as we took off. Forty-five minutes later, I exhaled as we landed at the airstrip on Kiriwina.

The itinerary from MTS promised, or warned, of the greeting we would receive upon landing in Kiriwina: "Touching down on the Kiriwina airstrip is an experience you'll never forget; typically, a hundred villagers meet each plane's arrival." This echoed Paul Theroux's experience in

Kiriwina a decade earlier, described in *The Happy Isles of Oceania: Paddling the Pacific*. Landing in Kiriwina (his collapsible kayak packed in the luggage hold like our kayaks were), Theroux's flight was met by about 200 people, gaping at the plane as it taxied to a stop. As he too noted, this was one of the group activities of Kiriwina—watching the plane land and take off.

Despite this advance notice, I failed to anticipate the intensity of the greeting. The crowd was friendly, but there were too many of them in the small space between the tarmac and the shed that served as the terminal. After their initial welcome to the *dim dims*—smiles and waves and greetings—about half the group (maybe a hundred) just stared at us. The other half (another hundred) wanted to help with our bags. We did not have a hundred bags. In all the chaos, I became a low-lying atoll in a sea of Trobriand Islanders. I could not see or hear the rest of our group. I kept smiling and moving forward, away from the plane and toward anything on the other side of the crowd.

When I surfaced on the other side of the shed, I saw David and Brock standing next to a truck. Public transport in Papua New Guinea is in so-called PMVs (public motor vehicles). A PMV is any vehicle—a rickety minibus or, in this case, a big truck, open in the back—that carries passengers. We were lucky that a PMV happened to be in Losuia at the airport and heading north when we wanted to go. It may have been the only transport that day, or that week. We loaded our gear, climbed up, and squeezed into the few openings between passengers already seated in the back.

I tried to strike up a conversation with two women seated next to me. In response, they just stared and laughed at the *dim dims*. Then, one of the women reached over and touched the relatively white skin of my bare leg. Before I could react, though, she spotted a pasty-white leg covered in freckles, and shifted her attention to Jana, a fellow paddler and even whiter *dim dim*. Just as I was thinking the day was getting better—the plane took off and landed safely, we found transport that could carry us and our gear, and my white-skinned leg was no longer interesting—it started to rain again. Okay, I could deal with riding in the back of an open truck in the pouring rain, not a problem. And then a tire blew. We all piled out of the truck and stood in the rain in the middle of the road, surrounded by staring locals, including two little girls who could not stop giggling, seeing the humor in our predicament that I could not appreciate. Luckily, the driver had a spare tire, and he made the swap. We all piled back into the truck and continued north. We were the last passengers on the transport when it stopped at Kaibola, a small village at the northern tip of Kiriwina.

The village headman greeted us with delight—his village was anxious for more tourists. How long could we stay? To make the offer more enticing, he directed several villagers to erect a huge Australian surplus tent that had arrived in the village as part of cyclone aid a few years earlier. It was a great shelter that protected us from the rain later during dinner. But first, the headman insisted, we needed to see a very famous and important cave. I put my raincoat on over my wet clothes and joined the others and a local guide.

Before we could proceed to the cave, however, we needed to obtain permission. The headman's invitation and permission (plus the cash David paid him) was not enough. We also needed permission from the landowner, an ancient, Yoda-like blind man squatting and hunched over into a tiny ball of sharp elbows, shoulders, and knees. Because of his position above me at the edge of his raised hut, I could not tell whether he was naked or wearing shorts. In response to David's request, the man spoke softly, keeping his head down between his knees. A young man, huge by comparison, translated and told us we had permission to visit the cave.

Walking toward and through the limestone cave was like walking over a dry coral reef covered in jungle growth. My foot was still sore from the sea-urchin stings, so I walked gingerly. The locals guiding us were barefoot, walking over limestone that would have shredded my sissy city feet. When we reached the cave, the local guides told us that the cave was part of a creation myth, the story of how people spread across the Pacific. But neither of the locals guiding us knew the full story. One hadn't even been to the cave before, which is why he volunteered to join us—he too wanted to see the mythical cave.

———— ꦠꦍꦤꦾꦠꦤꦠꦾ꧀ꦠ ————

Travel in the Trobriand Islands presented more challenges than travel in the Tufi area. The Trobriand Islands are a small archipelago of twenty-eight coral atolls, only a few feet above sea level. In sharp contrast to the lush fjords around Tufi, the Trobriand Islands are flat, hot, and humid, with a swampy lagoon in the middle of each atoll. Most of the 12,000 Trobriand Islanders lived on the island of Kiriwina, where our plane landed. The other islands had populations of a few hundred people or were uninhabited. Except for a single hotel on Kiriwina, the Trobriand Islands had no tourist infrastructure, not even simple guesthouses like the ones where we stayed around Tufi.

Fresh food was harder to find, except for pineapple, taro, and yams— lots of yams, growing everywhere. We often fell back on the freeze-dried food we carried with us, but I found it inedible and subsisted primarily on fresh pineapple and Luna bars. One day, I hit a breaking point—I needed to eat something different. I bought a giant watermelon from a woman in a village where we stopped to get fresh water. For the rest of that day, I paddled a small inflatable kiddie pool in the Solomon Sea with that watermelon secured under my knees—just so I could eat watermelon and Luna bars for dinner instead of pineapple and Luna bars.

The itinerary anticipated that we would camp on Kiriwina and other inhabited islands, where we could get fresh water and meet and interact with the people. These interactions became even more meaningful because we did not have to communicate only through smiles and pantomime. Although the native language of the Trobriand Islands is Kilivila, many villagers spoke English because Christian missionaries had established schools and taught English as part of their efforts to convert the Trobriand Islanders. Methodist missionaries arrived in the late nineteenth century, followed more recently by Catholic missionaries and Seventh-day Adventists.

When we camped in their villages, the people invited us to sit and "tell stories." And we did. The Trobriand Islanders wanted to know about America and peppered us with questions. "Does everyone in America wear oxygen masks?" "Are there giraffes in America?" "Does America have lakes? Fish?" I don't know if they believed the answers when we told them about frozen lakes and ice fishing. David had an inflatable globe—it might have been a beach ball—which worked to show where in the world Papua New Guinea is in relation to the US. But it still was not enough to explain ice fishing to people living on the Solomon Sea, just south of the equator.

Through music, we found something in common that spanned the latitudes. One evening, the church choir in a small Seventh-day Adventist village held a practice in the central hut. As they sang, Jack looked up. He knew the song. And as a former Whiffenpoof—the senior men's (now coed) a cappella singing group at Yale—Jack could sing. He joined the choir for that song, and then for the remainder of the choir practice.

The Polaroid camera continued to captivate and draw crowds. In Tauwema village on Kaileuna Island, I was arranging and posing groups of people who wanted a Polaroid when a woman came up to me, grabbed me by my wrist, and pulled me away. Everyone—tourists and locals alike—laughed as she dragged me across the village to a hut with a baby. She wanted me to take a picture of the baby. I did. And then she dragged me to the next baby, and the next. I took the photos, but babies and toddlers cried as soon as they saw me—a *dim dim*. (It was not just me; all of us *dim dims* made babies cry.) It was difficult to take a memorable photo with a screaming child in the center.

In a small village near Kaisiga, on the southern end of Kaileuna Island, a woman beckoned me over to where she stood with a friend, clearly wanting to have her picture taken with the Polaroid camera. As I raised the camera to take the photo, she put up her hand and yelled at me to stop. She spoke no English, but there was no doubt about what she meant. Confused, I lowered the camera. As I stood there, the woman yanked off her shirt. Next, she pulled off her friend's shirt. Then she donned the friend's shirt, smiled, and posed for her photo. When I handed her the developing Polaroid, she immediately handed it to her friend so that she could remove her friend's shirt and put her own back on. The friend, now wearing her own shirt, then posed and smiled in what must have been regarded as the nicer outfit.

I brought six cartridges of Polaroid film, ten shots each, to Papua New Guinea. I had suspected sixty photos would be too many, but even six hundred would not have been too many. That camera provided me with a wonderful way to say thank you for allowing us to camp in your village or refill our fresh water supply. (Of course, David also paid cash for these things.)

I felt fortunate to be on this exploratory trip when *dim dims* arriving in a village were a welcome surprise, not a biweekly event. In Kaisiga, other than Paul Theroux on the journey he recorded in *Happy Isles of Oceania*, we were the only *dim dims* to paddle in and stay. It was an experience that could not be repeated and one that I would not have missed. But at night, when we wanted to eat, sleep, or maybe somehow wash, it was difficult. We tried to find campsites away from the village center, where their homes, thatched huts on stilts, were built around a central square. We set up our tents close to the shore, where it was quieter, hoping for a bit more privacy. But no such luck. The only moments of privacy were in our tents—if the flaps were closed and zipped and we didn't use our flashlights.

We had come to the Trobriand Islands for the experience of meeting the people and camping in their villages, but we also needed relief from the unrelenting gaze and intense scrutiny of the villagers. At our break point, just before we might have started to act less graciously toward our hosts, we set off in our kayaks in search of some privacy, just for one night. This required paddling from the small village of Tauwema on the northern tip of Kaileuna Island to the uninhabited Burawdi Island.

The crossing between these two islands was about seven kilometers as the crow flies—which is not how we paddled—across open sea. It would have been challenging in our inflatable kayaks even under good conditions. We did not have good conditions. About halfway across, a violent storm blew in, bringing a strong headwind, high waves, and pelting rain. Seeing more than a few yards ahead became difficult. Moving more than a few yards forward was even harder.

During an earlier paddle, Brock had explained his "bubble strategy" for safety. It should not take him more than one minute of "Oh, shit"

paddling to get to someone in trouble. But now, during this open crossing—
in pounding rain, high waves, and strong headwinds—Brock and Jack burst
that bubble and raced ahead, paddling their kayak away from the group
and out of sight. What was Brock doing? How could he paddle away and
leave the rest of us in this potentially dangerous situation? Although angry
at their macho move and Brock's negligence as a guide, I was okay. Luckily,
it was my turn to paddle the Feathercraft, and although I was having a hard
time paddling a straight course to the island, progress was much easier for
me than for those in the inflatable kayaks. But our group was now missing
a skilled guide and a strong paddler, which we would need in an emergency.

I kept paddling, fighting the wind and waves, squinting into the
driving rain. I had no other choice. Despite my efforts, I did not seem
to be making progress. When our situation seemed at its worst, I looked
down and saw a huge bloom of giant jellyfish moving just beneath
the surface of the water, propelled by graceful contractions. I stopped
paddling. I called out to the others, who also stopped and saw the same
fantastic scene surrounding us. It was magical. Then, as fast as the storm
had blown in, it blew past. No longer fighting the elements, we sped up
and paddled to shore.

When we landed on the beach, instantly my frustration disappeared,
replaced by understanding and relief. Brock and Jack's kayak lay deflated
on the sand. Their sprint to the island had been lifesaving, not a show of
machismo. Jack had noticed bubbles near his feet, meaning that air was
escaping from the tube into the water at the bottom of the kayak. Jack
jammed his foot into the area where the bubbles appeared, hoping the
pressure would slow the rate at which the kayak was sinking. As Jack told
Brock about the leak, they both thought of the tiger sharks that swam and
fed in the waters around the deserted island we were paddling toward.
Tiger sharks are large and voracious with teeth designed for shearing their
food. They are one of the few sharks known to attack swimmers and
surfers unprovoked and are second only to the great white in the number
of reported attacks on humans. Not taking any time to convey what was
happening, Brock and Jack took off and paddled as hard and fast as they

could toward shore before their inflatable kayak deflated and sank in the tiger sharks' home turf.

They made the right choice to take off; it just would have been nice if they had shouted out before paddling away. If they had stayed with the group, more than one kayak might have sunk, and a tiger shark could have taken a bite out of someone. The Feathercraft I was paddling had a small circular cockpit that only one person could fit in. If either Jack or Brock had tried to lie across the canvas top, the kayak likely would have rolled and swamped. If any of the inflatable kayaks, already riding low in the water, could have managed to stay afloat with an extra passenger squeezed on board, I suspect no one could have paddled through that storm. Fortunately, we did not need to find out. Shaken by the averted disaster, Brock and David paced the beach, saying over and over, "We all made it. We all made it."

We set up camp at the tip of the island. As we had hoped, the island was deserted. No other human inhabitants. No one staring incessantly at us. But also no one to help us. No one to lend us a boat or give us a ride. However, with the storm gone, it was a lovely evening, disrupted only by groans, grunts, and an occasional obscenity as Brock and Dave attempted to glue patches on the rips in the kayak.

We slept well that night, with no roosters crowing hours before dawn. The next morning, it was evident that the kayak could not be repaired. After much discussion of logistics and options, Dave set off alone in the Feathercraft to paddle to Kaduaga, a larger village than Tauwema, on the west coast of Kaileuna Island, in search of a rescue boat. The rest of us explored the island, its beaches, and caves. As long as we did not focus on the fact that we were stranded, it was a great day.

Not long before sunset, Dave returned on a motorized fishing boat large enough to carry all of us, our boats, and our gear. He had paddled quickly to Kaduaga, but the negotiations to secure a boat had moved slowly. Before Dave could get to the point of discussing details of our rescue, he needed to sit and chew a large quantity of betel nuts, seeds that are wrapped in leaves coated with lime and chewed for their narcotic effect. Traveling in Asia, when you see someone with ruby-red gums and rotting red teeth, he is a heavy consumer of betel nuts. Dave's willingness to partake saved us (or at least saved MTS some money). Luckily, the negotiations concluded while the captain was still competent to navigate and motor his boat to Burawdi. The rescue boat carried a few extra "crew" on deck who came for the ride to see firsthand the dum-dum *dim dims* stranded on a deserted island. We did not disappoint.

By the end of the trip, sitting on the dirty pavement outside the Losuia Airport on Kiriwina, "I reached a Zen state regarding dirt, sweat, heat, and flies," as I wrote in my journal that day. With flies buzzing everywhere (the bug-less environment of drought-stricken Tufi had been replaced by steamy, buggy conditions in the Trobriand Islands) and surrounded by a crowd, I sat on the ground and played twenty questions as we waited to see what day a plane might arrive. I had never been so grody for this long. If the trip had had a motto, it would have been "The fungus among us."

Hungry and bored, I poured Purell over my hands in a futile attempt to remove some of the layers of DEET before I peeled a mango. "Sister, sister," someone called out from the crowd watching us. Apparently, my technique for peeling the mango was wrong. But I had not yet reached the point when I could let my critic peel my mango with her even dirtier hands. I quickly finished my inartful peeling before she could grab the fruit. I took a big bite and let the sweet, sticky juice cover my chin and drip down onto my damp, mildewed, dirty, stinky T-shirt.

Risk is hard to assess. Soon after 9/11, I made the choice to travel to Papua New Guinea, a country described in the *Wall Street Journal* story about my trip as "so crime-ridden the State Department has issued a 'primer on personal security' for US visitors." Then I chose to fly on an overloaded prop plane that took off in the rain from a soggy grass field that dropped off a cliff into the ocean. Yet, on November 12, 2001, I was alive and well, paddling my inflatable kayak in the Trobriand Islands.

That morning, at 9:13 EST, American Airlines flight 587 was cleared for takeoff from JFK Airport in New York, heading to Santo Domingo, Dominican Republic. The passengers taking off on that commercial jet from a major American airport probably were not worried about their safety. Two and a half minutes later, however, the plane crashed into the intersection of Beach 131st Street and Newport Avenue in the Belle Harbor neighborhood of Queens, New York. Pilot error, not another terrorist attack, caused the crash. No one on the plane survived.

What does this mean, other than that I am fortunate? Should I be more careful because you never know what might happen? Or should I take more risks because you never know what might happen? I did not take risks for the thrill of the risk. I took the risks necessary to go where I wanted to go and do what I wanted to do. I took the risks I felt were reasonable for me. That calculus changed completely, though, when I had a baby.

Owner of the sacred creation cave and his translator, Kaibola,
Kiriwina Island, Papua New Guinea

Courtesy of David Nitsch, reprinted with permission

Lancelot and his family in ceremonial dress, near Tufi, Papua New Guinea

Courtesy of Andrew Meissner, reprinted with permission

Margo and Jake in the klongs of Bangkok

Part II

AFTER

JAKE WAS BORN IN November 2004. Before he could roll over, walk, talk, or had any teeth, he was featured in an article in *The Wall Street Journal.* Why? For doing what his mama did best—taking a trip.

In 2005, bringing an infant to a business conference was not best practices, not the way to build a career, and definitely not a sign of devotion to the job. But it also did not seem newsworthy enough for the front page of the Weekend Journal section. Yet, on Friday, January 21, 2005, baby Jake's first trip featured in a *Wall Street Journal* story titled "The Parent Trip." The *WSJ* reported that when Margo Weinstein, a "partner at a top Chicago law firm, goes to a partners' weekend gathering later this month at the Biltmore in Arizona, she'll invite her mom along to look after her baby, 10-week-old Jake." Jake was famous. He achieved what some businesspeople strive a lifetime to obtain—his name in the *WSJ*. My mom, whose name did not appear in the story, enjoyed the attention she received when she pushed Jake around the resort's grounds in his stroller. Hotel staff and conference attendees recognized Jake as the baby featured in the *WSJ* and stopped to chat. My mom loves to chat.

I did not enjoy the weekend as much as my mom did. I spent the nights getting up every few hours to nurse and care for Jake, trying to do so silently in the dark so that we did not wake my mom. I spent the days in conference rooms pretending my brain could function at a high level on two hours of sleep and that I cared about the substance of the meetings. The low point came when I made a presentation to more than 100 of my partners, not knowing that I had baby spit up in my hair and down the back of one of the few shirts I owned that I could still button. These were not my finest days of parenting or lawyering. I struggled with both. In retrospect, traveling to Arizona (with my infant) to attend partners' weekend during my maternity leave was not the best move. But it provided my first lesson on how to (and how not to) combine motherhood and travel.

After Jake was born, I finally understood a one-minute encounter that at the time struck me as so odd that it stayed with me. In September 2000, I attended a talk and book signing by Steve McCurry, the photographer best known for his image of the young Afghan refugee girl with piercing green eyes that appeared on the cover of *National Geographic* in 1985. McCurry was in Chicago promoting his new book of striking photos taken in South and Southeast Asia, including images from Pakistan, India, Burma, Thailand, and Cambodia, all countries I recently had traveled through. Following a slide presentation that made me want to get on a plane and go, a woman raised her hand to ask McCurry a question.

"Do you have any children?"

"No, I don't," McCurry replied.

"I did not think so," she said. "If you did, I don't know how you could have traveled so much."

At the time, I rolled my eyes at her. Now, I was her, or at risk of becoming her.

I had the opportunity to continue with the same kind of adventure travel I had always done, now with Jake in tow. Dave, one of the guides on the exploratory kayaking trip in Papua New Guinea, invited Jake and me to join his family (including his toddler daughter) and others on a kayak trip in the Solomon Islands. Since toddlers cannot snorkel, scuba dive, or paddle a kayak, the parents would take turns traveling in a small motorboat with the toddlers while the other adults explored on and under the sea. I declined. If I had wanted to go, I could have made it work. But I did not want to go. I did not want to take that level of risk with Jake or be responsible for someone else's child under such conditions.

The tables had turned. Before Jake was born, when I took trips like the one Dave proposed in the Solomon Islands, many colleagues and some friends thought I was crazy. They would never take such a trip and could not understand why I wanted to. Now, I thought Dave was crazy. I could not understand why he wanted to bring his toddler daughter on this trip. After years of taking month-long vacations off the grid, my risk calculus had changed. My travel needed to change, too.

I went from camping on deserted beaches in Papua New Guinea and Palau to stays at all-inclusive beach resorts in Mexico, Jamaica, and the Cayman Islands. I traded steep mountain switchbacks in Nepal for flat city

boulevards in Paris. And I left the river rafts behind for Disney cruises—
two to the Caribbean and one to the Baltic. The trips were nice, and Jake
and I had fun, but they did not satisfy my wanderlust. This was not how
I wanted to travel and experience the world. I needed to figure out how
to travel to a different country and immerse myself in a different culture
in a way that accommodated Jake but still challenged and interested me.
How could I combine wanderlust and motherhood? Eventually, I found a
way. The path I stumbled upon led us first to Shanghai and then to Bali.

Margo and Jake falling for Shanghai

Chapter Seven

TEXARKANA TO SHANGHAI
TRAVEL SABBATICAL

I COVETED A SABBATICAL, a break, extended time someplace different.

By the winter of 2011, when Jake was in kindergarten, I had worked at the same law firm for twenty-three years, advancing from associate to equity partner. When I started there in the fall of 1988, just out of a federal appellate court clerkship, I assumed I would stay a year or two, gain some experience, make some money, and move on. But I liked the job and the firm. The work was challenging and paid well. My colleagues were smart, hardworking, and nerdy (even for lawyers). A few became lifelong friends. Although sex discrimination and gender bias were rampant in the legal profession, they did not seem as pervasive at my firm. And a stable job with a good salary and generous vacation benefits afforded me the freedom to travel on extended trips. So, I stayed—for decades.

Then the firm's management changed, and they changed the focus and nature of the firm in ways I disagreed with and did not want to be a part of. And as I became more senior, the gender discrimination I had managed to ignore became more overt. Succeeding as a woman handling major commercial litigation for Fortune 100 clients meant dealing with the sexist truth Bette Davis called out when she said, "When a man gives his opinion, he's a man. When a woman gives her opinion, she's a bitch."

I suspect I was referred to in this manner on multiple occasions behind my back, but it only happened once in an email that landed in my inbox. I was working on a class action lawsuit with hundreds of defendants represented by dozens of law firms and even more lawyers. Following a joint defense meeting where I gave my strong (and well-reasoned, I thought) opinion on the best strategy, a senior male partner for a different defendant sent an email that he mistakenly cc'ed to the entire service list of all defense lawyers on the case (including me). In the email, he referred to me as "that bitch."

In their book *What Works for Women at Work,* Joan C. Williams and Rachel Dempsey label this the "what-a-bitch" pattern. The more accomplished and, as a result, the more threatening women become, the more often they are called a bitch. Williams and Dempsey's research confirmed as a widespread phenomenon what I already knew from personal experience. For a successful woman, "being labeled a bitch is sometimes an unavoidable side effect of doing your job." After decades as a litigator, I was tired of waiting for structural change to eliminate sexism and bias in the workplace and tired of being called a bitch for doing my job. Something had to give.

At the firm's partners' weekend in February 2011, I hatched a plan that addressed my wanderlust and job frustration. The firm recently had opened small offices with a handful of lawyers in Hong Kong, Beijing, and Shanghai. These were early moves in an aggressive expansion that grew the firm to more than 12,000 lawyers in over eighty countries, the largest law firm in the world by head count. The firm now has over 5,000 lawyers and forty-six offices in China, but in 2011, there were just a few lawyers there, and the partners all flew to the US for the annual partners' weekend. I spent much of that weekend tracking them down, introducing myself, and learning about their offices.

My initial idea was to contrive a way to transfer to the new Hong Kong office for a year.

Hong Kong is one of my favorite cities in the world. Even after the return of Hong Kong to China a decade earlier, English was still widely spoken, and the British common-law system was still in effect. Hong Kong was a mecca for expats, and finding an international school for Jake would be easy. Living in Hong Kong for a year seemed exciting and doable. Or so I thought.

The lawyers from the Hong Kong office quickly dissuaded me. Housing in Hong Kong was prohibitively expensive, they said, and renting a decent-size apartment in a nice neighborhood near a school for Jake would cost more than I wanted to spend—if I could even find one. Beijing was out, too. In 2010, the US embassy in Beijing launched a Twitter feed—@BeijingAir—with hourly reports of the pollution readings taken from a monitoring station on the embassy roof. When the air quality index soared above 500, the top of the US scale, the US embassy's tweet described the air quality as "crazy bad." No, I did not want Jake (or me) breathing Beijing's air for months. I shifted my focus to the Shanghai office.

The main obstacle to my evolving plan was the lack of a legitimate business reason for me to work in Shanghai. I don't read or speak Mandarin, and I don't practice corporate or tax law, the two primary areas of American law of interest to Chinese clients seeking to do business in the United States. So, I came up with a proposal to do business development for class action cases filed in the US against Chinese companies. This plan passed the straight-face test, though just barely. In 2011, the Securities and Exchange Commission charged dozens of Chinese companies trading on US stock exchanges with accounting irregularities. Class action lawsuits by investors followed. That year also saw the beginning of litigation arising out of defective Chinese drywall used to rebuild homes after Hurricanes Rita and Katrina devastated the Gulf and East Coasts in 2010. This litigation, consolidating cases filed around the US, was not settled until 2019, when the defendant Chinese drywall manufacturers agreed to pay $248 million to homeowners.

In the end, it did not matter whether I had a plan or whether the plan was feasible. The new management of the firm seemed as exasperated with me as I was with them. They let me go to Shanghai. For the firm, there was not much downside. I kept my health insurance (switching to CIGNA, which provided both international and domestic coverage) and took a considerable reduction in my income, receiving only a small stipend until I returned to Chicago.

Although the firm did not oppose the plan, the newly opened Shanghai office would not be able to provide me with a work visa. My best option for living legally in Shanghai was to get a student visa, an "X" visa, and a residency permit. I needed to find a graduate school in Shanghai, with a program taught in English, that would admit me for the coming fall semester. It would be a bonus if the program taught a subject I was interested in at an advanced level. (I already had a BA in economics and political science from Yale College and a JD from Northwestern University School of Law.) Surprisingly, I found the perfect institution that fit all these criteria: Fudan University.

Although my plan bordered on ridiculous, Fudan University is no joke. Widely regarded as one of China's most prestigious universities, Fudan has 30,000 students on its Shanghai campus and exchange programs with more than 200 foreign universities. Fudan also offers a postgraduate program for international students taught in English by Chinese professors on the Shanghai campus. I did not intend to stay long enough, or plan to work hard enough, to earn a master's degree, so I applied for a non-degree program in Chinese history and culture. If I was admitted, the program would come with visas and residency permits for Jake and me. I set up an interview with the head of the history department for May 10, 2011, when Jake and I would be in Shanghai to explore our options.

Next, I needed to find a school for Jake, who would be in first grade in the fall of 2011. I considered three different international schools, in three different locations in the vast city, with three different education philosophies: YK Pao, Yew Chung International School of Shanghai (YCIS), and Shanghai American School (SAS), Puxi Campus. YK Pao had no spots in first grade for the 2011 to 2012 school year. I submitted applications for YCIS and SAS and set up interviews and tours at these schools for a few days after we arrived in Shanghai, giving us time to adjust to jet lag.

Other than my new law firm partners, whom I had just met at the partners' weekend conference, I knew no one in Shanghai. I had never even been there, though I had spent a month traveling in China in 1999. Fortunately, I had a friend (Bob) who had a friend (Peggy) whose husband worked for Chrysler, and their family, including a daughter several years older than Jake, had recently transferred to Shanghai. Although they received help from a relocation company paid for by Chrysler, they had just navigated a similar process to find a place to live in Shanghai and an international school for their daughter. Bob emailed Peggy and introduced me. I followed up with a long list of questions about schools and real estate brokers, and included the May dates when Jake and I would be in Shanghai, saying I would love to meet her if she had time. Peggy's substantive response was invaluable, including all the things she wished she had known and done before her look-see trip, which she called an exhausting disaster. Peggy also invited Jake and me to stay with her family while we were in Shanghai.

Peggy's generous offer would save me the cost of ten nights in a Shanghai hotel and give Jake and me a better idea of what expat life might be like in Shanghai. But could I accept? I considered the possibility that, after just a few months in China, Peggy had adopted Asian courtesy and made the polite offer knowing that the equally polite recipient would demur. Polite ambiguity could lead to a major misunderstanding. So, I asked directly. The invitation was genuine. I gratefully accepted and offered to bring a duffel bag full of items they could not find in Shanghai. Their modest list included four bottles of Neutrogena aerosol sunscreen, athlete's foot spray, and 5-hour Energy in tiny bottles. I threw in some nicer items as well, to be more of a gift and less the outcome of a trip to Walgreens.

On May 5, 2011, Jake and I boarded American Airlines flight 289 for the fourteen-hour nonstop flight from Chicago to Shanghai. Our return flight was May 16, 2011. With a day lost in travel and time zones, that gave me nine days to secure a place in a graduate program, a first-grade class for Jake, and a home for us, all to start in August.

———— เรานฐานเรา/\ ————

Peggy arranged for Joe's Chrysler-provided car and driver to pick us up at Pudong International Airport, Shanghai's main international airport for long-haul flights. Located on the far eastern edge of Shanghai, it's sixty-four kilometers from the Minhang district on the western side of Shanghai, where Peggy, Joe, and their daughter Grace lived. During that seemingly endless drive across Shanghai, everything was foggy from a combination of my jet-lagged brain, contacts that had been in my eyes far too long, and the yellow haze that often hung over the city.

The skyscrapers in the Pudong financial district of Shanghai—the Jin Mao Tower, Shanghai World Financial Center, and Shanghai Tower (just begun in 2011)—are world famous not only for their record-breaking height but for their innovative and unique architecture and structural engineering. But the architecture I remember from that first drive across Shanghai bore no resemblance to these icons. Instead, we drove past kilometer after kilometer of nondescript apartment blocks, rows and rows of them—clusters of twenty, thirty, or forty identical buildings. These massive housing blocks were cookie-cutter towers, distinguished from each other only by their color—the pink one, the blue one, the yellow one, the green one. In 2011, more people lived in the city of Shanghai than on the continent of Australia. They all needed housing.

Forest Manor, where Peggy, Joe, and Grace lived, bears no resemblance to these monolithic apartment blocks. Forest Manor is a gated community of palatial houses, many decorated with gleaming marble floors and walls and extravagant crystal chandeliers. I knew this before we arrived. While searching for ways to prepare Jake for a potential move to Shanghai, I found an episode of the reality television show *House Hunters International* (season twenty-two, episode three), in which a suburban Dallas family moves to Shanghai and hunts for a house. House number two was in Forest Manor. Watching the show, Jake and I could see the neighborhood and what the houses looked like. Our first morning in Shanghai, Jake and I woke up far too early because of the thirteen-hour time difference with Chicago. When the sun finally came up, we took a walk around the neighborhood. Just around the corner was house number two in the *House Hunters International* episode (the family had chosen house number three in a different neighborhood). Maybe it was the jet lag, but being in Shanghai did not feel real yet. It felt more like a reality show than our life.

For it to become our life, things needed to get real, fast. The top of my must-do list was getting a student visa and the residency permits it would provide. Without these, my plan would disintegrate, and we could not move to China. With this single goal in mind, I headed to Fudan University to meet with the chair of the history department and the program's administrator. Based on emails sent back and forth with my application materials, I was fairly confident I would be admitted. Although it is a stereotype, it is nonetheless true that many Chinese are extremely status-conscious, especially regarding education. Even at a prestigious university such as Fudan, the admissions office and the department head considered a Yale degree the pinnacle of academic achievement and status (except maybe a Harvard degree). The most likely reason I was admitted to Fudan on such short notice and without an apparent academic purpose is that I am a Yalie. It also helped that I could pay the full $3,000 tuition.

Next on my list was finding a school for Jake. Grace attended Shanghai American School. SAS has two campuses in Shanghai, fifty-seven kilometers apart at opposite ends of the city—one in Puxi and one in Pudong. On our first morning in Shanghai, Peggy took us on an informal tour of the Puxi campus, which was within walking distance of Forest Manor. In Chicago, Jake attended a small private school located in a loft building next to the el tracks in Chicago's River North neighborhood. For gym, the students played in the public park or used the nearby tennis courts and indoor swimming pool of Moody Bible College. From SAS's website, I knew to expect something different, but did not appreciate the scope of the school and the extent of the difference until we arrived.

The SAS Puxi campus is on twenty-nine acres, filled with a baseball field, softball field, playing fields, a 400m running track, and playgrounds appropriate for various ages. The multiple buildings house an "aquatics center" (not a pool) that was purportedly the premier swim facility in Shanghai, a Broadway-caliber performing arts center, multiple indoor gyms and workout rooms, a restaurant-style cafeteria, and bright open classrooms. What impressed me most was the library, which, combined with the Pudong campus, holds the largest collection of English-language books in all of mainland China. Jake and I were agog. Sign him up. I wanted to use that library, which was open to parents. But first, we still needed to see whether Jake would get in.

During the interview at SAS a few days later, the admissions officers were somewhat taken aback by our circumstances. Most American students at SAS were in Shanghai because a parent (usually the father) worked in Shanghai for a multinational company. In these cases, the student's exorbitant tuition was paid directly to SAS by the parent's company as a perk included in the standard expat package. SAS's tuition rivaled that charged by private schools in Manhattan. Companies were beginning to discriminate against employees with multiple children because of the high cost of international school tuition.

Jake and I did not fit the mold for Americans applying to Shanghai American School. Jake would be living in Shanghai because his mother wanted to live there, not because of her job. This baffled the admissions officer. "What about a visa?" she asked. (At the time, we were in Shanghai on tourist visas.) "Jake cannot enroll in SAS without a residency permit," she continued. Leaving out the details of how much I had grown to dislike my law firm and my plan to get a student visa from Fudan, where I had not yet been officially accepted, I reassured the admissions officer that Jake and I would have residency permits before school started in August, a mere three months later. Apparently convinced by my confidence, she finally stopped asking about our circumstances. By the time we left the interview and finished our tour, I was fairly certain Jake would be admitted. And he was before we even left Shanghai. Why was Jake accepted so quickly so late in the admissions cycle? I think, in large part, because the Shanghai *American* School needed *American* students. SAS gave priority in admission to overseas families, US passport holders, and those with stronger academic English proficiency. Jake was a threefer.

We still needed to find a place to live. If I had moved to Shanghai on my own, I likely would have looked at the new construction near Xintiandi, a district with enough expats and English to make it feasible but also with an interesting history and a great location. But I had six-year-old Jake to consider. Assuming at this point that Jake would be admitted to the Shanghai American School, I felt that living at the Shanghai Racquet Club (SRC), across the street from Forest Manor, made the most sense. Jake could then walk or bike to school with me. He could take tennis lessons, swim in the indoor and outdoor pools, and ride his bike without traffic. Plus, SRC's internet was routed through Hong Kong, so in the days before easily downloadable VPNs, we could skirt Chinese restrictions and freely use Google and Gmail, watch YouTube and Netflix, and I could read the *New York Times*. Living at SRC was the opposite of an immersion experience in Shanghai and Chinese life and culture, but it was the right choice for us at that time.

I arranged with an agent from the Shanghai Racquet Club to show us available apartments in the complex. Jake and I had already spent several days enjoying the club, swimming in the outdoor pool and ordering poolside meals and snacks with Peggy and Grace, who were members, but the SRC agent, a young Chinese woman, insisted on starting with a tour of the clubhouse and facilities. As we walked, she gestured with her arms and pointed toward the tennis courts, pool, spa, and restaurant. Her eyes, however, remained fixed on Jake's surfer-blond hair, blue eyes, and long, dark eyelashes. Annoyed by her staring, Jake stayed as far away from the agent as possible, weaving and bobbing to get out of her line of vision. When we entered a small elevator, finally on our way to see an apartment, Jake was trapped. Before he could hide behind me, the agent reached out and stroked Jake's blond hair. Jake recoiled, and shouted, "Don't." The woman quickly pulled her arm back, only slightly embarrassed. Finding her behavior odd but nothing more, I failed to recognize what it portended for Jake if we moved to China.

The first apartments the agent showed us were boxy, dark, and depressing.

I did not need (or want) the marble floors, vaulted ceilings, and crystal chandeliers of Forest Manor, but I hoped for some natural light. When I expressed this to the agent, she thought for a minute, made a call on her walkie-talkie, and led us to a different area of SRC. There, she showed us a big, bright, open three-bedroom corner unit with a huge wraparound terrace and light streaming in through a wall of windows. Located on the fourth floor of a centrally located building, it was apartment 4BD (a combined unit, which is why it was so big). The empty unit looked as though no one had lived there for a long time. Everything was covered in layers of dust. The unit needed repairs to the floor, walls, and appliances, and most of the furniture included in the rental package was missing. But Jake and I liked it. I agreed to lease 7G 4BD (7G was the building), subject to finalizing the lease (which a partner in the firm's Shanghai office agreed to work on for me) and completion of repairs and cleaning of the unit.

On the flight back to Chicago, I finally had time to read Deborah Fallows's book *Dreaming in Chinese,* which had been sitting on my nightstand at Peggy's house. I should have left it there. Fallows offered an ominous reason why apartment 4BD was unoccupied for so long: "The Chinese are very superstitious about their language. They consider the number 4 unlucky . . . because the word for 'four,' 四 *sì* sounds like the word for 'die,' *sì* 死." I put the book down and stared out the plane window. The apartment we planned to rent was on the fourth floor and had the number 4 nailed to its door. Is that why it had been vacant so long? Why would I move with Jake into an apartment with *death* marked on its door? Wait, what am I thinking? I am not Chinese. I don't speak Mandarin. I am not superstitious.

On August 11, 2011, Jake and I moved into building 7G, apartment 4BD, at the Shanghai Racquet Club.

Margo, Jake, and the Leshan Giant Buddah in Sichuan, China

Chapter Eight

CHINA WITH A TOWHEADED SIX-YEAR-OLD
TRAVEL TRANSFORMED

"MAKE SURE IT'S NOT grandma and grandpa in Ohio," said the speaker, only half in jest, as she walked us through the required forms during the new-parent orientation at Shanghai American School. Nervous laughter followed as parents realized they knew no one in Shanghai whom they could list as an emergency contact for their children. Luckily, I knew Peggy and could list her name and phone number in the space for Jake's emergency contact if I could not be reached. Later, I was surprised to discover that most of the parents of Jake's first-grade classmates did not have this quandary. They were Chinese. Grandma and grandpa lived in Shanghai or Beijing, not Detroit or Los Angeles.

Shanghai regulations restricted attendance at international schools to foreign passport holders or children of foreign passport holders, yet most of the students in Jake's class were Chinese. They had Chinese parents. They had lived in China their entire life—except when they were born. They spoke Chinese at home. They ate Chinese food and celebrated Chinese holidays. Ethnically and culturally, they were Chinese. Legally, however, they were US citizens. They had US passports. They were admitted to Shanghai American School as Americans.

But were they American, or just US citizens? Were those the same?

Our friend Lily came home one afternoon from her fourth-grade class at Shanghai American School and announced to her mother that these kids, born in the US but raised in China by Chinese parents, were not really American. It was not because of their race. Lily was born in Hunan Province to Chinese parents. She was adopted by an American couple and raised in New Jersey before the family moved to Shanghai for her father's job with a shipping company. Lily was American. For Lily, it was something else. It was cultural. The US-born Chinese students were not American because "they don't know who Martin Luther King is!"

Lily's comment about what it means to be an American stayed with me through the time Jake and I lived in China, later when we moved to Indonesia, and then living in the US again with the ongoing culture wars. What does it mean to be an American? My identification as an American was strongest when we lived overseas. "American" was the first thing people noticed about me from my clothes, my accent, my attitude. "American" was how they labeled me. What that meant precisely, beyond US citizenship, was less clear and varied depending on how the other person perceived the US, the US foreign policy toward their home country, and, sometimes, how much American television they watched.

As Americans living as expats in a foreign country, Jake and I learned from and adapted to our host country's culture and modified our behavior and activities, up to a point. That point did not extend to birthday party celebrations. Americans have big birthday parties for small children. For Jake's seventh birthday in November, he wanted to have a party at a laser tag facility. I made the arrangements and sent invitations to everyone in his class. Other than the Canadian who lived downstairs from us at the Shanghai Racquet Club, no one responded. Chinese families typically do not have American-style birthday parties for their kids, which I thought might explain the lack of responses. I went through the list of the kids in his class with Jake and asked whether each was Chinese (they all had assumed American names).

"I don't know," Jake replied for each one.

"What do you mean you don't know? Do they look Chinese?"

"I don't know."

"Do they speak Chinese?"

"I don't know. Everyone has to speak English in school."

Despite my frustration with the lack of RSVPs to Jake's birthday party, I was pleased that Jake did not see race or nationality when he looked at his classmates. Something I needed to learn from him. I also needed to adapt to cultural differences, so I called every child's parent to explain the invitation and arrange their attendance. All the kids—Chinese, Indian, and Canadian—came to this American kid's birthday party and had a great time. Apparently, shooting your friends with a laser light is multicultural.

Outside our expat bubble, China was not as multicultural or ethnically and racially diverse. Everywhere we went in China, people stared at Jake and took his picture. It was like traveling with a celebrity besieged by paparazzi. Some people photographed him surreptitiously. Others asked whether he minded if they took his photo—most of those requests were from those who wanted to pose with him. Typically, people were polite, but Jake was not gracious in return. If he realized someone was taking his photo, Jake would duck behind me or spin around. If someone politely requested to take his photo—in English or through gestures—Jake always rudely said, "NO," leaving me to explain politely. It was bad on the streets of Shanghai, but much worse in other Chinese cities where foreigners were even more scarce. It was the worst at tourist sites, where everyone had a camera. (Fortunately, this was just before smartphone cameras were in constant use by everyone everywhere and before the selfie stick became ubiquitous in China.)

Like most constant annoyances, Jake gradually grew accustomed to being photographed by strangers without his consent. On our first domestic flights in China, when someone took Jake's photo while we sat at the departure gate, we would need to get up and change seats, and sometimes even move to a different gate. We almost missed our flight to Beijing because I did not understand an announcement changing the boarding gate after we had moved from the original gate area to escape the paparazzi. On our last domestic flight in China, flying from Xi'an back to Shanghai, the woman sitting across from us in the boarding area kept snapping photos of Jake, despite my requests that she stop. I asked Jake if we had to move. His sensible reply was, "No, she will stop, and if we move to a new gate, someone else will just start."

Living at the Shanghai Racquet Club among other blond-haired, blue-eyed expat children gave Jake a break from the unwanted attention over his appearance. Few, if any, of the European families who lived at the Shanghai Racquet Club sent their kids to Shanghai American School. These European parents had no interest in American pedagogy or curriculum, and, except for the Brits, they did not want their kids taught in English. The European kids mostly attended the French School of Shanghai, the British International School, Shanghai German School, or the Western International School of Shanghai, all located close to SRC. But all of the kids played together at SRC, and Jake blended in, indistinguishable as he ran down the soccer field or swam in the pool.

Living at SRC also helped me navigate Shanghai, literally and figuratively. In 2011, Shanghai was significantly easier for foreigners to navigate than the rest of China, but it was still tricky if you could not read Chinese or speak more than a few words of Mandarin. To commute to Fudan University and get around the city, I depended on the Shanghai Taxi App. Google Maps did not (and still does not) work in China. Google and all of its products, including Google Maps, are blocked unless you have a workable VPN on your phone. There are Chinese apps for directions, but they are only in Chinese characters, not Pinyin (the system for writing Chinese characters in Latin letters based on pronunciation). With Pinyin, I could at least recognize the words. Without Pinyin, I was lost. The OCR function on Google Translate, where you scan or take a screenshot of any text and get its translation, did not exist until 2014, and it would have been blocked by the Chinese government anyway. So I used the Shanghai Taxi App, which was basic but worked. I could type in any location, and the address would appear in English and in Mandarin with Chinese characters, and then I could show the screen to the taxi driver.

One Saturday evening early in our stay in Shanghai, Jake and I were on the Bund, the historical district in central Shanghai along the Huangpu

River. We went to a hotel to find a taxi, rather than hailing one on the street, because I needed to find a taxi I was comfortable riding in with Jake. The back seats of most Shanghai taxis were covered in crisp white fabric, making it impossible to use the seat belts. This was not a problem for the Chinese, who seldom used seat belts anyway, and never while riding in the back. It was a problem for me. I preferred not to ride with Jake in a Shanghai taxi without seat belts, and I would not do so on a long ride at high speed on an expressway, such as we took going home from the Bund. I had not yet learned the Expo taxi trick, discussed below, so I opened the door of every taxi in the line at the hotel until I found one with usable seat belts or found a taxi driver willing to pull apart his back seat to pull out the seat belts and latches.

About fifteen cars down the line, I found a taxi driver willing to pull the seat belts out from under the seat cover. I used my Shanghai Taxi App to show the driver our address on Jinfeng Lu. He nodded yes. He knew where it was. Within minutes, though, I knew we were going the wrong way. The driver had taken the tunnel under the Huangpu River, and the taxi was heading east on the Pudong side of Shanghai. We should not have crossed the river. We needed to go west, to the Puxi side of Shanghai. I repeated the address to the driver, and he kept saying, "*Shi, shi, Jinfeng Lu*" ("Yes, yes, Jinfeng Road"). At the limits of my communication ability and rapidly traveling the wrong way, I called the Shanghai Racquet Club office, explained the situation, and asked for help. I then handed my phone to the driver. When the driver gave the phone back to me, the man in the office told me not to worry—the driver said he knew where he was going. But I was worried. It may seem like nothing, a cab going the wrong way, happens all the time. But when you are in a vast and still-unfamiliar foreign city where you do not speak the language and are traveling at night with a small child, being taken for a ride is scary.

Despite the reassurances from the man at SRC, the taxi continued to go the wrong way. I tried again to communicate directly with the driver—no change of direction. I considered calling the Shanghai call center hotline for help. The hotline number was posted in all Shanghai taxis and offered the same translation service and assistance to foreigners who do not speak Mandarin as SRC did for its residents. But the hotline operator might not have known where SRC was located, so I decided to call the SRC office again and hope a different person answered. Someone different answered. I explained the situation and handed the phone to the driver. Abruptly, the driver stopped talking on the phone and stopped the car in the middle of the highway, which was even scarier than driving in the wrong direction. The driver handed the phone back to me. As cars honked and screeched to a stop or careened around the taxi, the person at SRC explained. There are two roads named Jinfeng in Shanghai, forty-nine kilometers apart. The taxi was headed to the wrong Jinfeng Lu. We got off the highway and got back on going in the correct direction.

The next weekend, I learned about so-called Expo taxis, a holdover from Expo 2010, which Shanghai had hosted. Although the preparations for the Expo were not as extensive as they had been for the 2008 Beijing Olympics, significant changes had been made to accommodate and impress the expected foreign exhibitors and tourists. Shanghai opened new subway lines, built new ring roads, and added 4,000 brand-new taxis the month before the Expo opened. All these "Expo taxis" had useable seat belts. Apparently, I was not the only foreigner who insisted on seat belts—a fact recognized by the Chinese planners of Expo 2010. For the remainder of our time in Shanghai, I always requested or looked for an "Expo taxi." Seat belt problem solved.

Why didn't my expat friends in Shanghai tell me about the two Jinfeng roads? Almost all of them lived in Forest Manor or at SRC, both on Jinfeng Lu, and sent their kids to the Shanghai American School, also on Jinfeng Lu. Why didn't they tell me about the Expo taxis? They used seat belts for their kids, so why didn't they share this key advice? Likely, because they did not know. My expat friends all had drivers. Their expat packages included cars, drivers, and international school tuition for their children. Without a company-paid package, Jake and I navigated Shanghai by taxi, bicycle, foot, and, once we learned to handle the pressing crowds without feeling overwhelmed, subway. We learned to find our way, and in the process, got to know the city better.

──── ᩁᩣᩴᩅᩪ᩠ᩆᩣᩴ᩠ᩅᩁᩣᩘ᩠᩺ᩅᩁ ────

On the days I had an afternoon class, I would be on the other side of Shanghai at Fudan University when Jake got out of school. Jake could take the school bus the short distance to SRC, but I needed someone to meet him at the bus stop and watch him until I got home. I hired an *ayi*. The literal translation of *ayi* is "aunt," but the Chinese use *ayi* as a term of respect for a woman of your mother's generation and, in this context, to mean a housekeeper. Through word of mouth at the Shanghai Racquet Club, I met several women who had worked for other expat families and were interested in the part-time position. I liked Xi'e from our first meeting, facilitated and interpreted by the long-term expat family for whom she had worked previously. Among the things I liked about Xi'e was that she used her actual name rather than adopting a Western name, as most *ayis* did. I could learn to pronounce Xi'e; she did not need to pretend her name was Irene or Debbie for my convenience.

It was not just *ayis* who adopted Western names for dealings with Westerners. The Chinese lawyers in my firm's Shanghai office did the same. I asked one of the lawyers why he used an assumed Western name. Did he think Americans were too stupid or lazy to use his actual name? He shrugged and replied that it was easier. Part of me understood. When he used an assumed Western name, his American colleagues and clients were less likely to embarrass themselves by confusing his surname and his given name and less likely to mispronounce both. Chinese state their surname first and their given name last, the opposite of how Westerners state their names. But when dealing with Westerners, Chinese sometimes switch to the Western convention of using their given name first and their surname last. If I was introduced to Qin Chen, I might not know which was her first name and which was her last. Had she switched the order to accommodate Western norms? If I was introduced to Susie Chen, I would know to call her Ms. Chen, not Ms. Susie.

The confusion went both ways. Almost every written communication I received in English from Fudan University, SRC, and the Chinese company

I used to book travel addressed me as Mr. Margo. Not only did they not know which was my surname, but they could not figure out my gender. The exception was Shanghai American School, which in official correspondence referred to me as Mrs. Weinstein, correctly identifying my surname and gender but assuming I was married. Whatever anyone called me, I responded.

Xi'e worked afternoons. She kept the apartment clean, did laundry in our in-unit washer and dryer, bought fresh vegetables from the wet market at local prices, made delicious vegetarian dumplings, watched Jake when I was at Fudan, and was a crack shot with a nerf gun. Xi'e and Jake successfully communicated through a combination of Mandarin, English, and pantomime. When Xi'e tried to make Jake a grilled cheese sandwich in a wok with oil, he pulled out a frying pan and butter, and they figured it out together.

One day late in the term, I received an email from Jake's Mandarin teacher, asking that I call her. Concerned, I called the school immediately. It turned out that the teacher was disappointed that Jake was speaking Mandarin with a low-class, Sichuan accent—clearly learned from Xi'e—instead of the proper accent the teacher taught. I thanked Jake's teacher for the call and said I would speak with Jake. I did not. I was delighted. My child was speaking Mandarin with a Chinese accent.

My attempts at direct communication with Xi'e were not as successful as Jake's. I understood Xi'e's limited English better than Jake did, but my Mandarin was worse than Jake's and not improving over time as his was. For everything beyond the most basic communication, we called the SRC front desk, where the employees were used to translating between expats and their *ayis*. Before Xi'e left for the day, I would tell the SRC employee about the next day's schedule—what time I would be back from Fudan, what groceries we needed, what we would like for dinner. My requests were translated and conveyed to Xi'e. She would do the same, sharing her ideas for meals, household items we needed, and issues with the apartment. Our communication was not seamless. We both made mistakes based on misunderstandings, but the mistakes were mostly minor and sometimes funny. Overall, it worked.

——— ᨠᩣᩴᩮᨾᩨᩦᩢ ———

When I applied to Fudan, I wondered why this prestigious university had a small graduate program for international students taught in English by Chinese professors. After I had been at Fudan for a few months, I asked the head of the department this question. Simplified, his answer was that it would help China in the future and influence international relations favorably for China. As I learned more about my fellow students, I saw how this could work. Many of them were the recipients of scholarships offered by Fudan to the best and brightest students in their respective countries. These were serious students with lofty ambitions. They would go back to their home nations and become politicians, policy advisers, and ambassadors. The former students would bring to these roles an understanding of Chinese history, economics, culture, and politics shaped by Fudan.

I was one of the few international students in the program who spoke English as a first language. The other students were proficient in English, but it was their second or third language. The professors lectured and led class discussions in English, but their first language was Mandarin. One day in my modern Chinese history class, we considered the role of the Communist Party of the Soviet Union in establishing the Chinese Communist Party. The Chinese had long denied any Soviet involvement, but documents buried in archives and discovered when the Soviet Union collapsed proved the opposite. As the class discussed the implications of this trove of documents on how Chinese history would be taught and understood, accents and language barriers interfered. The Chinese professor could not understand the insightful comments made, in English, by a student who spoke with a strong foreign accent. The class stalled. I interrupted and, in my American accent, repeated the student's points. The discussion resumed. As the semester progressed, students and professors looked to me for help with English-to-English translation.

By the time I enrolled at Fudan, I was an experienced English-to-English translator. My training started on my first trip to China in 1999. I had landed in Beijing, groggy from jet lag, barely competent to take a taxi to my hotel, and ready to flop into my bed. But an Italian tourist and a Chinese desk clerk stood between me and the key to my hotel room. The Italian tourist, increasingly frustrated and clearly exhausted, was trying without success to check into her room. In Italian-accented English, she explained who she was and want she wanted. In Chinese-accented English, the indifferent desk clerk asked her who she was and what she wanted. Neither understood the other, but I understood them both.

When I could stand it no longer, I interrupted and asked if I could assist.

The Italian said, in English, "I would like to check in, please."

I repeated, changing only the pronoun, "She would like to check in, please."

The Chinese desk clerk responded, in English, "Is your reservation with a tour group?"

I repeated, "Is your reservation with a tour group?"

And so on. Both understood me. The impasse was broken. The Italian woman checked in, took her room key, and headed for the elevator. For my efforts, I hoped a grateful clerk might upgrade my room. Not in China, but I could finally check in to my standard room and climb into bed.

My skills in English-to-English translation would have been helpful in other Fudan classrooms. For example, the wife of a visiting American professor told me about her husband's experience teaching his first class at Fudan. A native of Mexico who spoke English with a Mexican accent, he was at Fudan for one semester to teach two graduate seminars and an undergraduate lecture course in English to Chinese students. He prepared and presented what he thought was an engaging and relatively basic first lecture. After the class, a group of students waited to speak to him.

"Thank you for taking the course," the professor said with enthusiasm. "I hope it will be a great semester. Do you have any questions from today's lecture?"

With some hesitancy, one of the students said, "Yes, we have a question. What language were you speaking?"

——— ᘓᘃᘏᘄᘃᘏᘄᘏᘄᘃᘏᘄᘏ ———

I enrolled in Fudan to get a student visa and residency permits for Jake and me. For my $3,000 tuition, I could have taken five classes in the fall semester. But I did not want to spend all day every day at Fudan or doing homework. I wanted free time so Jake and I could enjoy living in Shanghai. And I wanted the flexibility to travel on Shanghai American School holidays not otherwise observed in China—like Thanksgiving vacation when we volunteered at the Chengdu Panda Base. Plus, I was supposed to be doing business development for the firm's Shanghai office. I enrolled in just three classes.

Because I had been admitted to Fudan through the history department, I needed to take at least one history class. History is my favorite academic subject, but the offerings that semester were limited. I chose a class in modern Chinese history. I was interested in this dramatic period of revolutionary changes from the Opium Wars (which forced China to open to the West) to the Cultural Revolution (from 1966 until Mao Zedong's death in 1976), but I expected the course to be a review of material I knew. At Yale, I studied modern Chinese history and was taught by Jonathan Spence, the preeminent China scholar in the West. Spence's book *The Search for Modern China*, published after I graduated, grew out of these Yale lectures. When I reviewed the Fudan syllabus and saw that *The Search for Modern China* was the assigned text for the class, my expectations for learning something new diminished further. I was wrong. My eminent professor at Yale studied and wrote books about modern Chinese history. But my professor at Fudan lived modern Chinese history, at least the more recent parts of it. I learned more from the latter.

At Yale, I sat through lectures and read chapters about the Great Leap Forward and the Cultural Revolution. At Fudan, I learned about these subjects from a scholar who, as a teenager, was one of the millions of educated young people sent from the cities to the countryside to work on farms. He told us how he idolized and blindly followed Mao, falling totally for the cult of personality. Now, however, he saw Mao's ascendancy and control of the Chinese Communist Party as the worst thing to happen to China. At Yale, I had learned in the abstract how intellectuals were demonized as class enemies, turned in by their own children, and killed or sent to the reeducation camps in the countryside. But at Fudan, this became more concrete as I learned specifics of what occurred at that university. First came a spate of "suicides" by Fudan professors and students. Then people disappeared. Finally, the university was shut down. I was in the place where it happened, always the most meaningful way to learn and understand something.

When my parents visited Jake and me in Shanghai, I took them to my history class. I never took my parents to any of my college or law school classes, and it was a little strange taking them to this one. But I did. It was part of their tour of Shanghai. From the moment we walked in, the professor was gracious. He warmly greeted them, suggested that they sit in the front, and asked them a few questions before turning to the topic of the day, World War II. I had done the readings for the class, so I knew that we would be starting with the events leading up to September 18, 1931, when the Japanese invaded Manchuria, not September 1, 1939, when Hitler's army invaded Poland, or December 7, 1941, when the Japanese bombed Pearl Harbor. At first, my parents were confused. But as the class progressed, they received their own lesson in what I had been learning all semester—how differently the Chinese see the world and the twentieth century.

The second class I enrolled in was demographics, mostly taught by an engaging expert demographer, fluent in English, who played a key role in planning the needed and upcoming changes in China's disastrous one-child policy. I say it was mostly taught by him because he was in New York or Berlin as often as he was in Shanghai. Whenever he missed a class, he sent an interesting substitute, usually an international expert in demographics visiting Shanghai.

Years before China changed its one-child policy, I knew the change was coming and why. My demographics professor shared with the class the forthcoming changes he expected to be implemented and why the time had finally come. Leaving aside the morals and ethics of the policy and the horrible personal tragedies—the forced abortions and the murders of baby girls—the one-child policy was always doomed to fail and was never necessary to control the population. Populations drop when economies succeed. Just compare the population growth of the People's Republic of China (PRC) and the Republic of China (ROC, known as Taiwan). The consequences of this failed policy will be with China for decades, and generations will suffer.

An unintended yet obvious consequence of the one-child policy is the imbalance between the male and female populations in China. During strict enforcement of the one-child policy, across China, about 120 to 125 males were born for every hundred females. This average understates the problem and the skewed gender ratios. In Shanghai, where baby girls were, for the most part, allowed to be born and allowed to live, the ratio is standard, almost one to one. But in villages, the imbalance is severe, resulting from the abortion of female fetuses because of their gender and the murder of baby girls at birth. The 1.5-child policy, adopted in the mid-1980s, allowed rural families to have a second child if their first child was a girl. This reduced the appalling practices somewhat, but not enough.

Stepping away from the statistics, my professor drew a chart showing the practical consequences of the imbalance. At the top, he wrote "Men" and "Women." Beneath each heading, he put a column of the letters A, B, C, and D to indicate an objectification and hierarchy of persons. Drawing connecting lines between the columns, he stated that A men marry A and B women. B men marry B and C women. C men marry C and D women. D men marry any remaining D women or Vietnamese women (if they can afford to travel to Vietnam and pay her family). Who is then left without a spouse? Poor, uneducated D men and affluent, educated A women. Despite my objections to the explicit ranking of human beings on supposedly objective criteria like income, education, and class, the chart was supported by statistical evidence and reflected in the advertisements posted by desperate parents in the Shanghai Marriage Market.

Every Saturday afternoon, the Shanghai Marriage Market takes place in People's Park in People's Square in central Shanghai. Parents advertising their single children for marriage gather on a lane among the lush gardens and set out their listings. They describe their marriageable children on a single sheet of white paper. Photographs are rarely included. Parents clip these sheets, often with clothespins, to a gift bag or sturdy shopping bag and stand the bag in a long row of other similar bags atop a low stone wall that separates the lane from the gardens. Unable to read the Chinese, Jake and I tried to guess what each family was like from the bag chosen for the display. Was it from a luxury store? A convenience store? A simple gift bag?

One Saturday, Jake and I were in People's Park with a Chinese lawyer from my firm's Shanghai office, her husband, and her young daughter to see the "Pixar: 25 Years of Animation" exhibition at the Shanghai Museum of Contemporary Art. After touring the exhibit, my colleague's husband took the kids to the playground so that she could walk through the marriage market with me and translate the advertisements. The listings were not poetic or flowery. No descriptions of long walks on the beach, reading by the fire, or working out at the gym seven days a week. No mentions of favorite authors, music, films, or sports teams. No personality descriptions, such as outgoing, warm, friendly, lusty, or feisty. None of that, just the facts: age, zodiac sign, weight, height, job, education, any overseas study, personal income, and birthplace. For the parents advertising their sons, an additional key fact was the location, size, and value of the apartment he owned, if any. I asked my colleague to characterize the adult children who were being advertised. The largest groups were those my professor had defined as A women and D men.

The third class I took that semester had a promising title: Protest and Social Change. But the readings were dry, academic, and dull, and I remember nothing worth repeating. But it was the site of an ironic coincidence. One afternoon, when the professor was late for class, the only other American in the class, and one of the few Americans at Fudan, asked me what I was doing there. I was twice the age of the other students in that class, most of whom were part of a graduate program in which they spent one year studying in Paris and one year studying in Shanghai. This was their second year together, and, clearly, I was not part of that program. I told him I was a lawyer. We quickly figured out that he was the son of a state-court judge in Beaumont, Texas, who had presided over a case I litigated for years with no resolution until the Texas Supreme Court decided the dispositive legal issue in a different case. Not wanting to deal anymore with frustrating cases and biased judges was part of why I was in a classroom in Shanghai rather than a courtroom in Texas. I held my tongue and said only, "Wow, what a coincidence. Please tell the judge I said hello." Living in China, I had learned discretion.

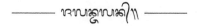

As the first semester at Shanghai American School was ending, I decided not to send Jake back after winter break. It had been a good experience for him, but academically, he was not learning much. The SAS facilities were unparalleled, but first grade is all about the teacher, and Jake's teacher fell short. New to Shanghai, new to SAS, and on her first international assignment, it seemed she had no clue how to teach reading to a class of students with a wide range of English proficiencies. At one end of the spectrum, a boy who lived near us at the Shanghai Racquet Club spoke fluent Chinese at home with his father and fluent Japanese at home with his mother, but he knew only a few words of English. At the other end of the spectrum, Jake, a native English speaker, had an extensive and advanced vocabulary from being raised by a loquacious lawyer mom. It felt like a waste of time and money for Jake to continue at SAS. I figured that Jake surely could learn more if we spent the next two months traveling around China.

We used our Shanghai apartment as a base for our travels. I had not yet heard the terms *world schooling* or *unschooling*, but without consciously joining a very self-conscious movement, that was what we did.

When we curled up on a lounge chair and read *Harry Potter and the Prisoner of Azkaban* on the beach in Sanya on Hainan Island, Jake learned literature. In Harbin, when the nighttime low reached negative forty degrees, Jake discovered that this is where Celsius and Fahrenheit temperatures are the same, and learned science and math. Jake learned ancient Chinese history and art in Xi'an while wandering the partially excavated pits and observing thousands of life-size terracotta warriors, each with a unique face. And Jake learned social studies when we joined the largest human migration on the planet—known as *Chunyun* (Spring Movement)—flying in and out of Shanghai's Hongqiao airport during the Chinese Lunar New Year, when an estimated three billion trips occur.

Most of the travelers leaving Shanghai (though not by plane) were migrant workers making their only trip that year back to their villages. When I researched Shanghai before moving there, I could not figure out if Shanghai's population was sixteen million or twenty-three million. That's a significant difference, and I saw both numbers in multiple sources. After I moved to Shanghai, I figured out that it depended on who was included in the count. Based on the 2010 census, Shanghai's total population was a little more than twenty-three million. Approximately nine million (39 percent) of the twenty-three million residents were long-term migrants with rural *hukou* (household registration). Sources reporting Shanghai's population as sixteen million omitted the migrants living in Shanghai without the corresponding urban *hukou* and the rights *hukou* conveyed for education, health care, housing subsidies, unemployment benefits, and retirement income.

As tens of millions of migrant workers left for the holiday, Jake and I flew back from Xi'an and spent the 2012 Lunar New Year in Shanghai. This was the Year of the Water Dragon, the most auspicious combination of animal and element in Chinese astrology. The Chinese astrological cycle has twelve animals and five elements, so each combination of animal and element occurs only once every sixty years. Of the animals, the dragon is the most revered. It is the only mythical creature and is used as an imperial icon. In Chinese astrology, children born under the sign of the dragon are deemed superior and powerful, and destined for good fortune, success, and wealth. Of the five elements, water is the source of life on earth, and is a symbol of intelligence, wisdom, optimism, and growth. Dragon children born under the water element also have characteristics such as sensitivity to others and patience that temper the egoism of the dragon and calm its recklessness.

A child born in the year of the water dragon is destined for greatness, and this advantage is something Chinese parents would like to provide their children. The twelve months from January 23, 2012, to February 9, 2013, was the only chance in 120 years (1953 to 2072) to have a water dragon child, preferably a son. Prospective parents delayed or moved forward their efforts to conceive their only child. Even with China's one-child restrictions, population experts predicted a 5 percent increase in babies born in China in 2012. In Hong Kong, without the one-child limitation, experts predicted a 20 percent increase in children born that year.

I celebrated the start of the Year of the Water Dragon in Shanghai with my wood monkey Jake, born in 2004 and destined to be adaptable, intelligent, determined, optimistic, industrious, warmhearted, and perennially happy. I am a metal rat, which, if I believed in the Chinese zodiac, would mean I am clever, energetic, honest, frank, and optimistic and have a strong environmental adaptability, but am also impatient, suspicious, and kind of vain.

The second semester at Fudan started in February after the Lunar New Year celebration. I decided not to enroll. Academically, Fudan exceeded my expectations. Rather than merely providing the needed residency permit, the classes ended up enriching my experience of living in China. But one semester was enough. I was too old to sit in classrooms with students half my age with twice my ambition. It was time to go back to work at the firm and see whether I could regain my enthusiasm for practicing law, or at least tolerate the new direction the firm was moving.

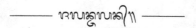

When Jake and I returned to Chicago in February 2012, we came home to the same house, same job, and same school that we had left six months earlier. Jake joined a first-grade class with the same kids he had known in kindergarten. I went back to the same office where I had worked for twenty-four years. In many ways, it was as though we had never left.

But our behavior and thinking had changed, and it emerged in little ways. One evening during rush hour, Jake and I were standing on a crowded platform waiting for the Brown-line el train. When the train arrived and the doors opened, a crowd exited. Instead of waiting until they had cleared the platform, seven-year-old Jake, who probably weighed forty-five pounds, started elbowing people and pushing his way onto the train. Because he was so small, no one pushed or punched back, but what was de rigueur in Shanghai could get you arrested for battery in Chicago.

On a gloomy, cold Saturday at the end of February, shortly after our return to Chicago, Jake and I went to the movies at the ShowPlace ICON Theatre on Roosevelt Road in the South Loop. Ever since it opened, this had been our go-to movie theater because the stadium seating allowed a small child and a short woman to see the film, regardless of who sat in front of us. Before moving to Shanghai, I had never paid much attention to the racial composition of the audience. Now, after living and traveling in a country with virtually no racial diversity, I could not stop staring at the people lined up at the concession stands to buy popcorn and junk food. Because of the theater's location and the eclectic mix of movies shown on its sixteen screens, it attracted audiences that matched the racial diversity of Chicago. It felt good to blend into the mix. No one looked at us twice. No one tried to take Jake's picture. We fit in rather than stood out. We were home. Until we left again.

Browsing at the Shanghai Marriage Market

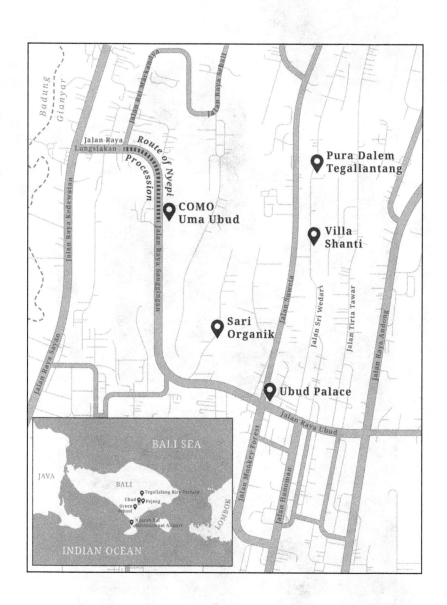

Margo, Jake, and *Ogoh-ogohs* in Lungsiakan, Bali

Chapter Nine

BALI RECONNAISSANCE TRIP
TRAVEL DEMONS

THE INITIAL SUGGESTION TO move to Bali, Indonesia, came from friends who visited Bali in the summer of 2013. When they returned to Chicago, they called me at my office when I was busy, focused on work, and had no time to talk. The catalyst for a move that changed my life was a phone conversation that lasted less than thirty seconds:

"Oh my god, you and Jake have to move to Bali. It's amazing!"

"No, we are not moving again."

"You know you would love living in Bali, and Jake would love Green School."

"Maybe, but we are not moving again. If you move to Bali, we'll come visit you. Sorry, I need to go. I will call you later. Bye."

I had recently left the global mega-firm where I worked for twenty-four years and joined a smaller, kinder law firm (if that's not an oxymoron). I was committed to giving my new firm a chance. Yet, after initially dismissing the suggestion out of hand, I found myself researching a possible move to Bali.

Like many of the parents who moved across the world to Bali and enrolled their children in Green School, I started the process by watching John Hardy's 2010 TED talk *My Green School Dream*. Wearing a sarong on a stage in Oxford, England, Hardy told the story of how he and his wife Cynthia founded Green School after watching *An Inconvenient Truth*, Al Gore's documentary about climate change. As Hardy spoke, he showed photos of the school, its dramatic and sustainable bamboo architecture an outward manifestation of the school's uniqueness. Within these extraordinary wall-less buildings, Hardy asserted that the school focused on educating kids for a future different from the past.

Listening to Hardy speak about educating the green leaders of the future, I remembered when I first learned about the environmental movement and became an environmentalist. It was the summer I turned fifteen, while on the Man and His Land Western trip. One of our vehicles, a retrofitted school bus, carried a small library. My environmentalism goes back to a book on that bus: *The Place No One Knew: Glen Canyon on the Colorado*. With stunning photos by Eliot Porter, the book shows what we all lost when Glen Canyon was flooded in arguably the most destructive and least useful water project ever constructed.

The Sierra Club and its executive director David Brower created the book as the first step in a decades-long *mea culpa* for the deal they cut to save Dinosaur National Monument on the Upper Colorado River, at the expense of the lesser-known Glen Canyon. After reaching this deal, Brower went to see Glen Canyon and realized his colossal error. Too late, Brower declared that flooding Glen Canyon would be America's most regretted environmental mistake. His last-ditch efforts to stop construction of the dam failed. Brower hoped the text of the book and Porter's photos would "serve [a] lasting purpose by in some way stepping up the pace with which mankind preserves what is left of the world's irreplaceables."

The book's environmental message stayed with me that summer as I hiked, rafted, camped, and climbed in national parks across the West. I even got to see the "damn dam" (as I called it in my journal) and what remained of Glen Canyon after more than ten years of flooding. (The flooding that transformed the canyon into Lake Powell began in 1963 but was not completed until 1980, five years after I saw it.) After that summer, I returned to Chicago committed to conserving energy and preserving "irreplaceables" like Glen Canyon.

Decades later, I was doing little to back up my environmental beliefs and my growing concern about climate change. My main contribution to stopping climate change and preserving the environment was being a vegetarian and raising a vegetarian child. But Jake ate a lot of cheese—grilled cheese and mac and cheese were staples of his diet—and cheese has a relatively high carbon footprint. And it is difficult to eat local produce in the winter when you live in Chicago. Our somewhat fresh vegetables traveled far from farm to table, creating carbon emissions. Also, I never attempted to do the math, but the carbon emissions we saved by not eating beef, pork, or poultry likely were less than the carbon we expended when we traveled by plane around the world. On balance, beyond monetary contributions to environmental groups, I was not acting on my environmental beliefs and concerns. If Jake went to Green School, a school focused on the environment, maybe he would learn more than I did after reading just one seminal book and spending a summer in national parks. Maybe when he grew up, Jake would do more to protect the environment than I had. The chant we joined in once in Bali—"People Change, Not Climate Change"—was a good reason to join the Green School community.

Another good reason would be that it would eliminate a major obstacle to our legally living outside the US—the need for a visa. I did not intend to enroll in another graduate school, as I did to get our visas and residency permits to live in China. Once was enough. And I would not need to if we moved to Bali. Green School had an in-house visa consultant to walk families through the process and secure visas. As an international student at Green School, Jake could get KITAS (*Kartu Izin Tinggal Terbatas*), a temporary residency permit good for one year and renewable. As Jake's resident parent, I could get a visa valid for twelve months, although it would require me to leave Indonesia every sixty days for a "visa run."

The travel requirement was a bonus, not a hardship. When we moved to Bali, my required visa runs usually aligned with a Green School vacation. Jake and I traveled to Laos, Vietnam, Thailand, Malaysia, Japan, Australia, and Hong Kong (twice), satisfying my visa requirements with each departure and return. We also took a few quick weekend trips to

Singapore when the timing was off and I had to do a visa run before the next school holiday. I recognized the environmental impact of these visa runs, but Indonesia is a country of 17,000 islands, so driving or taking a train across an international border was not an option. I tried to offset the carbon emissions from our travels in other ways.

Green School's focus on the environment, experiential learning and the assistance offered in obtaining visas and residency permits were reasons for Jake to attend Green School if we moved to Bali, but they were not the reasons I wanted to move to Bali. I spent three weeks in Java and Bali in March 1994, and in all my travels, no place had matched Bali's combination of kind people, vibrant culture, year-round warm weather, large expat community, and gorgeous landscape of volcanoes, beaches, and terraced rice fields.

And then there was the magic of Bali, which I had a glimpse of on that first trip. I happened to be in Ubud on an auspicious day under the Balinese calendar, appropriate for scheduling one of the most elaborate and dramatic ceremonies in Bali—the cremation of a prince. Abandoning our touring plans, my parents, childhood friend Lauren, and I donned sarongs and sashes and spent the day absorbing the spectacle of this amazing event. As we watched, dozens of men—wearing matching sarongs and T-shirts printed with the name of the deceased prince and the date of the cremation—lifted bamboo frames supporting a tall cremation tower (holding the prince's body) and the still-empty, black, bull-shaped sarcophagus, and started moving slowly down the street. A gamelan orchestra accompanied the procession, its gong seeming to set the pace. We joined the procession, merging into the crowd as it moved toward the cemetery. We stayed to watch the ritual cremation, transfixed as flames consumed the bull-shaped sarcophagus and the prince within it. Even without understanding the religious and societal aspect of the cremation, it was a powerful experience. The indelible images stayed with me.

More concretely, so did Indonesian shadow puppets (*wayang kulit*) of the principal characters in the *Ramayana*. The *Ramayana* is the epic story of Prince Rama's quest to rescue his wife, Sita, from the clutches of Ravana. It has been retold for centuries in many forms, including the most successful TV show in Indian history—seventy-eight weekly forty-five-minute episodes shown on Indian television on Sunday mornings in 1987 and 1988 that drew eighty to a hundred million viewers per episode. (During the 2020 COVID-19 lockdown in India, 170 million viewers watched reruns of the first four episodes of the 1980s *Ramayana* series.)

In Indonesia, the *Ramayana* is told with intricately designed and carved flat leather puppets that throw shadows for the audience watching on the other side of a screen. Entranced by the flickering flames and the shadows cast by the puppets, I purchased several fine examples as souvenirs to bring the magic back to Chicago. Rama, Sita, Ravana, and Hanuman (the monkey god who helps Rama and the namesake of a major street in Ubud) hung on my living-room wall for the next twenty years, tangible, daily reminders of Bali.

I weighed all of these factors in reaching my decision. But the clincher was the weather. Over the December 2013 to January 2014 winter break, Jake and I traveled around Nicaragua, ending our trip on the warm beaches of San Juan del Sur. On our return to Chicago, we stepped out of the international terminal at 1 a.m., and we were hit by a blast of negative-sixteen-degree air and a wind chill of negative fifty degrees. On the short dash to the waiting shuttle, we froze without our winter gear. Then we froze at home too. The downstairs furnace in our house was out, and we could see our breath as we screamed and headed for the coat closet. Bundled up, Jake headed upstairs, where the remaining furnace managed to keep the temperature at fifty degrees. I headed to the basement. I tried to relight the pilot on the basement furnace by using a blow dryer on the condensation. No go. It would have to wait until morning when I could call our frequent visitors from the HVAC service company. Climbing up to the relative warmth of the second floor, I called out to Jake, "That's it! We are moving to Bali."

I was ready to go, but I was not financially or professionally ready to stop working entirely, and working remotely was iffy. When Jake was a baby, I had worked from home rather than from my office in the Sears

Tower. In 2005, remote work was not common, especially for lawyers, and it was frowned upon. But working remotely was the only possible way that I, as a single mom, could juggle a demanding full-time job and a nursing baby who did not sleep through the night. So that's what I did.

I worked in my home office with the door closed. A nanny watched Jake during business hours, but I could step out of my office to nurse Jake and play with him. And I was not stressed about racing home before the nanny left for the day. I only had to open my home office door to transition. I also saved at least ten to fifteen hours every week—a full (lawyer) workday—by not having to spend valuable time grooming, dressing, and commuting. (This was fifteen years before the COVID-19 pandemic forced lawyers out of their offices, and they, too, learned the time-management benefits of working from home in pajamas.) When necessary, I could don a suit, put on makeup, and leave my house to attend firm meetings, client meetings, depositions, and court hearings in Chicago. I could also get on a plane and, within a few hours, travel anywhere in the US for a client or court.

By early 2014, the concept of working as a digital nomad had just started moving into the mainstream. Co-working spaces for digital nomads were opening around the world, including several in Bali. But these digital nomads were mostly freelancers or gig workers, not tied to set business hours in a particular time zone, and their work did not demand in-person appearances. The COVID-19 pandemic forced the archaic legal industry to adapt or cease functioning. Zoom court hearings, Zoom depositions, and Zoom meetings allowed cases to proceed virtually. But neither this technology nor the flexibility existed in 2014. Then, the practice of law was not set up for remote work. Judges demanded in-person appearances, even for minor status hearings that took less than five minutes. All but the most mundane depositions were taken in person, face-to-face across a conference room table. Plus, the time difference between Bali and the US made synchronous communication difficult—9 a.m. in Chicago was 11 p.m. or midnight in Bali, which does not switch to daylight saving time.

If Jake and I moved to Bali, I would need to cut back on my practice.

I could still participate in meetings by telephone, if I could schedule the calls for first thing in the US morning. I could do tasks not dependent on time zone or working with others, but would have to delegate the parts of my practice I enjoyed most—appearing in court, arguing motions, trying cases, deposing witnesses, and working with others. The upshot? My practice would be less interesting, and I would earn less money, but I might be able to figure out a way to work remotely from Bali. And it might be worth the hit to my career and income.

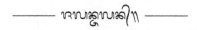

Despite my declaration on that below-freezing January night, before committing to the move and all that it involved for my job and our lives, Jake and I needed to make a reconnaissance trip to Bali. We wanted to check out Green School to see those bamboo buildings in person, get a feel for the atmosphere, learn more about the curriculum (me), and sit in on some classes (Jake). We also wanted to visit Ubud, where I thought we would live if we moved to Bali, but which I suspected was no longer the peaceful village that had enchanted me twenty years earlier. And as long as we were flying to Asia, we wanted to stop in Shanghai for a few days to visit our friends still living there.

Our stopover in Shanghai necessitated a change in the usual airline routing from Chicago to Bali. Using American Airlines miles through the Oneworld alliance, I snagged free round-trip business-class tickets on Malaysia Airlines. At the time, the only downside was a long, middle-of-the-night layover in Kuala Lumpur. Then, on March 8, 2014, less than two weeks before we were scheduled to leave Chicago, Malaysia Airlines Flight 370 disappeared on a flight that departed Kuala Lumpur International Airport (KLIA) in the middle of the night. The plane vanished without a trace. Was it terrorism or an accident? Was it the fault of Malaysia Airlines pilots or maintenance? Was it the fault of KLIA ground crews or air traffic control? As the speculation spread and fear increased, I looked for a different option that avoided flying Malaysia Airlines and a stopover in Kuala Lumpur. The choices were limited, inconvenient, and expensive. I decided it was irrational to avoid Malaysia Airlines just because of the missing plane. Whatever happened to MH370 was too odd, too mysterious to happen again.

Twenty years after my first trip to Bali and not long after MH370 disappeared, Jake and I flew Malaysia Airlines from Shanghai to Bali, with a layover in Kuala Lumpur. As we boarded the plane in Shanghai, mystery still surrounded the loss of MH370. Twenty-six countries were involved in a massive operation searching the Indian Ocean, the South China Sea, the Gulf of Thailand, China, India, and Central Asia. Speculation and blame filled newspapers and television in a never-ending news cycle. Not surprisingly, the atmosphere on our flight to Kuala Lumpur was tense. Passenger worry was palpable. The shaken flight crew announced that their thoughts and prayers were with the missing crew and passengers, raising the tension on board even higher.

Luckily, Jake was wearing his headphones during this announcement. Before we left Chicago, I had done my best to shield him from the news of the missing aircraft and its 239 passengers and crew, all presumed dead. Most mornings, I listened to NPR's *Morning Edition* as I made breakfast and got us ready to head out the door to the office and third grade. Whenever the news shifted to the missing plane, I grabbed the controller to turn off the radio. I did not want Jake to learn about the missing plane when we had four Malaysia Airlines flights ahead of us.

The flight to KLIA landed on time at 9:50 p.m. We had a five-hour layover before our flight departed for Denpasar, Bali, at 3 a.m., so we headed to the Malaysia Airlines business-class lounge, open round the clock. I had researched the lounge's amenities in advance and knew it had a so-called relaxation room in the back with beds, where I hoped Jake would sleep through the layover. On our way through the lounge, I carefully steered him away from the magazine rack that dominated the center of the lounge. Without considering its impact on nervous travelers, someone had neatly arranged a display of at least forty copies of *TIME* magazine's Asia edition, with its "Mystery of Flight 370" cover story. Some of the missing passengers probably had sat in this lounge waiting for that flight. It was unsettling.

The "relaxation room" was not relaxing. A nearby door swung open and shut repeatedly as a stream of waiters carried in trays of dirty dishes and dropped them on a counter or into the sink of the dishwashing room, located just behind the relaxation room. Frequent flight announcements in Bahasa Melayu (the language of Malaysia), repeated in English and often in a third language (usually Mandarin), were loud enough to ensure that they wouldn't be missed by passengers wearing headphones and watching Netflix. During our first forty-five minutes in the room, six different people came in to ask me for our boarding passes and scribble something on a clipboard. Relaxation was impossible unless you were an exhausted little boy. With a bed to lie on, Jake slept soundly, blissfully unaware of the noisy surroundings or the missing plane.

Four hours later, with a pit in my stomach, I dragged a sleepy Jake through security and to the gate for another Malaysia Airlines flight leaving Kuala Lumpur in the middle of the night. Part of my sleep-deprived brain shouted, *You are crazy and irresponsible to take Jake on this flight.* Another part of my sleep-deprived brain countered, *You are even crazier to worry. Whatever happened to MH370 was not systemic. Nothing will happen to another Malaysia Airlines flight.* (Of course, it did just that three months later, when Malaysia Airlines Flight 17 was shot down over Ukraine by a surface-to-air missile, killing all 298 passengers and crew.) Practicality won over superstition. We boarded the plane. Three hours later, the plane landed safely in Denpasar.

Jake and I left our hotel in Ubud early the next morning and, after only a few wrong turns, arrived at the campus we had seen in John Hardy's TED talk and on the slick website. In person, the buildings were even more awe-inspiring. I had no idea whether Hardy could run a school, but this former jewelry designer could design and build fantastical buildings. I was impressed. I was also dripping sweat, and it was only eight in the morning.

Bali's warm weather was the clincher that had brought us there, and I was not deterred by a little heat and humidity-induced sweat. (The day we visited Green School was exceptionally hot and humid, and everyone on the campus was sticky and sweaty.) I was, however, pleased to see that the small vegan café at the campus entrance sold chilled fresh coconut water. I guzzled several bottles. Unfortunately, I did not sweat out all the excess fluid, and I needed to visit the composting toilets that Hardy had boasted about during his TED talk.

Instructions with demonstrative pictures were posted on the stall door. One hole in the ground with a toilet seat was for pee—only pee. The other hole in the ground with a toilet seat was only for everything else—no pee. The composting system (and the posted signs) demanded no mixing of waste. This required standing up and switching holes mid-visit, which might be simple for John Hardy and other males, but it was not for me, and not for most females. Per the instructions: After using the first hole, the toilet paper went into a basket. After using the second hole, the toilet paper went into the hole. Then scoops of sawdust went into one hole, but not into the other. This was taking way too long. I just wanted to get out of the stall. I found the composting toilets disgusting, much worse than a porta-potty at an outdoor music festival. I began to wonder whether I was too urban and too prissy for Green School and Bali.

I was not. After Jake started at Green School, I learned that almost everyone except John Hardy hated the composting dual-toilet system, which could not handle the volume of waste. A portion of the high school curriculum and significant administrative time were devoted to developing or finding and purchasing a sustainable alternative. The Green School website described the project as follows: "With access to the world's most beautiful and innovative bamboo architects, students have a vision for an architecturally beautiful and sustainably made structure employing the latest eco toilet technology. This project has the ambitious goal of being the most beautiful, sustainable, and eco-friendly toilet system in the world." Jake and I had a more a modest objective: a toilet that was not a gag-inducing biohazard.

Jake spent the morning visiting a third-grade classroom with the students who would be his classmates if he joined Green School the next year. It did not go well. When I saw Jake, I reminded him that this was to be expected. The admissions office had urged us to come on a different day because the day we planned to visit would not be typical. In the morning, the lower-school students would be putting the final touches on their class *Ogoh-ogohs* (effigies of demons meant to drive away evil spirits). In the afternoon, students, teachers, and parents would celebrate Nyepi, a Balinese holiday, by parading their *Ogoh-ogohs* through the neighboring village. Jake would not get to see a class in session, and we would not get a sense of what a normal school day was like. But this was the only day we could visit. A day earlier would have required us to go straight to Green School from the airport after our overnight flight from Shanghai. A day later and Green School would be closed for its two-week spring break. We decided to see what we could and make the best of it.

While Jake visited the classroom, I met with the on-site visa agent to find out about securing a residence permit for Jake and a visa for me. I also met with a few administrators and teachers and tried to suss out information on the curriculum. The visa process was clear and straightforward. The curriculum and pedagogy were not. Following our discussions, I still had no idea what they taught or how. I didn't think they knew either. I later learned that in the six years between when Green School opened in 2008 and when Jake started there, Green School adopted, implemented, and dropped at least five different educational philosophies and curricula. As a former principal succinctly put it, it was "the chaos curriculum."

Based on what I heard, I had some concerns about the quality of the academics and teaching. But the head of Jake's school in Chicago had assured me that fourth grade was not an important year academically—nine-year-old brains were not yet ready for the next big developmental leap. Jake would come to Green School (if he did) for its environmental and experimental focus, not its strength in reading, writing, and math. If Jake learned nothing in the core academic subjects for the coming school year, it would not matter in the long run. And he would still be learning, just

other things. Jake could learn about the environment and sustainability—
this was the *Green* School. And instead of a Western-focused education, he
could learn about the world from a different perspective. Indeed, on the
large world map in the classroom Jake visited, Indonesia and Australia sat
prominently in the center, not falling off the right edge—a tangible sign
of a different world view. And wasn't that the point of making a change?
Things should be different. Beautiful, open, experimental Green School
in the Bali jungle was definitely different from the academically rigorous
classical school Jake attended in a small loft building in the crowded River
North area of Chicago.

When I planned our reconnaissance trip to Bali, I knew we would be
there during Nyepi, the Balinese New Year, when a day of silence follows
a night devoted to driving evil spirits off the island. However, other than
being restricted to the hotel property for twenty-four hours, I knew little
about what to expect on Nyepi. We started to get an idea as soon as we
arrived.

For Nyepi, the Balinese create monstrous effigies, *Ogoh-ogohs*, from
papier-mâché or, more commonly now, Styrofoam, to drive the evil spirits
off the island. Some *Ogoh-ogohs* represent powerful gods, mythical beings,
or demons. Some are poised, ready for battle, alone, or part of multifigure
tableaus. Everywhere Jake and I traveled around the island, we saw people
putting the final touches on their *Ogoh-ogohs*.

In Junjungan, near a villa we considered renting, we watched artists
file Styrofoam teeth and spray-paint lurid skin tones on an *Ogoh-ogoh*.
Under a makeshift bamboo shed on Jalan Monkey Forest, a road on the
edge of the Ubud soccer field, we watched artisans attach (fake) jewels to
the crown adorning a demon's head, apply hair to the demon's curling toes,
and drizzle red paint to look like blood on the pile of skulls beneath the
demon's feet. Balinese artistic tradition pervades these carved Styrofoam
and spray-painted monsters. No detail is too small. Curved toenails cover

disgusting toes. Fangs drip blood. Nothing is too vulgar, too outrageous, or too frightening. The more, the better.

Excited to see the parade of these *Ogoh-ogohs* on Nyepi eve, I tried to figure out the logistics. When did it start? Where should we go?

Jake and I were staying at the Como Uma Ubud, a hotel on Jalan Raya Sanggingan, 2.5 kilometers from the center of Ubud. When I asked a front desk clerk for information about the *Ogoh-ogoh* parades, the hotel manager stepped in and suggested that Jake and I might find the parade and festivities in Ubud Center a bit overwhelming. He recommended the smaller celebration in the local village, Lungsiakan, and a tour he had arranged for the hotel's guests. This seemed a great way to see the celebrations and learn more about the holiday. I signed us up for the tour.

At the appointed time, Jake and I showed up in the lobby, where at least twenty other guests awaited the guide. When he arrived, we piled into three vans and drove a very short distance. Six *Ogoh-ogohs* were lined up on the street. Each one was centered on a checkerboard frame made from long bamboo poles strapped together. The design allowed twenty to thirty men to each stand in separate squares within the frame and then together lift and carry the bamboo frame and mounted *Ogoh-ogoh*. When I turned to the guide for some explanation, he mumbled a few things I had already gleaned from a quick Google search. Jake and I headed down the line for a closer look.

The first *Ogoh-ogoh* was the largest—easily twenty-five feet tall, with fiery red skin. On his matted chest hair, and interlaced with his dreadlocks, he wore a necklace of human skulls and held a freshly severed human head still wet with blood (artistically rendered, not real; this was not that kind of ritual). A purple sarong hung under his bulbous belly and wrapped his big butt. The next demon in line was an impressive double-decker, with one demon balanced on the other's head. The lower demon had midnight-black skin, a face that was more warthog than human (with teeth to match), and a blue *tilak* (Hindu mark) in the middle of its forehead. The dominant feature of the upper demon was a long tongue hanging down to its huge sagging breasts and erect nipples. Behind were four smaller but equally gross *Ogoh-ogohs* surrounded by groups of young boys, probably the creators of these figures. Jake and I posed for pictures imitating the *Ogoh-ogohs'* threatening postures and waited for something to happen. We waited a long time, too long. I think the hotel manager worried that if we had departed from the hotel later, the van would not have been able to get through the crowds.

Finally, as it got dark, more Balinese started to arrive. The young men who would carry the *Ogoh-ogohs* took their positions near the bamboo frames. Young women with torches gathered in a circle. I looked for the guide to get an explanation, but he had vanished. As the crowd got bigger and bigger, I pulled Jake onto the sidewalk, and he climbed up on a low wall for a better view. Then the noise started. The marching band version of a gamelan orchestra—mostly gongs and drums—started playing right in front of us. Teenage boys set off bamboo cannons that created surprisingly powerful noises. Unlike the gongs and drums that had a rhythm, the cannon explosions occurred at odd intervals and took us by surprise. The cacophony vibrated through my body and hurt Jake's ears. An older woman turned to face me and pointed to the cotton in her ears. When I nodded and smiled, she pointed to a store on the corner. "*Terima kasih,*" I said, thanking her with one of the dozen Bahasa expressions I had learned. Jake jumped off the wall, and we edged our way through the crowd to the Alfamart convenience store on the opposite corner. Inside, when I pointed to my ear, the clerk knowingly pulled out a small bag of cotton balls. Jake and I stuffed cotton in our ears and headed back out to the street.

By this time, dozens of men and boys had taken their places in the bamboo platforms. The smallest *Ogoh-ogoh* had twelve boys lined up in the squares made by the overlapping bamboo frame. The largest *Ogoh-ogoh*, with at least thirty men positioned to carry it, rose into the air, wobbling side to side and back to front as the men struggled to hold the weight and balance the load. The men, the bamboo frames, and the *Ogoh-ogoh* high in the air lurched across the street, not yet under control. I grabbed Jake, and we both scrambled up a small wall. Things were starting to happen, but I had no idea what. Again, I looked for the guide. Again, he was nowhere I could see from my perch above the crowd.

Noise is an integral part of the ceremony—it drives the demons away. But the yelling, the gongs, the drums, and those bamboo cannons were too much for Jake. The cotton provided scant protection, and his ears hurt. He wanted to go back to the hotel, and I did not blame him. We had experienced enough—time to go. I checked Google Maps, and the hotel was only a kilometer away. But the *Ogoh-ogohs*, the gamelan players, and the crowd filled the street and the sidewalk from one side to the other, and there was no room to squeeze by. To get to the hotel, we would have to become part of the procession and move with the crowd.

Progress was slow. Kids stopped to get leverage to shoot off their cannons, causing the crowd to shift or stop abruptly to avoid them. When the dozens of men carrying the largest *Ogoh-ogoh* tried to execute a 360-degree turn and lost control, the procession stopped as everyone scrambled to get out of the way. And the entire procession stopped every time a power line crossed the road—which happened often. The largest *Ogoh-ogoh* and the two-tiered *Ogoh-ogoh* were too tall to pass under the power lines. The system to get around this was simple, but eventually effective. A tall pole with a V-shaped piece on top was placed under the power line and lifted until the line was high enough for the *Ogoh-ogoh* to pass underneath. This did not always work the first time, but the crowd did not care. The procession was the point, not getting to the end. But Jake and I wanted to get to our hotel.

Finally, I spotted the wall surrounding the Uma Ubud and saw the sign for the hotel about 200 meters ahead. Holding tightly to Jake's hand, I moved us from the center of the street onto the sidewalk. The large *Ogoh-ogoh* approached another power line, and the procession stopped. Trying to keep moving by hugging the wall, I spotted an opening on the sidewalk and moved toward it. I stepped forward with my right leg, which went straight down a gaping hole. My left leg, now several feet above my right leg, collapsed underneath me. Stunned, I just sat there on the ground, one leg in a hole. Because the procession had stopped for the power line, no one tripped over or walked into me. Two men pulled me up slowly, careful not to further scrape my leg against the sides of the hole. I was wearing a dress, so my leg was scraped and bloody from the fall. Despite all the blood, the wounds were superficial, and I could walk. When the crowd moved forward again, we soon reached the hotel entrance.

I limped into the long driveway of the Uma Ubud, blood dripping down my leg. Jake, his face smeared with my blood from touching my leg and then touching his face, served as my crutch. As we approached the serene lobby area, the manager saw us stumbling in, bloody and without the guide. Shocked, he rushed over and asked what had happened. Jake and I just wanted to get to our room, so I explained briefly. The manager apologized profusely, saying that the hotel's regular guide had decided to participate in the ceremony in his own village, so someone from the hotel staff had filled in. Then so many guests wanted to join, and he did not want to disappoint anyone. Of course, he added, the hotel would refund what we paid for the guide, and he would send some first aid supplies to our room. "Are you sure you do not need a doctor? Do you need anything else?" the manager asked, genuinely concerned. After reassuring him that a refund and bandages were all I needed, Jake and I headed down the stone path to our room. As soon as we walked in, Jake climbed under the mosquito netting and collapsed onto the bed's crisp white sheets in our quiet, air-conditioned room. After washing off the blood and applying bandages, I joined him. We looked forward to the coming Day of Silence.

On Nyepi, Bali is silent for twenty-four hours. No cars, motorbikes, or people are allowed on the roads. No one is allowed outside their family compound. No electricity, no cooking, and no noise are allowed within the family compounds. *Pecalang*—security officers from the *banjar* (the local village administration)—patrol the streets on foot to enforce compliance. The silence tricks the evil spirits driven from the island the previous night into believing that the population had also left Bali, so the evil spirits have no reason to return.

To maintain the façade for the evil spirits, Ngurah Rai International Airport in Bali closes for twenty-four hours—from six the morning after the *Ogoh-ogohs* scare away the evil spirits until six the next morning. Hundreds of international and domestic flights are canceled. Under the Balinese lunar calendar, Nyepi occurs on the day after the dark moon of the vernal equinox, which falls on different dates, but usually in March. Western holidays tied to the vernal equinox—such as Passover and Easter—similarly fall on different dates in different years. Nonetheless, every year, foreign airlines fail to adjust their schedules to the Balinese lunar calendar and sell tickets for travel on Nyepi, stranding uninformed tourists in Bali or at their last connection before Bali.

Despite the strict enforcement of the Day of Silence, tourist hotels not visible from the road are afforded some leeway in adherence to the rules of Nyepi. Perhaps the exception exists because these hotels are concealed from the demons, or perhaps because tourism, defined broadly to include related businesses, dominates and sustains the Balinese economy, representing almost seventy percent of the island's economy in 2014. The hotel staff arrive before 6 a.m. and stay on the property until 6 a.m. the next day. On the hotel property, electricity is allowed, meals are cooked and served, rooms are cleaned, and the spa is open.

Jake and I spent most of Nyepi swimming and lounging at the pool. From a comfortable poolside chaise, I dipped into more of the books I downloaded before leaving Chicago—books about Bali, books about moving to Bali, books about moving abroad with children, books about sabbaticals, and a book titled *f**k it: the ultimate spiritual way.* I was ready to move, ready for a change. But was it doable in Ubud as an expat, as a single woman with a child?

Cat Wheeler, a long-term Canadian expat in Ubud, wrote in her book *Bali Daze: Freefall off the Tourist Trail,* "Ubud is unique in many ways, one of which is the high expat population of accomplished single women. Generally speaking, I've never met a group of happier, more positive and grateful people anywhere." I thought that sounded promising. At Green School, I hoped to find a community of people who did not think it outrageous to leave your job, home, family, and friends, and move with a child to a small island on the other side of the world. Virtually everyone at Green School had made that journey. And we already had friends. Not our friends in Chicago who had raised the idea—they never moved to Bali, and never even visited us. But friends of theirs—Wen and Corky and their children, Eamon and Lucy—who became our first friends in Bali, sharing poolside pizzas with us after that long, hot, and humid day checking out Green School.

A few days after Nyepi, Jake and I sat at a small table on the front porch of our hotel room while I typed an email to the broker with our best and last offer for a one-year lease for Villa Shanti, the house we had chosen to rent. When I finished, Jake and I looked at each other. I handed him the iPad. His hand hovered over the screen as he decided what to do. Slowly he reached down and hit "Send." We smiled, pleased with the decision. Later that day, Jake talked about "when we move to Bali." He then made a point of asking me whether I noticed that he had said "when," not "if." I noticed.

After ten whirlwind days in Bali, we were again at an airport in the middle of the night. Our Malaysia Airlines flight from Bali to Kuala Lumpur was scheduled to depart at 4:25 a.m. We stayed at an airport hotel the night before and arrived at the airport at about 2:15 a.m. As the hotel shuttle pulled up to the deserted drop-off area, the driver read the departure board and shook his head. A few minutes later, when the board switched from Bahasa Indonesia to English, I shook my head too. Our flight was canceled. I left our bags in the shuttle and asked the driver to wait, please. The driver was not happy about it, but he agreed to wait. Jake and I walked into the empty airport and up to the Malaysia Airlines check-in counter.

The ticket agent informed me that the entire airport was closed for five hours, from 1 a.m. until 6 a.m. No flights could land or take off during this time. The closure had been scheduled; there was no emergency. Apparently, all the passengers on our flight (and every other flight)—except for Jake and me and three twenty-something European backpackers—had been contacted and reticketed for different flights. Maybe the airline did not contact me because I had booked with American Airlines miles, but the reason hardly mattered at that point. Even if we took the first flight to Kuala Lumpur once the airport opened, we would miss our connections to Shanghai and on to Los Angeles. I stood at the counter in the deserted airport with two Malaysia Airlines employees who did not know what to do. While they called Kuala Lumpur for instructions, I wasn't paying attention to Jake. The airport was empty, except for the seven of us and a few security guards. I could see Jake out of the corner of my eye but didn't focus on what he was doing. He was watching CNN.

"Mommy, did you know that a Malaysia Airlines flight disappeared?"

"Oh, really? Hmm."

"Yeah, I was just watching it on TV. It left Kuala Lumpur at night and just disappeared. They don't know where it is."

So much for the weeks of shielding Jake from the news of MH370. At the Malaysia Airlines counter, in the middle of the night, he discovered the tragic news.

I turned back to the ticket agents, who had no solution. The best they could do was to book Jake and me on the first Malaysia Airlines flight to Kuala Lumpur once the airport reopened. When we arrived at KLIA, I would have to figure out how to get to Los Angeles. Jake and I headed back to the waiting airport shuttle, back to the hotel, back to the room we had left, and back to sleep. Early that afternoon, we flew to Kuala Lumpur. Although it took hours to accomplish, the agents at KLIA came through for us in the end. They booked us on Malaysia Airlines all the way back to the US—flying the next day from Kuala Lumpur to Tokyo and then Tokyo to Los Angeles. The airline also booked and paid for a room for Jake and me at the Sama-Sama Hotel, connected to the airport by a sky bridge.

On our way to the Sama-Sama Hotel, we rode in a golf cart with a public relations guy working on coordinating and communicating with the families of MH370 passengers. He told me we were lucky to get a room at the hotel. For weeks, the hotel had been fully booked with grieving relatives of MH370's passengers (flown to Kuala Lumpur and put up at the hotel by the airline), media from around the world, airline officials, and investigators. A meeting room at the Sama-Sama Hotel had been turned into a crisis management center, and a media center was set up in the hotel's basement. The day before, with virtually no hope left of finding survivors, the crisis management center moved into the city, and the media center shut down. The families flew back to their respective homes (mostly Beijing, where MH370 had been headed), and the reporters and television crews moved on to other stories. Overnight, the Sama-Sama reverted to a transit hotel with available rooms, but the sadness remained.

After two more flights on Malaysia Airlines, Jake and I finally landed at LAX. It had been a long few days of delayed and rerouted travel back through sixteen time zones. "Just a little further," I mumbled as we got into the back seat of a town car for the drive to Palm Springs to visit my parents before flying home to Chicago. Crawling through LA traffic, I closed my eyes and tried to will my body clock into flipping to Pacific Daylight Time. Jake nudged me.

"Mom, are we going to lose two days with Nana and Papa in Palm Springs because of the messed-up flights?"

"Yes," I replied, "but it could have been worse. Our flight could have been canceled the day before we arrived in Bali instead of the day we left, and then we would have missed the only chance to visit Green School before it closed for spring break."

What I really thought—and did not say to my nine-year-old child— was that it could have been far worse. One of the five Malaysia Airlines planes we took could have disappeared over an ocean with us in it. Our close encounters with some of the aftereffects of the MH370 disappearance reinforced how lucky we were in life and in our travels.

Spending the Nyepi Day of Silence on Bali had forced Jake and me to stop moving, sit still, and contemplate our lives. After that, we decided to make the leap. To change our lives. To move to Bali. It would take a few more Nyepis to connect to the power of Bali and the magic of the island, but we were on our way.

Jake thrilled to be at a ceremony at Pura Gunung Lebah
in Campuhan, Ubud

Chapter Ten

"I HATE IT HERE"
EXPAT TRAVEL

IMMEDIATELY AFTER I LISTED our house in Chicago for rent, an otherwise ideal tenant agreed to pay the asking price (pegged at the top of the market) but conditioned his offer on a June 15 move-in date—six weeks before Jake and I planned to leave for Bali. I hesitated. But "rent the house" was by far the most pressing item on my "to-do" list, second only to finding available appointment times for the multidose vaccinations (including Japanese encephalitis and rabies) Jake and I needed before leaving the US. Plus, six bonus weeks' rent might compensate for the hassle of moving out early. (I conditioned an early start date on an extension of the lease term by six weeks so that it would still cover the entire year I planned to be in Bali.) I started packing.

The tenant agreed to rent the house furnished, but I still needed to pack and store Jake's and my personal belongings, including thousands of books. I hired my nephew Jason, home from college for the summer, to help me. Sweaty and grimy, we climbed up and down the stairs, packing boxes and stacking them in the dusty, unfinished basement of the 110-year-old house. We finished on time, and I turned our home over to the tenant. (Jake and I stayed in my parents' home in the suburbs for the next six weeks.)

Moving with a child from Chicago to a small island in a Muslim country on the other side of the world was not for everyone. I understood this. But as we prepared to leave for Bali, I was still surprised by the level of opposition I confronted from colleagues, friends, and acquaintances who questioned the wisdom of the move and challenged me. Some reproaches took the form of backhanded compliments from people who purported to admire my sense of adventure and regretted that their fear of terrorism, disease, and Third World living conditions prevented them for doing the same. I often heard statements such as, "I would love to do something like that, but ____." Fill in the blank with your particular prejudice, deepest fear, or favorite pet that cannot be left behind. Others were direct. One colleague told me, with great concern, about a grandniece who died when her mother took her to some exotic location. A former good friend and colleague—no longer in touch since I moved to Bali—droned on and on about how I would ruin my career and finances. As it turned out, he was right about my legal career. But by the time I realized that this career was over, I was done with it anyway. Fortunately, my family and close friends supported the move and were excited for us—or were wise enough to say nothing to the contrary.

On July 29, 2014, I picked up Jake—who sat cross-legged on the floor of my parents' house and refused to walk to the van waiting to drive us to the airport—and we left for Bali. Thirty-six hours later, after a sixteen-hour flight to Hong Kong, a sleepless few hours at a Hong Kong airport hotel, a five-hour flight to Bali, and a nerve-racking nighttime drive to Ubud through Bali's chaotic traffic, we arrived at our new home. As the staff carried in our bags, I collapsed on the porch of Villa Shanti, our aptly named villa—*shanti* means peace in Sanskrit. Gazing out at the rice paddies, illuminated by the hotel next door, I took a deep breath. All the doubt evaporated. I was home, at peace and happy.

Villa Shanti is in Tegallantang, a small village two kilometers uphill from the main temple and commercial area of Ubud Center. Tegallalang—"la lang" not "lan tang"—a different village about seven kilometers farther uphill, is world famous for its spectacular rice terraces. Once I got the hang of shifting gears on a steep hill—I had always lived in a flat city—and got used to the traffic flow, I often rode my bicycle uphill from Tegallantang to the Tegallalang rice terraces. After the hard ride in a low gear, I would sit at a café, look at the justifiably famous terraces, and cool down with a glass of ice-cold, fresh coconut water. When I told people in Bali that I lived in Tegallantang, they often thought that I lived in Tegallalang and could not correctly pronounce, or did not know, the name of the place where I lived for two years.

Although I instantly felt at home in Tegallantang, Jake did not. In our early days there, Jake reminded me of someone who would buy a guidebook written by Macon Leary, the protagonist of Anne Tyler's novel *The Accidental Tourist*, who wrote guidebooks for people who, when forced to travel, wanted to feel like they had never left home. We had an infinity pool in our backyard, rice terraces off our back porch, and an entire island of rich local culture and world-famous beaches to explore. Yet Jake did everything he could to behave exactly as he would have done in Chicago. When his new friend Eamon came over, the two boys watched each other's Minecraft videos and played on the Wii. Nonetheless, at least three times a day, Jake said, "I hate it here! I want to go home to Chicago!" I remained convinced that Jake would like Bali and Green School if he just gave it a chance. As it turned out, a series of unfortunate events conspired against us.

Jake's first two months in Bali did not go well, not well at all.

The first day at Green School started with great fanfare, a ceremony blessing the school and the students and making offerings to ensure a good year. The school administration asked the students to wear the traditional Balinese ceremonial outfit. For the new students (and their parents who needed to find the items), the school provided details of what the kids should wear. Boys should wear a sarong, a sash, a white button-down shirt, and an *udeng* (a headcloth Balinese men fold and tie around their heads and wear during ceremonies). I bought Jake a pre-folded *udeng* (akin to having a pre-knotted, clip-on bowtie). All he had to do was wrap it around his head and tie a knot in the front. Jake did not want to wear these clothes on his way to school, but he said he would change before the ceremony. I folded the clothes neatly and put them into his backpack with his lunch.

I wanted to see the ceremony, too. Didn't everyone need a blessing to start the school year? I rode along. When we arrived at school, I asked Jake if he wanted me to go with him to his classroom. He responded with an unequivocal "No." He had spotted Eamon and was already halfway out of the car to meet him. Good. I was relieved. Maybe the day would go well. Maybe the year would.

About an hour later, students, teachers, staff, and parents gathered for the ceremony in the Heart of School. The soaring bamboo Heart of School is like no other school building in the world and like no other building I had ever seen before coming to Bali. The roof, in the shape of three nautiluses spiraling into one another, is supported by three massive bamboo towers. The design is grand and dramatic yet light and airy. Constructed totally from bamboo, the building shouts sustainability and serves as the iconic image of Green School. Or that is what I saw and felt this first day of school. Jake saw only a building without walls and without air-conditioning.

I searched for Jake in the crowd of hundreds of kids in varying levels of Balinese ceremonial dress. Some wore just a T-shirt and sarong. Others, mostly little girls, wore the full ceremonial dress. I searched for Jake's white *udeng* with its black-and-gold trim. I looked into all the little boys' faces under their *udengs*. No Jake. Finally, I spotted him, wearing only his blue T-shirt, khaki shorts, and flip-flops. At least he was sitting with his class. Jake smiled at me. I smiled back and blew him a kiss.

As the crowd moved around the Heart of School, I lost sight of Jake again among the bamboo pillars and hundreds of kids. But then he found me. Sobbing, he held his palm over his right eye. As part of the ceremony, the teachers and students each received a traditional offering of flowers, rice, and a stick of smoking incense wrapped in a banana leaf. Sarita, the theater teacher, had been standing near Jake, holding the offering in her hand, the incense stick right at Jake's eye level. He turned, or Sarita moved, and the smoldering incense poked Jake in the eye.

While the ceremony continued, Jake and I and the Balinese teacher from his classroom made our way to the nurse's office. The small bamboo building was poorly located for dealing with emergencies. It was down several steep flights of uneven and slippery wooden planks dug into the dirt on the side of the hill. Even when you could see out of both eyes and were not sobbing, the path was tough to navigate. The nurse, of course, was not there. He was at the ceremony. The teacher rushed back to the Heart of School to find him.

While we waited, I convinced Jake to remove his hand from his eye so I could see his injury. Fortunately, he had been struck in the eyelid, not in the eye. A burning stick of incense in the eye would have been a major problem, given the limited medical facilities at this jungle school—and, for that matter, on the island of Bali. When the nurse arrived, he washed the incense and ash from Jake's eye. Instantly, Jake was in less pain and stopped sobbing. I refused to take the experience as a sign of anything bad. Maybe, I told myself, an incense stick in the eyelid is better than the proverbial stick in the eye. We went back up to the Heart of School, where the ceremony was still underway. After a few pleas to go home—this time to Villa Shanti, not Chicago—Jake rejoined his class.

The rest of that first week of school passed uneventfully, and I planned a fun and busy weekend to cheer up Jake. We spent Saturday with friends at Waterbom, an Australian-run waterpark in Kuta, popular with Balinese, expats, and tourists. Jake had a blast. I had fun, too. The water park was well run, the lines for the water slides moved quickly, and a lazy river floated through palm trees and tropical flowers. Waterbom was far less tacky than the many water parks we had visited in the Wisconsin Dells, the self-proclaimed "Water Park Capital of the World," and the tropical plants and burkini-clad Muslim women swooping down the water slides were vivid reminders that we were not in Wisconsin anymore.

Although Bali is a major international tourist destination, it receives more domestic than international tourists. Most of the domestic tourists come from neighboring Java, which, like the rest of Indonesia (except Bali), is predominately Muslim. It was easy to spot the Javanese tourists, at least the women, because many of them wore burkinis. I had never seen a burkini before and quickly realized the beauty of the design. Unlike the burkas that completely hid the Muslim Pakistani women and kept them from participating in society, the burkinis allowed the Javanese Muslim women to join in. Wearing burkinis, the Muslim women could fly down the waterslides and float down the lazy river with their families and friends without risking being dragged under by their clothing. Unlike the burka, the burkini frees and empowers women. And I could tell that several women who almost lost their bikinis at the bottom of a water slide were tempted to try a burkini next time.

After a relaxing and fun weekend, I stopped worrying about Jake. Too soon, as it turned out.

Jake and I both love watching the reality TV show *The Amazing Race*. If he were older and I were younger, we could see ourselves as a powerful team, racing around the world to the million-dollar prize. Jake's favorite parts of the show were the crazy physical challenges, like walking a tightrope between the towers at Marina Bay Sands in Singapore. I liked the cultural challenges, especially when they suited the location. In an episode we watched before moving to Bali, the contestants arrive at the airport in Denpasar and rush to Ubud, where they are given the choice of building an elaborate ceremonial offering or dredging volcanic sand from the bottom of the river and carrying it on their head up to the riverbank. The show's producers did not invent these activities. They copied them from the Balinese.

One evening not long after the opening ceremony at Green School, Jake and I looked for an episode of *The Amazing Race* to watch. We typically cherry-picked episodes, finding ones in which the contestants raced to and around cities where we had been or planned to go. Jake found an episode in Tokyo, a good choice because we planned to spend spring break in Japan, starting in Tokyo. We purchased season fifteen from Amazon Prime Video and started watching the first episode.

After about twenty minutes, Jake paused the episode, freezing contestants midbite as they played a Japanese game show called "sushi roulette," in which they had to eat a wasabi-filled roll to get the next clue.

During the day, we kept the house open to the outdoors. In the evening, about an hour before bedtime, Jake would shut his bedroom door, close his windows, and turn on his air conditioner so his room would cool off before he climbed under the mosquito net and into bed. Jake did not want to miss anything while he ran up the outdoor staircase to his room to turn on the air-conditioning. An instant after he disappeared from sight, I heard Jake yell, "Mommy!"

He ran back into the family room. "Snake! On my steps!"

A snake on the steps was beyond my frame of reference for bedtime preparations. We needed help. I took Jake's hand, and we hurried down the stone path to the staff house at the front of the property. Hearing our approach, Nyoman, our night security guard, met us on the path. Made, from the day staff, who was hanging out in the staff house watching TV, joined him.

"How big is the snake?" Made asked.

"About two meters," Jake answered.

"Black?"

"No," Jake said. "Beige."

Beige was not one of the English words Made or Nyoman knew, but what seemed important was that the large snake was not black. Based on Jake's response, Made and Nyoman were even less concerned, almost nonchalant.

We all walked back to the main house. Nyoman directed Jake and me into the family room while he and Made headed to the staircase. I started closing all of the French doors. A huge snake on the outside steps was bad enough. I did not want it in the house. Through the glass, I saw Made and Nyoman head toward the staircase and out of sight. Seconds later, they walked through the main house and back toward the staff house without saying a word. When they returned, they were not as casual—they were armed with long sticks and a scythe. Apparently, Made and Nyoman thought Jake, the American city kid, had exaggerated the snake's size. He had not.

"Should we kill it?" Made asked me.

I eyed the scythe he held, wondering how it would be used to kill the snake. Chop its head off?

"Is it poisonous?" I asked.

Made's response was muddled by the language barrier, but I thought his answer was that the snake would not kill us, but it could kill our cats. He set down the scythe and gestured with both arms, demonstrating how the snake could coil around a cat and suffocate it. I had never had a snake in my home before and had no idea what to do. Gesturing with the scythe, Made and Nyoman suggested what they would do. Later—too late for this snake—I learned that there is a British expat in Bali, Ron Lilley, who will come to your house, identify the snake, and remove it if it is dangerous (or you just want it out of the house). After this, I kept Lilley's number handy in my phone under "Snake." But with this first encounter, I regret I responded, "Kill the snake."

About a week later, Jake and I decided to watch the second episode of *The Amazing Race* season we had purchased. In that episode, the contestants traveled to Ho Chi Minh City and the Mekong Delta in Vietnam. Jake and I planned to travel both places during our upcoming vacation in Vietnam over winter break. No, we did not plan our vacations that year to align with season fifteen of *The Amazing Race*. It just happened that the show started that season in Asia, and Jake and I planned to travel throughout Asia on my required "visa runs."

Because it was getting late, I asked Jake to take a shower and get ready for bed before we watched the episode. Jake headed to his bathroom, which was open to the outdoors. An outdoor shower may seem exotic on vacation, but not so much when it's your everyday shower and not at all after that evening. Shortly after Jake left, I heard him howl and shriek. He ran out of the bathroom, dripping wet, screaming, and clutching his foot.

I rushed to him. "What happened?"

"Don't know. Ow, ow, OW!"

I half-lifted, half-pulled Jake to the couch. Sitting next to him, I examined his heel. Given his gasps of pain, I expected to see a puncture wound gushing blood. But there was nothing. When I touched his heel, he screamed even louder. All I could see was what might be a tiny hole. Neither one of us could figure out why he was in so much pain.

Stopping first at the front door to grab a pair of flip-flops to protect my feet from whatever Jake stepped on, I headed to his bathroom to investigate. Walking on his left foot and the toe of his right to avoid putting weight on his throbbing heel, Jake followed me. Cautiously, we walked over to the outdoor shower, which was blocked from outside view by a three-quarter-height wall topped with a row of plants. It was a pitch-black night, the lighting in the bathroom was dim, and the shower floor was made from dark stone. I could not see anything. I went back into the house and got a flashlight from the kitchen pantry. With the faint beam, I searched the wet, stone shower floor, looking for anything sharp Jake could have stepped on. I spotted nothing. Then, out of the corner of my eye, I saw something move on the shower wall. Next to the shower tap, I saw a mouth, pincers, and a long, light-brown tail. Instantly, I realized that a scorpion had stung Jake. Before I could find something to grab it or kill it, the scorpion disappeared into a crack between the rocks of the shower wall.

Now I knew what had happened, but I had no idea how serious a scorpion sting was or how to treat the sting. Still in a lot of pain, Jake curled up on the lounge chair in the family room and screamed. I needed to figure out what to do but could not focus or function while he continued screaming. After Jake's encounter with the huge snake the week before, I'd researched what to do if bitten by a poisonous snake. Remaining calm was essential to slow the spread of venom. It seemed logical that the same would be true for the venom from a scorpion sting. So there were two reasons for Jake to calm down: his physical well-being and my mental competence.

I took a deep breath and turned to Jake. "I'm going to help you," I said, "but first, you need to calm down so I can figure out our next step."

Even injured, Jake is pragmatic—he's my kid. Jake breathed deeply, relaxed, and stopped yelling. I grabbed my iPad and googled "scorpion stings." I scanned the search results, ranking them in my mind by the credibility of the source. The site sponsored by the US National Library of Medicine, National Institutes of Health, seemed like a reasonable and responsible place to start.

NIH's cover page began, "Scorpion stings kill more people than any other animal, except snakes (snakebites)." That was scary and unhelpful. I clicked on the Mayo Clinic site: "Scorpion stings—although painful—are mostly harmless." Better. My heart rate slowed a bit.

The Mayo site further advised that only about 30 of the 1,500 known species of scorpions can inflict potentially fatal stings, and these species are located predominantly in the Southwest United States, Mexico, South America, parts of Africa, the Middle East, and India. Indonesia was not on the list. While the site stated that healthy adults usually don't need treatment for scorpion stings, it urged, "If your child is stung, seek immediate medical care."

Good advice, but where would I seek immediate medical care? In Chicago—if we had scorpions there—I could have hopped in my car, driven ten minutes, and been at one of the premier children's hospitals in the world. I did not yet know where to go in Ubud. Scrolling through the contacts in my phone, I called the few people I knew in Bali. No one answered. So I opened the Green School Facebook page and typed, "Help, please. A scorpion stung my nine-year-old son. We are in Ubud. Where should I take him?"

The response was immediate, from new friends as well as strangers. Some of the advice I received from the Facebook posts was practical: wash the area, apply ice, take an antihistamine and pain medicine, and watch for signs of an allergic reaction. As expected from Green School parents, several people suggested various homeopaths and homeopathic remedies. Two people suggested the following remedy: kill the scorpion, cut it in two, cut off the stinger, smash the dead scorpion, and put the smashed body on the sting to pull out the poison. (The CDC says this folk remedy does not work. Besides, the scorpion had already escaped.)

I followed a tip to call a twenty-four-seven medical clinic in Nyuh Kunning, a village down the hill. Within thirty minutes, a doctor, nurse, and driver arrived for a house call, bringing medicine and advice: ice, Benadryl, anti-inflammatories, and antibiotics. (In Bali, antibiotics are prescribed for everything, whether bacterial or not.) Jake suffered no adverse reaction to the venom, or the treatment, only localized pain and swelling. By the next day, he felt fine, and we headed to the beach in Amed on the northeast coast of Bali for a weekend of snorkeling.

We both learned something that night. Jake learned to wear flip-flops when he showered outdoors at night—that is, after he finally agreed to use that shower again, which took a few weeks. We both learned that the scorpion stings in Bali are excruciating but not as dangerous as those in the United States. I learned that the US medical website I initially consulted was not at all helpful in Indonesia. And I discovered I was not alone with my child in a foreign country that lacked advanced medical care. Instead, we were lucky to have joined a community that was ready, willing, and able to help when we needed it, even though we still would have to fly to Singapore if we required any major medical care.

The following week, Jake and I sat down to watch yet another episode of *The Amazing Race*, this time selected at random and not based on a planned vacation. The contestants traveled to Botswana and flew to the Kalahari Desert. Their roadblock required the teams to accompany Kalahari Bushmen into the bush and dig up and capture a scorpion. They were aided by a Bushman, who put the scorpion in his mouth. Several contestants were frightened, one so much so that he flapped his arms and screamed, "I don't want to die." Jake smirked and sat back with a look on his face that said, "Been there, done that."

Not everyone adapts well to the drastic change in lifestyle from living indoors in the northern hemisphere to living outdoors in the tropics. Living in Bali meant living with bugs (so many kinds of bugs), reptiles (geckos on the ceiling and walls, as well as the snakes), frogs and toads (which mostly stayed outdoors), rats (which is why almost everyone we knew had at least one cat), bats (which eat the bugs), and more. Those who cannot acclimate leave. For those who can acclimate, you don't notice as things that once sent shivers down your spine become the fabric of everyday life, the new norm.

I became hardened but not immune to things that creep and creepy things. One evening, a few months after we moved to Bali, I walked through the door from my bedroom to my outdoor bathroom and jumped. On the wall between the door and my hanging medicine cabinet was a spider the size of my fist, with a massive body and long, hinged legs that arched up above its back. After this involuntary jump, my first voluntary reaction was to call Jake so he could see it too.

Jake arrived and was unimpressed.

"Look, that spider is huge; isn't it amazing?" I said.

"Oh, I've seen lots of those."

"No, we have not had one of these spiders in the house before."

"I know. There are a lot of them at school."

"Well, I have not seen one before. I want to take a picture. Wait here," I said, as I walked back into my bedroom to grab my phone.

Phone camera ready, I instructed my assistant. "Jake, put your fist next to the spider so the picture will show how huge it is."

Jake was willing, but the spider would not cooperate. The lights around the bathroom mirrors created a shadow next to the medicine cabinet, and the spider moved into the shadow. It was either hiding out of fear or getting ready to pounce on our faces if we got too close.

Once the picture plan failed, I was not sure what to do with the spider.

"Kill it," Jake suggested.

"No, I can't."

I have no trouble killing mosquitoes and ants, but this spider was so big it was more like a creature than a bug. I did not want to kill it. Also, I worried about how I would kill it and what would happen if I succeeded. I did not want a smashed dead spider all over my bathroom wall.

"Throw it into the bush," Jake suggested.

"I can't." I did not know what to use to scoop it up and throw it and did not want it falling on me in the process. I considered calling our night security guard, but decided it was too ridiculous to call for help with a spider.

"Well, what are you going to do?" Jake asked.

"Nothing. Go inside."

Several hours later, I went back outside to the bathroom to brush my teeth before bed. The spider was still in the shadow of the medicine cabinet, and I needed my dental floss and toothpaste. Slowly and carefully, I opened the door to the cabinet. The spider did not move. I quickly grabbed what I needed and brushed my teeth at the second sink at the far end of the vanity. When I returned to my bedroom, before going to sleep, I looked under the bed, pulled the mosquito netting down to the floor, and double-checked that the openings where the net overlapped were all closed tight. Maybe the spider would be gone by morning.

The next morning, while I was still in bed, Jake went into my bathroom.

"Jake, is the spider gone?"

"Yeah."

"Good."

"Mom?"

"What?"

"There's a gecko in the toilet."

Acclimated to life in the tropics, Jake relaxing at one of Bali's five-star resorts, the Ritz-Carlton in Nusa Dua

Celebrating Nyepi at Green School

Chapter Eleven

PUTU, PUTU, MADE, MADE, NYOMAN, NYOMAN, NYOMAN, KOMANG, AND KETUT

LIVING TRAVEL AT VILLA SHANTI

MY PARENTS DID NOT discourage me from moving to Bali with Jake, but I knew they would miss him, their youngest grandchild. As soon as I confirmed the move, my mom started planning my parents' visit to us (really Jake) in Bali. They arrived in time for the Nyepi celebrations at Green School and in Ubud.

Without the opportunity for Jake to attend the renowned Green School, we might not have moved to Bali. But during the 2014–15 school year, Green School was in transition—again. If the school had had any walls and doors, the door for the head of school's office would have been a revolving one. In August 2014, another new head of school (whom many of the founding families despised from the get-go and many of the rest of us grew to dislike during the first semester) replaced the popular head from the previous year. These academic and organizational changes did not stop the school's growth. From 97 students in 2008, its inaugural year, by 2014, enrollment had grown to 410 students in pre-K through twelfth grade. Jake was one of approximately a hundred new students that year, a 30 percent increase over the previous year.

With the influx of so many new students, a new head of school intent on changing everything, and no coherent pedagogy, the academic year did not start strong. The so-called proficiency frame—math, English, science, and social studies—was weak and far below grade level. Within one week of classes starting, I moved Jake from fourth grade (where he would have been in Chicago) to fifth grade. Fortuitously, I also moved him from a class with numerous uncontrolled bullies to a class of nice kids who got along well. Jake formed a group of friends he still keeps in contact with.

The better part of Green School, the reason I enrolled Jake there, was the "experiential frame"—the hands-on, getting-dirty part of the school. For Nyepi, the experiential frame worked well, teaching a range of academic, social-emotional, and cultural lessons while having fun.

Each primary class spent weeks building an *Ogoh-ogoh*. The size and gruesomeness of the *Ogoh-ogohs* increased along with the grade level, from pre-K through fifth. The father of one of Jake's Balinese classmates helped Jake's class (5B) with the overall design and construction of their *Ogoh-ogoh* and likely built the *Ogoh-ogoh*'s impressive head. Working with the Balinese school staff, the kids made the bamboo frame to carry the *Ogoh-ogoh*, and the staff securely mounted the *Ogoh-ogoh* to the frame.

Green School modified the *Ogoh-ogohs* and the procession to respect the Balinese culture but align with the Green School values of environmental sustainability and gender equality. The Balinese build their *Ogoh-ogohs* from Styrofoam, which cannot be recycled, is not biodegradable, takes 500 years to decompose, and is likely to persist in the environment for more than a million years. The Green School students built their *Ogoh-ogohs* from recycled or recyclable materials, no Styrofoam allowed. Although women perform essential roles in Balinese ceremonies, including the daily responsibility for offerings made around every home and business, Balinese women and girls do not design and build *Ogoh-ogohs* and do not carry the bamboo frame and parade their *banjar*'s *Ogoh-ogoh*. At Green School, girls and boys designed and built the *Ogoh-ogohs,* and girls and boys carried the bamboo frames and paraded the *Ogoh-ogohs* through the village. The kids accepted these changes as the norm.

For the day of the procession, Jake's class had T-shirts made that followed the same design protocols as those worn by the men carrying the *Ogoh-ogohs* for Nyepi (and other ceremonies). The T-shirts stated the ceremony, the year, and, instead of displaying their *banjar*, the kids' T-shirts stated their class, "5B." Like the Balinese, the kids wore their matching T-shirts with matching sarongs, sashes, and *udengs*. Looking like the real deal, Jake and his fifteen classmates took their positions in the grid of the bamboo frame.

Slowly, they lifted the frame off the ground. As the *Ogoh-ogoh* rose into the air, it swayed to the left, then to the right, and almost tipped over before a teacher and parent grabbed hold to steady the frame. Class 5B's *Ogoh-ogoh* was the largest in the parade. The younger grades had smaller *Ogoh-ogohs* and a lot of parental assistance. They seemed okay carrying and maneuvering their *Ogoh-ogohs*. But the ten- and eleven-year-olds in 5B struggled. Their *Ogoh-ogoh* was too large and too heavy for them to handle. As they left the open field of Green School and turned down the road toward the neighboring village of Sibang Kaja, 5B could not maintain control. The bamboo frame was wider than the road, and the kids in the grid's outer squares were forced into the brush on the side. Then the road entered a wooded area, and 5B's *Ogoh-ogoh* started to hit the lower branches of the trees. The kids could not master the moves necessary to avoid the trees and stay on the path.

As the procession continued, 5B's *Ogoh-ogoh* felt heavier and heavier. The kids stopped every twenty or thirty yards and lowered the *Ogoh-ogoh* to the ground so they could swap positions, thinking that would somehow lighten the load. Of course, it didn't. To keep the procession moving, and avoid a collision or collapse, parents stepped into the bamboo frame to help. When it was my turn, I could barely hold up my sixteenth of the weight. I suspected that the kids were no longer carrying their share of the load but only taking up space standing in the frame. By the end of the procession, two tall, strong fathers of Jake's classmates carried the bulk of the weight and kept the *Ogoh-ogoh* level. As soon as the *Ogoh-ogoh* cleared the school gate and was back on the soccer field, the kids dropped the frame and *Ogoh-ogoh* onto the grass and collapsed into a sweaty, laughing heap. 5B's *Ogoh-ogoh* had been a huge success.

From my brief time in the bamboo frame, I gained an immense appreciation for the Balinese men who carry the *Ogoh-ogohs* on Nyepi eve. And 5B's *Ogoh-ogoh* was small and light compared to the elaborate monsters and gods they carry. This brief experience also informed my plan to keep my parents out of the path of the *Ogoh-ogohs* in Ubud Center the next evening.

Unlike the year before, when we had had no idea where we were, this year the main event in Ubud Center occurred at an intersection Jake and I knew well, just two kilometers down the hill from Villa Shanti at a spot we passed multiple times every day. This was my parents' first, and likely only, opportunity to see a Nyepi procession, and I wanted them to experience the big one in Ubud Center that Jake and I had missed the previous year. I knew exactly where to sit to get a good view while staying out of range of the surging crowd and precariously balanced *Ogoh-ogohs*. And I now knew a back-road route to get out and go home if the event became overwhelming.

We headed down early and grabbed spots across from the Royal Palace on a platform several feet above street level. I even snagged plastic chairs for my parents. We had the best seats in the house to watch the procession, like sitting in the viewing stands for the Macy's Thanksgiving Day Parade. We could watch the *Ogoh-ogohs* come west on Jalan Raya Ubud, turn the corner on Jalan Suweta, and pass right in front of us.

The impressive *Ogoh-ogohs* that year included the usual gods and monsters, huge and grotesque, sure to scare away the evil spirits. Lord Krishna, the blue-skinned god, rode a chariot bursting with flames and pulled by a white steed. Hanuman, the leader of the monkey army in the *Ramayana* and namesake of a main street in Ubud Center, flew high. Variants of demons with huge saggy breasts and long curly tongues, wearing necklaces and ankle bracelets made of skulls, accompanied the gods.

From our perch above the fray, I could see why the Uma Ubud Hotel's manager had suggested the previous year that we not go to Ubud Center. At the intersection of Jalan Raya Ubud and Jalan Suweta, where the procession made a turn to the north, it was mayhem—primarily caused by tourists behaving badly. Nyepi is not a show for the tourists. Although not holy like Melasti, the purification ritual before Nyepi, the

Ogoh-ogoh parade is still part of a meaningful ceremony for Bali's Hindus. Non-Hindus are welcome to watch and join the procession. However, from our raised seats, we saw how tourists took advantage of the Balinese welcome and acted as though they were the stars of the event put on for their enjoyment, rather than guests who belonged on the sidelines of a Balinese ceremony. I wanted to shout at the photographers, professional and amateur, whose only goal was grabbing prizeworthy angles for their shots. Dangling from the tops of temples and standing in the path of difficult-to-control *Ogoh-ogohs*, they endangered themselves and the ceremony. Worst of all were the parents who threw themselves into the mix with toddlers on their shoulders, putting their children inches from the swaying bamboo platforms and *Ogoh-ogohs*.

Through speakers mounted at the intersection, polite announcements (in English) requested spectators not climb on the temples and back out of the way of the moving *Ogoh-ogohs* struggling to make the turn. At one point, the announcer identified a particularly egregious and ridiculous parent with a young child by the writing on the man's T-shirt and asked him to move away from the *Ogoh-ogoh*. None of the tourists complied. The outsize impact of tourism on Bali's economy may be why the Balinese do not take firmer measures to stop this disruptive and possibly dangerous behavior by tourists.

For this second *Ogoh-ogoh* procession, Jake and I were more informed observers than the witless participants we had been the previous year. Yet the experience was not as powerful. Although we now understood the ceremony, sitting removed from the crowd and simply watching the parade go by, we were not caught up in the energy, so it lost some of the magic. But we certainly were safer. Jake was just ten and still small. My eighty-four-year-old father needed knee replacements. My seventy-eight-year-old mother had never regained good balance after having had polio as a child. And I was claustrophobic in crowds after being smashed and almost suffocated in the security line to get onto the Capitol grounds to hear Barak Obama sworn in as president. Clearly, the best spot for us was on the sidelines.

After the procession ended, we went home to Villa Shanti, and, like the rest of Bali, stayed home to observe the Day of Silence. Because of my parents' ages, the staff were very solicitous and willing to bend the rules. Although we could not leave the villa, the staff said electricity and cooking would be fine, as long as we were quiet and did not use any lights in the front of the house. We spent Nyepi reading, playing cards, and watching illegally copied DVDs—the only kind you can buy in Bali.

That Nyepi, our staff worked in the house day and night. I did not think to give them the day off, although I did the following year. Looking back, it did not occur to me that first year because I did not draw up (or even know in advance) the staffs' schedules and was still learning about Bali. That first year, in many ways, we were still tourists.

———— ᬳᬭᬧᬳᬭᬡᬧᬭᬟ᭟᭟ ————

Although many expats in Bali have staff who work in their homes, and most of the families I knew did, our staff was unusually large, too large for us, and, at first, strangely ill suited to our needs. If I had hired the staff myself, I would have hired a driver, a *pembantu*—the Balinese word for the housekeeper/nanny position called *ayi* in Shanghai—and a gardener to maintain the lush grounds and pool. But I did not hire the staff. My landlord did that, and an off-site manager trained the staff, dictated their duties, and set their schedules.

My lease specified the number of staff and their jobs and stated that the staff would work throughout the lease term. Even though I indirectly paid the cost of their salaries through my rent, per the contract, the salaries were set and paid by my landlord, not me. Before I rented Villa Shanti, the number of staff, their schedule, and duties were set up to run a guesthouse with a constant flow of up to ten tourists per night during the high season. Neither the staffing numbers nor the twenty-four-seven schedule changed when I rented Villa Shanti for the year for a family of two and our visiting friends and relatives. Even if I could have fired the staff we did not need, I would not have. I did not want to deprive them (and their extended families) of this good income during the period Villa Shanti was our home instead of a busy guesthouse.

Not only did I lack control over the number of staff and the hours they worked, but I had limited control over the scope of their duties. My lease provided, "The Second Party [me] is strictly prohibited from soliciting or using any of the house staff . . . for her own private purposes or for things that have nothing to do with the care or maintenance of this property or for things *which are not within their normal scope of duties for caring for the Second Party [me]*." The lease also expressly stated that if I needed a nanny, cook, or driver, that was outside the scope of the house staff's duties, and I would have to hire additional staff for these jobs. What, then, was within the "normal scope of duties for caring" for us? That ambiguity gave me the latitude to change some things over time.

Slowly, I made changes in the staff's routine to accommodate Jake and me, to transition Villa Shanti from a guesthouse to a home, and to save money. First, I asked the staff to stop changing sheets and towels daily and to stop placing clean towels twice per day on the ground in front of every sink. I also stopped sending the linens out to be cleaned and ironed. I bought a washer and dryer (which I sold when we left Bali), and linens were changed once per week and washed and dried on the premises.

When I received the first monthly electric bill of $300—almost double what any of the staff earned in a month—I investigated why we were using so much electricity and looked for ways to slash the electric bill and conserve energy. The most obvious reason was a carryover from when Villa Shanti was a guesthouse. At dusk, around 6 p.m. year-round—Bali is just south of the equator—the staff turned on every single light in the house and on the grounds to illuminate the villa and make the property look beautiful and welcoming for short-term guests. Stopping this practice was an easy change to lower our electric bill.

The air-conditioning units clearly used a lot of electricity, but we only ran them in the bedrooms and only while we were sleeping. Although I would have been comfortable sleeping without air-conditioning, Jake would not have been. And the air-conditioning served other essential purposes—drying the air to keep our clothes and bedding from getting moldy and protecting our electronics from rot. (When we were looking for a home to rent in Ubud, we saw one villa that had air-conditioning only in a large walk-in closet. I did not understand the design until I moved to Bali and realized it was ingenious.) The air-conditioning units would stay on at night. However, after a little googling and asking around, I discovered another way to cut an even more excessive waste of electricity. Our pool filter ran twenty-four seven. It only needed to run eight to twelve hours per day, depending on whether it had rained. Making all these changes slashed the electric bill.

After an initial period when the staff did not know what to make of us, and after they realized how much less work they had with just Jake and me instead of a stream of tourists, the staff began helping me with tasks likely well outside the scope of what my lease specified. Under the lease terms, decorating and preparing the villa and grounds for Hindu holidays was the responsibility of the staff, but decorating and preparing for pagan and American holidays was not. Yet, in October, they helped carve pumpkins and set up fake cobwebs, ghosts, and goblins for our Halloween party. In early November, they hung the piñata for Jake's birthday party. And by late November, they offered to bring over extra tables, chairs, plates, glasses, and flatware from a smaller guesthouse on the property (which I did not lease) so we could host a big Thanksgiving dinner for our new American friends in Bali. As to the nanny and driver positions, no one babysat Jake, but with little work to do in the evenings, the staff sometimes played with him, especially a Balinese game that involved popsicle sticks. And the only member of the house staff with a license to drive a car—as opposed to the motorbikes everyone drove—eventually also helped with driving when our driver was off duty.

In addition to the day staff, who worked in shifts from 8 a.m. to 8 p.m., night security staff took over from 8 p.m. to 8 a.m. I don't know whether we or the villa required this level of security, but again, the staff came with the villa, and the team was set up to service a small hotel, not a home. Every hour, from 8 p.m. to 8 a.m., the night security guard walked the grounds and checked that everything looked all right. The rest of the time, he hung out in the staff house and slept or watched TV. Sweeping the grounds once per hour did not provide much security. Anyone could have easily climbed over the low wall separating our backyard from the rice fields and entered the property and the main house without being seen during the fifty-five minutes per hour the security guard was in the staff house. Villa Shanti's primary security came from employing Nyoman as the head night security guard. Nyoman lived in Tegallantang and served as *pecalang*, security for the *banjar*. It was unlikely that anyone from the *banjar* would have robbed or damaged the villa or harmed us. Such an offense by a member of the *banjar* would not go undetected. Any risk to our property and safety likely would have come from Javanese men who worked construction projects in Bali, unscrupulous foreign tourists, or foreigners who prey on tourists.

When we arrived in Bali in July 2014, I asked for a key for the front gate and the front door. A reasonable and straightforward request, I thought. It took four days to get a key. And then I never used it. The gate and house were open all day and evening and only locked from the inside late at night by security (the gate) and me (the house). We only had one intruder. She was an Australian whose friends had stayed at Villa Shanti when it was a guesthouse. She walked in—which required going through an outer gate and private parking pad, through the door at a second gate, down steps, through another gate, and along a path to the front door—to check out the property. When I told her Villa Shanti was my home now and asked her to leave, she still wanted to tour the grounds and only left when one of our staff escorted her out.

Despite the sizable staff already working at the villa, I realized within a few days of arriving in Bali that we needed a driver. In Shanghai, Jake and I had managed fine without a driver. But we lived close to Jake's school, and Shanghai has public transit and readily available, reasonably priced taxis. None of that applied in Bali. Ubud has no public transit. Unlike the Ngurah Rai Airport and towns in the south of the island, Ubud has no metered taxis. Thinking they were protecting local jobs, the *banjars* prohibited metered taxis and later banned Uber when it tried to operate in Ubud.

We lived north of Ubud Center, and getting to and from Green School required driving through town. The most direct route was down the hill on Jalan Suweta and onto Jalan Raya Ubud, the main crossroad in Ubud. But this was also the biggest and most frequent bottleneck. For days before a royal cremation, Jalan Suweta was a staging ground to build the bamboo frames used to carry the cremation tower and bull sarcophagus and then decorate the tower and sarcophagus. The road was closed; drivers had to find another way. We usually knew about these major road closures, at least after the first day, but other ceremonies blocked roads for hours without notice. We might turn a corner and be stuck behind hundreds of motorbikes waiting for the procession to pass. If we were not delayed by a ceremony, we'd hit a traffic jam caused by one of the massive tour buses that often blocked the steep, narrow streets when the driver could not make a turn or back out of a driveway.

Green School was only thirteen kilometers (eight miles) from where we lived in Tegallantang, but it took thirty to forty minutes to drive there early in the morning, when we seldom encountered ceremonies or tour buses, and often twice as long on the way home, when we frequently encountered both. Although most Green School families chose to live south of Ubud Center to avoid this traffic, a few families lived in our area on Jalan Sri Wedari and Jalan Tirta Tawar and had a preexisting carpool. Even if Jake could have squeezed into their cars, it would have added fifteen to twenty minutes each way to his already too-long commute.

Two things stopped me from driving Jake myself. I did not come to Bali to spend two or three hours per day driving Jake back and forth to school. And I was a terrible driver in Bali. I can confidently and quickly merge onto a twelve-lane highway at 70 mph. I can drive in the snow on unplowed streets and control a spin on black ice. But I could not drive in Bali.

Before moving to Bali, I drove on the "wrong" (left) side of the road in New Zealand, but there were more sheep than cars on the roads and no motorbikes. In no way did that prepare me for driving on the left side of the road in Bali. Nor did decades of driving in Chicago, where the terrain is flat and the roads are wide, straight, and well lit at night. Most of Bali is volcanic. The roads in Ubud are narrow, steep, winding, and unlit. As if driving at night was not hard enough (for me, at least), the Balinese frequently dumped loads of black volcanic ash onto the road in front of houses and temples under construction—a huge dark hazard on the unlit streets just waiting for me to run into it. Swerving around the volcanic ash—as well as the dogs, chickens, motorbikes, and children in the road—was not always possible. There was nowhere to go. Bali's extensive and brilliant irrigation system (the *subak*) includes ditches on both sides of the narrow roads, leaving no margin for error when rounding a curve or avoiding obstacles. Then, there is the rainy season, which lasts for months. In heavy rain, Ubud's steep roads turn into fast-flowing streams, causing cars and motorbikes to hydroplane. Last, but not least, were the motorbikes, which passed my car on the left and right simultaneously, merging together and emerging suddenly in front of my windshield.

When I drove in Bali, I did so with my shoulders hunched, teeth clenched, and a death grip on the steering wheel. I was not worried that I, in my big car, would be injured in an accident. Traffic never moved more than 30 mph. I was afraid I would injure or kill someone, possibly an entire family of five riding on one motorbike. Despite my fear, I never hit a person or a moving vehicle. I did hit a parked motorbike while swerving to avoid a dog lying in the road and a chicken crossing the road, but the bike and the animals survived. No, I was not going to drive Jake to and from school every day.

I hired Komang to drive for us. His salary of 2,500,000 Indonesian rupiah (IDR) per month was at the upper end of the 2014 going rate for a full-time driver without a car. Depending on the exchange rate, which was very favorable for US dollars, that came to $160 to $180 per month, plus payment for a "thirteenth month." Payment of salary for a thirteenth month is required by Indonesian law and is paid once per year on a date determined by the religion of the employee. Muslims receive this payment on Idul Fitri (the end of Ramadan). Christians are paid in December around Christmas. Hindus (most Balinese) either can be paid the full amount on Nyepi, or the thirteenth-month salary can be split, with half being paid on Galungan, which occurs twice in a year (every 210 days). The salary I paid Komang was the most he had ever earned, and, according to him, it was the best (i.e., the easiest) job he had ever had. Komang still messages me frequently, just checking in. I send him photos of Jake and he sends me photos of his daughters.

I also hired two cooks who worked alternating days. I found them in a slightly devious, partly serendipitous fashion. After finishing my lunch at Sari Organik, a vegetarian restaurant along my favorite walking path in the rice paddies behind Ubud Center, I went down the stairs to use the restroom before walking home. The restrooms are right next to the kitchen, and I could see the chefs slicing and dicing organic produce. I wanted someone like them to cook for us at home. So, I asked. I leaned my head into the kitchen and asked if the owner was there. If she was, I was not going to try and poach an employee in front of her. The owner was not in. I asked if anyone was interested in working part-time in the evenings, cooking dinner for a family. Two of the chefs were interested. For the next two years, they worked for us part-time, supplementing their income by cooking for Jake and me on nights when they were not working at the restaurant. On Thanksgiving, when I hosted a dinner for our American friends in Bali, the chefs both asked for the day off from the restaurant and came to help prepare the meal and celebrate a traditional American holiday.

After these additional hires, Jake and I had a staff of nine: Putu, Putu, Made, Made, Nyoman, Nyoman, Nyoman, Komang, and Ketut. This repetition of names is typical in Bali and makes sense once you understand the caste system and naming conventions.

In Bali, there are four castes, in order of ascending privilege: Sudra, Wesya, Ksatryia, and Brahmana. Unlike Hindu India, Bali never had a fifth caste: Dalit, the "untouchables." All Balinese belong to a caste, and approximately 95 percent of them belong to the lowest caste, Sudra. Trying to understand Bali's caste system, I turned to Putu, my best in-house source. Putu is smart, speaks excellent English (he was majoring in English in college), and was always willing to stop cleaning the house or pool to talk. According to Putu, it is illegal to discriminate based on caste in Bali. Going further, Putu insisted that in modern Bali, you cannot distinguish between castes based on education, political power, or job.

But name conventions and language protocols still divide the population by caste. Balinese parents give their children names specific to their caste. Our staff all belonged to the Sudra caste, in which parents name the firstborn child Wayan or Putu; the second child Made or Kadek; the third child Nyoman or Komang; and the fourth child Ketut. The same names are used for both boys and girls. In a large family, the cycle repeats. The parents name the fifth child Wayan or Putu again, and she or he may be called Wayan Balik (loosely translated, "another Wayan"), and so on. Although we did not have any Wayans on the staff, my phone contact list is full of Wayans, distinguished by their job or how I knew them—"Wayan Juice Bar" owns a popular juice bar in Penestanan (another Ubud village) and is a cousin of Putu, the wife of our driver Komang.

In Bali, your caste can change—if you are female. Jero, the woman who left offerings at Villa Shanti every day, was born into the Sudra caste. When she married Gusti, she assumed his higher caste. She also changed her name to a Wesya name, to reflect her new caste. If her husband had been a lower caste than she, Jero would have moved down to his caste. Her husband would not have moved up to her caste.

Having staff was a pleasure and a luxury, but it was only temporary. Eventually, we would return to reality. Shortly after Jake and I arrived in Bali, on that first visit to Waterbom, I met and spoke with a German family (friends of friends) who were visiting Bali. After years of living in Bali with their young children, they had moved back to Germany, in part so that their children would learn how to make their own beds, load and unload a dishwasher, put away their laundry, and take public transit. At the time, Jake and I had not been in Bali long enough for me to appreciate the longer-term impact of life with staff, but their comments stuck with me. I tried to get Jake to at least clear the table and pick up his things, but the staff always did it for him. Jake's excuse was, "Nyoman [or Putu or Made or Ketut] did it before I could." I knew Jake was in for a rude awakening when we moved back to Chicago.

Having staff also provided an entrée to Balinese society and culture. When Nyoman (night staff) and his daughter danced in a ceremony at their temple in Tegallantang, Jake and I walked up to the temple to watch and silently cheer. When Putu's (house staff) aunt Ketut was cremated along with 165 others who had died in their *banjar* over the previous five years, Putu took me to the massive daylong cremation, introduced me to his extended family, and explained the ceremony to me. Nyoman (house staff) helped me figure out and manage the bureaucracy of the corrupt Indonesian government and eventually landed us the fastest internet in Ubud at the time—5 Mb/sec (that is not a typo).

When we moved to Bali, I told my small law firm that it was just for one year. I told Jake the same thing. But by Nyepi 2015, I had decided to stay a second year, at least. I contacted the firm to discuss my options. Simply put, my partners were not pleased. It certainly had not been seamless to try to work remotely with unreliable internet service and a fourteen-hour time difference (thirteen hours when daylight time was in effect in the US). And from my porch in Ubud, I could not develop any new business in the US, which they had hired me to do. Bottom line: if I stayed in Bali, I could not continue at the new firm.

For decades, if you asked me who I was, I would have replied, "I am a lawyer." Lawyer remained my prime identity even after I became "Jake's mom." In too many ways, being a lawyer defined me. I thought like a lawyer. I spoke like a lawyer. I argued like a lawyer. I worked lawyer hours—when not on vacation or living in Ubud. And I earned a lawyer's income. I had been a practicing lawyer for more than half my life and all of my working life. Yet, living in Ubud, among the Balinese and unemployed and underemployed expats, I could not imagine going back to the way things had been. My reluctance a year earlier to abandon my career and income was overcome by my experience in Bali.

I told the firm I was staying in Bali. We agreed that I would continue to work remotely through August, when my resignation from the firm would become effective.

Although I could simply inform the firm of the decision I made and deal with the consequences, with Jake, I wanted his buy-in. I broached the subject slowly over time, usually while floating in the pool. I offered a range of bribes for when we returned, including turning the guest bedroom in our Chicago house into a game room with huge monitors. (In fact, we never moved back into that big house, and the apartment we rented instead was much smaller, with no guest bedroom.) However, what ultimately convinced Jake to return to Bali for a second year was not the string of bribes (which he never collected) but the fact that, after a very rough start, Bali had grown on him. And Jake had grown in Bali, in mind and body—his feet were four sizes larger than when we had arrived a year earlier. More significantly, Jake was open to living in a different culture. As non-Hindus and *bules* (foreigners), we would never fit in, but it was a culture that we could enjoy, adapt to, and appreciate. Jake did not yet love living in Bali, as I did, but he reluctantly agreed to try it for another year.

Putu and Jake at the Tegallalang rice terraces

Two of many sarcophagi burning during a cremation ceremony in Ubud

Our car, now blessed

Chapter Twelve

IN BALI, THERE'S ALWAYS A CEREMONY
INWARD TRAVEL

DURING THE FOUR WEEKS Jake and I spent in the US over the 2015 summer break, our culture shock shocked me. We were back home. Why did everything seem off?

Jake and I went to a party at my sister's house in a Chicago suburb. In Bali, you know you are walking into a good party when you see sixty flip-flops piled haphazardly outside the door. As Jake kicked off his shoes, he noticed the absence of such a pile and said, "We must be the first ones here." We were the last to arrive. Everyone else at the party kept their shoes on.

I went to my firm's office in downtown Chicago to meet with my partners and plan how to wrap up or transition my work by the end of August. As I strolled along the smooth, level sidewalk along LaSalle Street, appreciating the lack of gaping holes for me to fall through, everyone else seemed to walk so fast and, based on their loud phone conversations, be working on such important matters. Going to an office to end a decades-long legal career seemed inconsequential by comparison. It was a warm July day, so I wore what I did most days in Bali, a sundress and flip-flops. In Bali, everyone wears flip-flops everywhere, except indoors, where they go barefoot. In Chicago, no one but me wore flip-flops in a law office or on the downtown streets. I could keep wearing the flip-flops, but I needed to shake off the Bali attitude and amp up the Bali pace. I had a lot to accomplish in a limited time.

The substantial rent I received for my house in Chicago covered the mortgage and taxes on that house and the rent for Villa Shanti, including all the staff salaries. My first tenant did not renew his lease, which expired on July 31. I needed to quickly find a new tenant to cover these expenses, especially since I had just quit my job. The new tenants (a family of five) were not as ideal as the prior tenant (a divorcing man who was never home and had a housekeeper), but they were willing to pay the asking price and provided a security deposit equal to sixty days' rent to cover the extra damage risk. The first tenant moved out a little early, and I had several days to get the house ready before the new tenants moved in on August 1. Without Putu, Nyoman, Made, or Ketut to help me, I paid my nephews to help me pack up the kitchen and move more boxes and furniture to the basement. I hired movers to transport my most valuable and favorite paintings and other artwork to my parents' house. I did not trust the new tenant's young kids not to destroy my art. This was a smart move, as they repeatedly broke the dishwasher by dropping chopsticks and marbles into the drain.

After a year of buying very few consumer products, I went on a shopping spree for Jake and me and for friends staying in Bali over summer break who had given me shopping lists. I bought all new shoes and clothes for Jake—nothing still fit him. I filled two huge shopping carts at Target with massive quantities of items unavailable in Bali—e.g., reef-safe sunblock, toothpaste with fluoride, and bug spray with DEET. Yes, thank you, I know DEET is poison. DEET is very unpopular with the Green School expat families who prefer essential oils and candles—which don't work. But the DEET was for sweet-smelling me, not Jake, who never got bit. Living outdoors in the tropics, on the edge of a rice paddy, I decided that a little toxic chemical was better than contracting dengue, which was endemic on Bali. After Target, I headed to the Apple store. I bought a new MacBook Pro that a friend had asked me to get for her son and a stack of iPad minis to give as gifts for the staff. (Apple products are cheaper in the US, and you don't have to worry about counterfeits.)

Jake and I did not have time to see all the family and friends we missed, but we checked everything else off our to-do list. With absolutely no drama, Jake and I headed to the airport and boarded the plane for our flight to Hong Kong. While we waited in the Hong Kong International Airport for our connecting flight to Bali, Jake took off his headphones, looked up from his laptop, and surprised me by saying, "I thought I would be upset about leaving Chicago, like last year. But I am not." Our departure had been so smooth that I had been unconsciously (metaphorically) holding my breath, waiting for Jake to lose it. With this one comment from him, I consciously and literally exhaled.

Arriving on Bali felt utterly different this time. Instead of the anticipation, uncertainty, excitement, and fear I had experienced a year earlier, I was filled with an overwhelming sense of belonging. After clearing customs, we easily dodged the phalanx of taxi drivers and found Komang grinning from ear to ear and ready to drive us home. The traffic on the now-familiar route to Ubud no longer fazed me. The house staff seemed glad to welcome us back, perhaps aided by the gifts of the iPad minis or simply in comparison to a month of tourists coming and going. (While Jake and I were in the US, I rented Villa Shanti to tourists through Airbnb.) Our arrival this year did not have the excitement of going somewhere new, but it had the pleasure of returning somewhere special. When we arrived at Villa Shanti, Jake and I were back home.

Green School was better, too. Unlike the previous year, there was no new head of school or large influx of new students. After the head of school left abruptly in the spring of 2015, the board of directors did not replace him. For the time being, the school operated more smoothly with no one in charge trying to change everything—including what worked. Because of turmoil during the 2014–15 school year, some families had chosen not to have their children return to Green School. At the same time, the school administration had decided not to fill these student vacancies, thus reducing the number of new students to integrate. With less upheaval, the 2015–16 school year was already off to a better start.

Still advanced a year (he would go back a grade when we returned to Chicago), Jake moved up to middle school and finally learned something from the proficiency frame. Jake placed into a class supposedly learning "high school math" taught by an excellent teacher. My sister, a high school math teacher, looked at the curriculum when she visited us in Bali. She confirmed it was not high school math as taught in a good American high school, but it was an advanced version of sixth-grade math, perfect for ten-year-old Jake.

Jake joined a band, playing the keyboard. The band performed at Green School events, played a gig at Old Man's (a club on Batu Bolong beach in Canggu), and competed as the youngest contestants in the Bali Battle of the Bands. Jake's initial misery on this small island—real and then feigned—had been the only damper on my happiness living in Bali. With Jake happy, busy, and learning—no more cries of "I hate it here!"—I no longer had to worry about having dragged him to Bali. I could, and did, fully embrace and enjoy our experience.

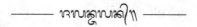

In Bali, ceremonies, and the extensive preparations for them, take precedence over mundane things like school and work. When Green School students are late for school, their excuse, whether true or not: "There was a ceremony blocking the road." When a Balinese misses a day of work, his reason: "I had a ceremony to attend." In case I, a non-Hindu newcomer to Bali, was not respectful enough of these ceremonies, my lease contained a specific provision granting persons acting on behalf of my landlord permission to perform traditional Balinese ceremonies around the property as per the calendar requirements.

Twelve years before Jake and I moved to Bali, my landlord, an American from California, leased the land Villa Shanti is built on for a term of thirty years from a Balinese man named Gusti. Although Gusti's family no longer occupied the land, their ancestors still did. The spirits of their ancestors are very real and very important to the Balinese. Ancestors ward off evil spirits and provide health, prosperity, and success to their descendants. But if ancestors are forgotten and neglected, they may retaliate against their descendants and cause—or fail to prevent—sickness, death, financial ruin, and other troubles. To respect their ancestors and stay in their good graces, the women in the family make daily offerings and maintain the family shrines, even when the ancestral land is leased to a non-Hindu foreigner.

Our first morning in Bali, I headed into the kitchen to make coffee and encountered a strange woman standing near the sink, lighting incense. After my initial surprise, I realized she was placing an offering, but who was she and why was she in my kitchen? It was Gusti's wife, Jero, and she was there to honor her husband's ancestors. Almost every day, Jero would place beautiful, handmade offerings of flower petals, burning incense, fruit, and sweets in more than a dozen separate locations throughout the grounds and villa. She left offerings at the small ancestral shrine next to our swimming pool, the shrine at the main entrance gate, at the front entrance to the villa, on the kitchen counter, next to the Wi-Fi router, in the driveway where our car's tires smashed the offering while backing out, and elsewhere. As she carefully placed each offering, Jero prayed in a ceremony that included sprinkling holy water and wafting the smoke from the incense to the gods and Gusti's ancestors. Jero never seemed rushed or annoyed praying to her husband's ancestors in my house. It was the responsibility and burden of being a Hindu woman in Bali. She carried it out with grace—every day.

Other than the offerings placed at the shrines, the front gate, and the entrance to the house, I could not figure out the rationale for the placement of the other offerings. Was the offering next to the Wi-Fi router to improve our service? I am not being snide or cynical—our Wi-Fi service needed all the help it could get. And the Balinese bless mechanical things; they even have a holiday devoted to this celebration. The holiday Tumpek Landep has evolved from blessing weapons of war, farming implements, and plows to blessing modern metal objects. Every 210 days, Balinese across the island now bless cars, motorbikes, computers, and other technology, like Wi-Fi routers. The purpose of the holiday remains the same: to bless the tools integral to people's work and livelihoods, to keep their tools—including people's minds—sharp (*landep* means sharp or keen), and to gain knowledge.

One of the first ceremonies Jake and I attended in Bali was for our car. I was not confident that I could drive on the left side of Bali's steep winding roads, and there was no way I could do so using a clutch and a left-hand stick shift. I needed a car with an automatic transmission, which was hard to find and priced accordingly for the foreigners who wanted them. With the help of Wayan, a driver and budding entrepreneur I met through my local real estate broker, I found a reasonably priced used car with an automatic transmission. However, before I could drive it, the car had to be blessed. Since I needed all the help I could get for driving that vehicle in Bali, I asked Wayan whether Jake and I could join him for the blessing ceremony. Wayan was surprised but pleased, and he quickly agreed.

For the ceremony, the freshly washed car was parked on the street in front of Wayan's family compound in Penestanan, a village down the hill from Villa Shanti, on the other side of Ubud Center. The car's hood was covered in white-and-gold cloths, atop which Wayan's mother placed several baskets full of offerings of flower petals, fruit, sweets, and money. Additional offerings were placed on the road in front of the car. Wayan's mother dressed for the ceremony in a sarong, sash, and *kebaya*—the traditional ceremonial costume for women. Wayan wore boardshorts, a pink T-shirt, and sunglasses. His father wore shorts, a T-shirt, and a baseball cap. Everyone wore flip-flops. The ceremony itself consisted of prayers said by Wayan's mother while she spread holy water around the car. The car was blessed and ready to drive—when I was ready to drive it.

Many more ceremonies followed, including some we chose to participate in and some we were caught behind, usually while driving. Balinese Hindu ceremonies, large and small, were all around us—in our home, in our village, throughout the island. Nothing about Balinese Hinduism—its ceremonies, magic, and mysticism—fit into my frame of reference or, more broadly, Western logic. And Balinese Hinduism is complicated and interwoven into every aspect of Balinese life. To learn about and try to understand the culture that enveloped us, I read and reread volumes I and II of Fred B. Eiseman Jr.'s *Bali: Sekala and Niskala* and other books by Westerners about Bali. I also tried to learn from the Balinese through observation and direct questions. I listened carefully to their answers, trying to parse what was left unsaid or assumed. After two years of living in Bali, I still barely understand Balinese culture and religion. But this did not stop me from sensing Bali's energy and power. I felt it. I benefitted from it.

Others tried to sell it. A lot of spurious spirituality is sold by and to Westerners, especially in Ubud. Having lunch at a vegan restaurant one day, I noticed offerings on posted flyers that included, "Crystal Bowls, Hanging Drum, and BreathLight Sound Meditation," "Shamanic Sound Activation," "Sacred Song Circle," and "Youthing classes." Or you could sign up for a ThetaHealing® Course, either the Basic or Advanced DNA Course or "Manifesting & Abundance." Or you could try "Butterfly therapy," which, according to its practitioner, Luise from Copenhagen, "offers an opportunity to get in deep contact with your intuition, higher self, and probably even your guardian angels or other loving spiritual connections." These modern snake-oil salespeople missed the true and deep spirituality of the Balinese and the power of Bali. But they were small-time compared to industry spawned by the popularity of *Eat Pray Love*, the book by Elizabeth Gilbert and the subsequent film starring Julia Roberts. *Eat Pray Love* inspired a sustained spike in tourism in Bali, which the island needed. Tourism had not yet recovered from the impact of the bombings in October 2002, which targeted busy tourist hotspots and killed 202 people.

Inspired by the book and movie, Western women traveled to Ubud seeking balance and looking for Ketut—likely not realizing the proportion of the Balinese population named Ketut. As if "balance" can be packaged, it seemed like every resort in Ubud offered an "*Eat Pray Love* Experience." Bliss Sanctuary for Women offered a retreat package that included a day trip to Ketut Liyer's house for a reading and a visit to Wayan, the healer from *Eat Pray Love*. In the very fine print, the terms and conditions noted that Ketut Liyer had passed away, that his son had taken over the family business of palm readings in the same family compound as seen in the movie, and that Ketut's son and Wayan sometimes ran on "Bali time," so a visit and reading were not guaranteed. The package also included an ecobike tour around Ubud, as seen in the film. The terms and conditions failed to note that biking on Bali's roads is not for the uninitiated. The bike accident portrayed in the movie was likely to befall them as well, except the person running them off the road probably would not be a handsome Brazilian and their future husband.

For the Balinese, spirituality, mystical powers, and magical forces are not courses you sign up for on Wednesday evenings and are not found on a weeklong retreat at an ecolodge. Magical powers, good and evil, define and structure their world. They adjust their homes, conduct, and lives based on mystical powers, supernatural forces, and unexplained energies. Western logic, my logic, often conflicted with these forces. Sometimes the conflict led to disagreements with the staff about how and when some mundane household chore would be handled. For me, laundry is simple—throw the darks in one load and the lights in another load. Done. The staff saw it differently. The main point of contention came over underwear and napkins, and whether they could be washed with other clothes. I turned to *Bali: Sekala and Niskala* and searched for an explanation. Apparently, clothing that has touched sexual organs is charged with dangerous power. That explained the underwear, but not the napkins.

For the Balinese, spirits control not only these mundane details but also life and death. Since I don't have the depth of knowledge to explain the intricacies of Balinese beliefs and practices, perhaps the best way to share a sense of the Balinese world is with an example of life and death, science and evil spirits. Ni Ketut Murni's death is such a story.

Ketut's story was told to me by her nephew Putu. At the time of the telling, Putu was a twenty-three-year-old college student, majoring in English, taking evening classes at Saraswati University in Denpasar after working at Villa Shanti during the day. Unless there was a ceremony, Putu wore cut-off jean shorts and a T-shirt most days. With the iPad mini we brought back from Chicago, Putu posted on Facebook, played video games, and streamed YouTube. In the midst of this surface appearance of Western modernity, Putu told me with profound sadness and sincerity that a *leyak*, an evil spirit, had killed his aunt Ketut with powerful black magic.

Ketut had been like a second mother to Putu. They had lived together with twenty-eight to thirty members of their extended family in the family compound. Putu's paternal grandparents had eight children, four sons and four daughters. As adults, the sons (including Putu's father and Ketut's husband, Made), with their wives and children, all lived in the family compound. (The adult daughters moved to their husbands' family compounds.) Ketut and Made had six children: Wayan, Made (who died at birth), Komang, Ketut, Wayan (again), and Kadek. With so many family members living together, privacy is hard to find in a Balinese family compound. However, close relationships like that between Putu and Ketut often develop across generations and nuclear families.

When Ketut got sick, she went to a medical doctor, who diagnosed a stroke. Ketut then visited a *balian*, a traditional healer with a sixth sense, the ability to see into the mystical world and communicate with spirits, like a shaman. He told Ketut that an evil spirit had attacked her. She knew how and why—because of a fight with her next-door neighbor over payments for a tooth-filing ceremony known as *metatah*.

The many ceremonies their religion requires the Balinese to celebrate are expensive and difficult for individuals to afford. For one ceremony per month, every person in Ketut's *banjar* contributed 100,000 Indonesian rupiah, about seven US dollars, to the person holding the ceremony. This was a significant sum—more than the minimum daily wage mandated by the Bali Provincial Government. More than one ceremony could occur each month in the *banjar*, but only the first ceremony received these contributions. Ketut coordinated ceremonies for the *banjar*. She decided which ceremony went first and thus received the contributions.

The month before Ketut became ill, two people in the *banjar* planned a ceremony. One of them, Dayu, planned a tooth-filing ceremony for a grandchild. Tooth filing is an important coming-of-age ritual. The filing dulls the points on the cuspids (canine teeth), which the Balinese consider coarse and evil—think of the fangs on the monstrous *Ogoh-ogohs*. Fangs are considered evil and ugly, so the filing of the canine teeth is both symbolic and aesthetic. For a tooth-filing ceremony, the family must make offerings; purchase and wear new clothes; hire musicians; buy, prepare, and serve food; and accommodate visiting guests. Expenses add up quickly.

Ketut scheduled the tooth-filing ceremony to be the second ceremony that month. Her rationale was that Dayu, who was from the highest caste, the Brahmana, had enough money to pay for the tooth-filing ceremony herself. She did not need the contributions. Also, Dayu was from a different *banjar* and had only recently bought the land next door to Ketut. Because Dayu's ceremony was the second ceremony that month, neither Ketut nor anyone else in the *banjar* contributed any money to Dayu for the tooth-filing ceremony. Just a few days later, Ketut got sick.

Ketut and her entire extended family believed that Dayu had unleashed a *leyak* that made Ketut ill and killed her. But none of them said anything about the attack to anyone else in the *banjar*. The family did not want the neighbors to get angry and send more evil spirits. Ketut and her family did not blame Dayu. They did not believe Dayu deliberately unleashed the *leyak*. It was simply too powerful for Dayu to control. Indeed, after the *leyak* attacked Ketut, it attacked Dayu, who then died before Ketut. I asked Putu what had happened to Dayu.

"Evil spirits fight with other evil spirits to get to the next level," Putu explained. "Dayu got caught in the cross fire between two evil spirits, and it killed her."

After the *balian* told Ketut about the evil spirit, he prescribed a remedy. He gave Ketut traditional medicine and sent her to a *melukat*, a purification ceremony, at a water temple to cleanse her body and soul with holy water and drive out the evil spirit. Ketut tried hard to rid herself of the evil spirit. She performed purification ceremonies at three water temples—two water temples near Ubud (Tirta Empul and Gunung Kawi Sebatu) and a water temple near Bangli in the Kintamani highlands (Pura Taman Pecampuhan).

In addition to seeing the *balian* and performing the purification ceremonies, Ketut went back to the medical doctor. According to Putu, both the *balian* and the medical doctor were necessary for Ketut to recover. But neither could cure her. Unfortunately, at age sixty-two, Ketut passed away.

Ketut died in 2012, but her cremation ceremony did not occur until September 13, 2015. When she died, her body was covered with fabric and buried in a wooden coffin in the cemetery after a simple ceremony. Three years later, her family exhumed her remains for the cremation. The reason for the delay was the same reason Dayu unknowingly unleashed the *leyak* that killed Ketut—the high cost of ceremonies. Cremations, and the many related ceremonies, are expensive. The costs of preparing offerings, building structures and a sarcophagus, feeding guests, paying the priest, hiring musicians, and renting chairs are too high for most Balinese families to afford to pay on their own. In some communities, families wait until a wealthy person dies and then join the scheduled cremation, allowing the wealthy family to bear most of the expense.

Pejeng, Putu and Ketut's village, found a communal solution. Several *banjars* that share the same temple and cemetery combine to have a massive cremation for everyone who has died in the previous few years, typically every three years. But to save money, they tried waiting longer. In 2015, the cremation was for everyone in those *banjars* who had died in the previous five years: 165 people, including Ketut. This produced too many sarcophagi and too many pyres. The resulting conflagration was overwhelming and almost burned completely out of control. The ceremonies had to be cut short, and everyone except those operating the fire truck retreated beyond the stone walls. After the cremation ceremony, it took me days, multiple showers, and essential oils to remove the residue and smell of the smoke and soot (the remains of those 165 people) from my hair, skin, eyes, nose, and mouth. After 2015, the Pejeng *banjars* reverted to holding a cremation every three years.

Before the cremation, Putu helped his uncle Made with the preparations. First, they needed to consult a *balian*. To determine which *balian*, they looked at the Balinese calendar to see which direction to go. (I did not understand how a calendar could show a cardinal direction, but the Balinese calendar is too complex for Putu to explain or for me to figure out.) The best direction was south, so that meant Batuan, the village directly south of Pejeng. Only one *balian* lived there, a seventy-year-old woman, which was exceptional, since most *balians* are men. On the way to see this *balian*, Putu and Made stopped at the Pura Dalem (the Death Temple). There, they made an offering and picked up Ketut's soul to accompany them to the *balian*.

Ketut's soul entered the *balian's* body and communicated with Putu and Made through the *balian*. I asked Putu how he knew it was Ketut speaking to him, not the balian.

He replied, "She sounds like my auntie. We know because the character is different from the healer, like my auntie's character."

When Ketut spoke, she said hello to her husband, her children, and her daughter-in-law. She missed them. She told Putu and Made she was sad that she had died. Then the conversation turned to the reason for the visit to the *balian*—to ask Ketut her preferences for her cremation. Ketut's soul told Putu that Ketut wanted to wear a yellow sarong and a white *kebaya* and headcloth for her cremation. For her sarcophagus, Ketut wanted a temple, not an animal. (Depending on the length of time between death and cremation, some families cremate bodies, and some cremate bones. The bodies needed a larger sarcophagus—often a bull or pig, depending on caste. If only bones remain, a smaller sarcophagus can be used, but a larger sarcophagus could still be used if that was what the deceased's soul requested.) Made and Putu made the arrangements for Ketut's cremation according to her request, as communicated by her soul through the *balian*.

As I listened to Putu describe his conversation with Ketut's soul, the always-present gap between our belief systems became a chasm. I had asked Putu to talk about his aunt Ketut's death and cremation because I wanted to understand and show respect for the woman whose cremation I attended and to learn and understand more about Balinese religion and culture. The questions I asked Putu were factual. I tried not to challenge the underlying premise or belief. But I could not fathom the circumscribed scope of the conversation Putu and Made had with Ketut's soul. How could Putu and Made only ask superficial and practical questions about earthly things? I would have seized the opportunity to ask fundamental questions about death and life, and so much more. Trying to respect Putu and his beliefs, I still had to ask.

"Putu, did you ask your aunt's soul about anything else?"

"No."

"If I had the chance to speak to the soul of someone who had died, I think I would ask deep philosophical questions. I would ask about death. I would ask about the meaning of life. I would not only ask, 'What do you want to wear at your cremation?'"

Looking at me like I was crazy, Putu said, "That's unusual."

As our third Nyepi in Bali approached, I still had no control over the staff's weekly work schedule, but I understood Bali better and knew the staff better. Without asking the villa manager, I told the staff that they did not need to come to work on Nyepi eve or Nyepi. Nyoman (night security) was a *pecalang* for the *banjar*, and, in that capacity, he would be patrolling our street to ensure compliance with the Nyepi rules. When he offered to check the grounds of Villa Shanti during his patrols, I accepted and thanked him, as it would not interfere with his celebration and observance of Nyepi. Everyone else, except for Nyoman (day staff), happily accepted the time off. Nyoman was the most senior and most responsible member of the staff. I could tell he was torn. He wanted to celebrate Nyepi at home with his family, but he was reluctant to leave the villa unstaffed for thirty-six hours. Nyoman's concern was unwarranted. Although Nyoman had never seen evidence of it, I could wash my own dishes and make my own bed. Promising that I would take full financial and moral responsibility for any catastrophe, I insisted the staff take time off for the holiday. Reluctantly, Nyoman agreed.

In the afternoon before Nyepi eve, Jake and I headed down the hill to Ubud Center to see the *Ogoh-ogohs* waiting on the main soccer field.

We stopped for frozen yogurt and then wandered around the dusty field, admiring the craftsmanship and creativity and pointing out the most disgusting and clever features. Before the gathering crowd grew too big and the procession began, we headed home. We walked uphill on Jalan Suweta through Taman Kelod, the *banjar* just down the hill from Villa Shanti and just up the hill from the intersection where we had watched the *Ogoh-ogoh* procession the previous year. As they got organized for their procession, Jake and I weaved through the crowd and came face-to-face with their main *Ogoh-ogoh*. The menacing head, claws, body, and wings of a dragon sat on the main bamboo frame, carried by dozens of men. The impressive body, extending about fifty yards beyond the frame, was held up with bamboo poles carried by a line of dozens of men. Having never before seen such an extension on an *Ogoh-ogoh*, I wondered how the men carrying the long body would keep pace with the head while maneuvering through the crowd. Glad we would not be caught on the street behind this spectacular-looking and impractical *Ogoh-ogoh* once it started moving, Jake and I picked up the pace to get home before the road became impassable.

Around dusk, I put on a sarong, *kebaya*, and sash over my sundress. I never perfected the art of tying a sarong so that it adequately covered me and did not fall off, and I had no safety pins handy. I also did not own the corset Balinese women wear under their fitted and revealing lace *kebaya*. It was too hot and constricting. My solid-color sundress did double duty as an underlayer. No one would mistake me for one of the graceful Balinese women who can walk down the street balancing a multitiered offering on her head while wearing a corset, a tightly wrapped sarong, and high heels, but it would do on a dark night. I convinced Jake to wrap a sarong over his shorts and tie on a sash. Semi-dressed for the occasion, we headed out. We walked up the hill to the Pura Dalem Tegallantang (the temple), where the residents of our *banjar* would start and end their parade of *Ogoh-ogohs* to scare away the demons for the coming year. No tourists or photographers lined the street or interfered with the procession. We stood on the side of the road with our neighbors and watched the kids and young men parade their monstrous creations to the banging of drums and clanging of gongs.

We stayed to watch the burning of the non-Styrofoam portions of *Ogoh-ogohs*, and then walked home, slipping off our traditional clothing as soon as we were out of sight of the ceremony.

In a remarkable confluence of power and mystery, the next day, March 9, 2016, was Nyepi and a total solar eclipse over Bali. If the Day of Silence did not convince the evil spirits that Bali was uninhabited and not worth returning to, the disappearing sun and resulting darkness midmorning certainly would.

Cardboard eclipse glasses, purportedly "safe for direct solar viewing," were for sale all over Ubud in the weeks and days before Nyepi. The fact that the glasses were labeled as ISO and CE-certified safe was meaningless. If you can make fake glasses, it is just as easy to add a phony certification sticker on the side. The store at Green School sold eclipse glasses ordered directly from Australia. I had a stash of my own, ordered from the US and brought to Bali by visiting friends earlier in the year. I kept pairs for Jake and me and gave the rest to the staff for their families.

Jake and I had a perfect viewing platform for the eclipse—the Villa Shanti patio, which ran the width of the house and faced east, where the sun would rise and then disappear. The patio was where we spent most of our waking hours when we were home. On one end, with French doors to the family room, there was a seating area with a wicker couch and two wicker lounge chairs with ottomans, all with forest-green cushions and batik throw pillows. An extra-long dining table dominated the middle of the porch, opposite windows to the kitchen. The other end, with French doors to the living room, held two chaise lounges and a massive Buddha head taller and broader than Jake with his arms raised to his sides. Like many buildings in Bali (though not the rest of the villa), the patio was covered by a corrugated plastic roof. When it rained, the thundering noise of the rain pounding on the plastic would drown out all conversations and the dialogue of anything we were watching on our computer or iPad. If I was on a phone conference for work, I could not hear a thing. But since the plastic roof also leaked in a downpour, we had to move inside anyway.

From the patio, the panorama took in terraced rice paddies, a ravine, and palm trees. The only better view was from the landing upstairs outside Jake's bedroom door, from where you could also see Mount Batur, an active volcano in Kintamani north of Ubud. The view from the porch is what had sold me on the house.

Nyepi morning, still in our pajamas, Jake and I lay back on the chaise lounges on the patio and had front-row seats for the eclipse. For hours, through our goofy protective cardboard glasses, we watched the sun slowly disappear and then reappear. In keeping with the rules and message of Nyepi, we were still and quiet. I cannot remember another time when Jake remained as peaceful for so long. It was almost as if our energy dissipated and recharged with the sun's passage.

Even after letting go of my career, my rational brain—educated and trained for decades to dissect and analyze—remained skeptical. I did not accept that the *Ogoh-ogohs* drove evil spirits from the island. I did not accept that *leyaks* cause strokes that kill. I did not believe in the rituals and black magic that shape Balinese life or the West's New Age crystal bowls and sound circles. I did not buy the theories that Bali's magical powers come from ley lines, dragon lines, spirit lines, or dream lines, which intersect on Bali and create an energy vortex. Nonetheless, despite all the things my rational brain rejected, I felt an energy and a power on Bali. It was almost like faith, something you can feel but cannot see or explain. I felt it most strongly that Nyepi morning while watching the solar eclipse from the porch of our silent house.

The following morning, the day staff returned to work. They may have expected to find Villa Shanti in shambles, if it still stood, and Jake's and my dead bodies floating in the pool. Instead, we were on the porch, eating breakfast.

"*Salamat Pagi*" (Good morning), said Nyoman as he walked in, looking around.

"*Pagi*," Jake and I each responded.

"*Apa kabar?*" (How are you?), Nyoman asked, glancing in the kitchen and obviously surprised to see no dishes stacked in the sink and no garbage overflowing the bin.

"*Baik, baik*" (Fine), I replied, trying to suppress a grin.

Villa Shanti had survived thirty-six hours without staff.

Jake and I more than survived that Nyepi. The power of Bali and the power of the eclipse brought together our travels, our experiences in foreign countries with foreign cultures, and our friends around the world. It pulled together what we had learned and how much we had changed and grown. On that Day of Silence, reflecting on all Jake and I had done together, I knew that through our travels and our openness to change, we had become better people. That Nyepi, we thrived.

Epilogue

TRAVEL STOPPED

TOO SOON FOR ME, but at the right time for Jake, we moved back to Chicago. Unlike when we returned from Shanghai, we did not step back into our old life. We couldn't. It didn't fit anymore. Living in Bali, our priorities and lives shifted. Forced to slow down and stop for Hindu ceremonies—which constantly blocked the roads and occasionally shuttered Ubud or the entire island—we absorbed some of the power of Bali. We remained practical Westerners but with an appreciation for the possibilities in a spiritual center.

Hanging out with international expats—digital nomads, world schoolers, and those just looking for a different way of life—gave me a different frame of reference, and a definition of success not tied to a traditional career trajectory and fourteen-hour workdays. Clearly, I already was headed in that direction, or I would never have moved to Bali in the first place, but I had fallen off the cliff, and there was no way back. Some of the changes faded as we reintegrated into US culture and society, but some I will try to hold forever and incorporate into who I am and how I live my life.

I hope Jake will too, but I am not sure he will or even wants to. After the first few dramatic months—a burning incense stick in the eye, a huge snake on his bedroom staircase, a scorpion in his shower, and a jungle school with pit toilets and no walls—Jake happily settled into life in Bali. But Bali never suited Jake the way it suited me. Jake missed what he perceived as "modern," which he defined as cities, tall buildings, fast internet, and indoor showers. When we moved back to Chicago, Jake got "modern."

We did not move back into the historic house I owned in Lincoln Park, which Jake considered "home" before moving to Bali. Instead, Jake and I rented an apartment on the sixty-second floor of a high-rise in the Chicago Loop with floor-to-ceiling windows and sweeping views of Lake Michigan, Monroe Harbor, Millennium Park, and the Chicago skyline. In our glass-enclosed box high in the sky, there were no snakes, no scorpions, no rats, no bats, no dengue mosquitos, and no giant spiders. All 3.5 baths were totally indoors. Jake adored it. Then his dishes started to pile up in the sink, his dirty laundry lay on his bathroom floor, his clean laundry stayed in the dryer, and no one waited to drive him wherever he wanted to go. Jake's modern apartment did not come with household staff. No Putu, Nyoman, Made, Ketut, or Komang to make life easier for us.

Jake barely noticed. He did not care about laundry or dishes, and did not need a driver because he walked to his new school. Jake cared about internet speed. When we moved to Ubud, Villa Shanti's internet speed was two megabits. We were thrilled when a new cable improved the speed to five megabits, the fastest in Ubud at the time. In Chicago, the internet speed in our new apartment was one gigabit—a megabit is a *million* bits per second, and a gigabit is a *billion* bits per second. Jake could play online games with his Bali friends (then living in Bali, Australia, and California) at faster speeds than he could when they all lived in Bali. Jake had fast friends and fast internet. What else could a preteen want or need?

When we left for Bali, I had not been ready to give up my job and the career I worked so long and hard to build. But when we returned to Chicago, I had zero interest in resuming that work and life. What else could I do? I considered my skill set and experience. I am a competent person and can do many things, but working as a lawyer is where I add value, doing what others are not trained or licensed to do. Since no amount of money could induce me to go back to working at a law firm, I started volunteering at a nonprofit that works on behalf of people with disabilities. I helped them draft and litigate a class action against Chicago Public Schools for failure to comply with the Individuals with Disabilities Education Act.

And, of course, Jake and I kept traveling. For 2020, we had a spring break trip planned in the Galapagos Islands and a summer vacation planned in Italy. Then, international travel stopped. Almost everything stopped. We were living through the COVID-19 pandemic.

Sitting at home with nowhere to go and nothing to do, I pulled out boxes and file folders full of trip itineraries, notes, photos, videotapes, and journals I had kept over the decades and started writing this book. Ironically, as I wrote about traveling the world, I barely left my high-rise condo. In some ways, it was an extension of Nyepi. Forced to stay home, I reflected, and the result is a book I otherwise might never have sat down to write.

On Nyepi, Ngurah Rai Airport closes, and Bali stops for the Day of Silence and for reflection. With COVID-19, worldwide travel and much of life stopped for much longer. I hope it's enough to keep the demons away when ordinary life resumes.

Acknowledgments

ONE OF THE JOYS of writing this book was the excuse it gave me to reach out to friends, guides, and fellow travelers I met along the way. Without them, I would have no stories to tell. Special thanks to the following: Andrew Meissner, whom I met trekking in the Khumbu region of Nepal, was always ready to explore another remote destination. Mike Speaks, my guide through Pakistan, Bhutan, and above the Arctic Circle, confirmed my descriptions of the rapids and helped me map out our route. David Nitsch and Brock Tabor guided me through Papua New Guinea, reminded me of what I blocked from my memory (stepping on a bed of sea urchins), and helped me recreate the routes we paddled along the Tufi Coast and through the Trobriand Islands. Peggy Currier invited Jake and me to stay with her family on our exploratory trip to Shanghai and became our first friend there. Margaret Guthrie, our second friend in Shanghai and our first visitor in Bali, laughed over the details of our shared time in Shanghai. I Putu Eka Putra helped me understand and appreciate Balinese culture and religion and allowed me to share the story of his aunt Ni Ketut Murni, who was killed by an evil spirit. Our staff in Bali taught us the way and took care of us, I Nengha Barwa (Nyoman), I Made Sukartono, I Ketut Suardana, I Made Tingu, I Nyoman Sloki, Ni Nyoman Wati Cantik, Ni Putu, and, last but far from least, I Komang Arta Dipa, our always cheerful driver who enabled our exploration of the island.

I sent early drafts of the manuscript to friends and family, asking for their honest assessment. Their comments helped me move forward with the story, and they may not recognize the final book. I am grateful to them all. Katherine Gehl found time in her overloaded schedule to read the entire manuscript twice and marked "Ha Ha" in the margins where it made her laugh. Diane Zabich, my friend since before I climbed Mount Rainier, exclaimed, "You need maps!" Sarah Katherman's honest comments led me to delete an entire chapter that did not fit the book's tone. Lisa Lilly was with me from the beginning, and I learned much from her writing expertise. Steve Levy was the first to comment on the earliest draft and the last to comment by proofing the final version. Tom Luz nicely asked the critical question, "What's the narrative arc?" while encouraging me to finish the book he always thought I should write. Julia Reidhead generously gave her professional opinion and referred me to a wonderful editor. Emily Buss encouraged me by sharing that her law students were heartened by my efforts to practice law and still have an interesting life.

I am grateful to my friends and family who read drafts of the manuscript and offered encouragement: my sister Becky Charous, my brother-in-law Steve Charous, my sister-in-law Janice Weinstein, my aunt Janet Ohlhausen, my cousin Daniella Rosenthal, and my friends Claudia Allen, Sally Strauss, Caroline Luz, Lixi Michaelis, and Sandy Hauser. And thanks to Joe Horiskey of RMI Expeditions, a stranger, who corrected technical details about climbing Mount Rainier and provided history and background on the practice of leaving exhausted climbers in a sleeping bag staked to a glacier.

To the Yale Women Writers Group, thank you. When the group formed early in the pandemic, I was barely a writer and not yet an author. I am glad that I presumptuously logged into Zoom for that first meeting. Joining you every second and fourth Monday was educational, inspirational, and fun. Thanks to Helen Mao for reading an early draft and recognizing the China I describe, and Lisa Fabish for her astute comments on a later draft and encouragement through the process.

In addition to friends and family who advised and encouraged me, I had professional help to turn my travels into this book. I appreciate (and needed) their assistance. My editor Kathy Brandt, a traveler herself and travel-book writer, shares my sensibility and never questioned why I would go there and why I would do that. John Koehler, Joe Coccaro, Miranda Dillon, Lauren Sheldon, and Hannah Woodlan of Koehler Books turned my manuscript into a well-crafted book.

Most of all, thanks to my parents, Marjie and Bernie Weinstein, who sent me off on that first Man and His Land trip. Someday I hope to travel to as many countries as you have. And thank you, Jake, for letting me tell our story, even when it differs from your memories. I love you.

CPSIA information can be obtained
at www.ICGtesting.com
Printed in the USA
BVHW081800200322
631576BV00003B/15